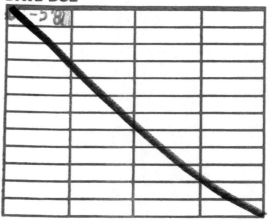

Invitation to
Lifelong Learning

Invitation to Lifelong Learning

Edited by Ronald Gross

Follett Publishing Company
Chicago, Illinois

Atlanta, Georgia • Dallas, Texas
Sacramento, California • Warrensburg, Missouri

Designed by Karen A. Yops

Library of Congress Cataloging in Publication Data
Main entry under title:

Invitation to lifelong learning.

1. Continuing education—Addresses, essays, lectures.
2. Learning—Addresses, essays, lectures. I. Gross, Ronald.
LC5215.I6   374   81-19410
ISBN 0-695-81660-8   AACR2

First Printing

This book is dedicated to the American Association for Adult and Continuing Education, a fresh force for lifelong learning.

Contents

Part I THE GREAT TRADITION

The Ordeal and Ecstasy of Learning

Plato **28**

The most powerful metaphor for education in the Western tradition, Plato's parable of the cave dramatizes the harrowing experience by which we free our minds from illusion and accept responsibility for helping others do so.

We Humans Must Create Ourselves

Pico della Mirandola **36**

The glory of being human is that one's essence is not given *a priori* but must be forged afresh by each person, throughout his or her life.

The Founding of the Junto

Benjamin Franklin **42**

The father of American adult education tells how and why he and his friends initiated a classic experiment, presaging a form of lifelong learning that now pervades our society.

Reaffirming a Great Tradition

Robert McClintock **46**

The mainstream of educational theory and practice in the West, argues a distinguished philosopher, lies not in schooling but in "study"—a lifelong course in which individuals use all the resources available.

Part III UNDERSTANDING ADULT LEARNING

Illuminating insights into the basic motivations of those who engage in continuing education are presented by one of the nation's leading researchers.

The key concept in contemporary adult education is defined by its creator.

Only one-fifth of what adults learn comes about as the result of being taught. How does the rest occur?

The stages and crisis points of change throughout adult life spur individuals to engage in educational activities, this recent study revealed.

What is the role of learning for its own sweet sake in the lives of adults? Is it prevalent? functional? necessary? Is it . . . happiness?

Part V A FUTURE LEARNING WORLD

Bridging the "Human Gap"
James Botkin, Mahdi Elmandjra, and Mircea Malitza 252

The internationally acclaimed Club of Rome report proclaims that mental development is the only unlimited resource left in the world and describes what kind of education is needed for tomorrow's global society.

The Worldwide Struggle for Adult Education

Frank Spikes 262

Principles and goals for lifelong learning developed by adult educators worldwide provide a global basis for public policy.

Lifelong Learning as Nightmare

Basic Choices 272

The prospect that an entire adult population might be compelled to go back to school has been raised, and contested, by an intrepid group of American adult educators.

Using Technology to Break the Shell of "Permitted Ignorance"
Buckminster Fuller 276

"We . . . are going to have to pay our whole population to go to school and pay it to stay at school."

Welcome to the Invisible College

Kenneth Boulding 282

"There is in the world today an 'invisible college' of people in many different countries and many different cultures, who have this vision of the nature of the transition through which we are passing and who are determined to devote their lives to contributing toward its successful fulfillment."

Preface

Lifelong learning is an international enterprise to which our colleagues from Western Europe, the socialist countries, and the Third World have made enormous contributions. In many areas of thought and practice, they excel us and provide models that we would do well to ponder. I have seen such programs at first hand and have met such colleagues during visits over the past five years to nonformal education projects in the Far East, Western Europe, and Israel.

This book does take account of such programs in its presentation of the UNESCO declaration and in its internationally oriented selections, such as those by Botkin and his socialist and Third World co-authors; by Boulding, with his worldwide vision of an "invisible college"; and by Fuller, with his global perspective. However, with the exception of Paulo Freire, these pages do not include *authors* from abroad. A collection of such works would be valuable to the profession, and it is hoped that such a book is forthcoming to enrich the readings for adult educators.

Moreover, these writings do not focus directly on the problems of deprivation, such as illiteracy and undereducation, toward which much of the effort, particularly in federally supported adult education, is quite rightly directed. Most adult education students are well exposed to those issues, problems, and techniques in their professional preparation. The effort here is to fill a less well served need: for readings that reveal the basic humanistic principles inherent in thinking clearly about lifelong learning.

Although this book was originally conceived and planned by myself, Beatrice Gross's contributions to refining the concept; to finding, selecting, and editing the pieces; and to supervising the processes of assembly, clearance of permissions, and so on, fully justified her being designated as co-editor. She disagreed, however. It is the only aspect of the work on which we did not concur.

RONALD GROSS
GREAT NECK, N.Y.

13

Acknowledgments

The selections in this book are reproduced by permission of the authors, their publishers, or the sponsoring organizations.

"The Ordeal and Ecstasy of Learning," by Plato. In the public domain.

"We Humans Must Create Ourselves," by Pico della Mirandola. From "On the Dignity of Man." Copyright © 1940, Charles Glenn Wallis.

"The Founding of the Junto," by Benjamin Franklin. Reprinted by permission of the publisher from C. Hartley Grattan's *American Ideas About Adult Education, 1710–1951* (New York: Teachers College Press). Copyright © 1959 by Teachers College, Columbia University. All rights reserved.

"Reaffirming a Great Tradition," by Robert McClintock. Reprinted by permission of the publisher from "Toward a Place for Study," by Robert McClintock. Copyright © 1971 by *Teachers College Record,* Teachers College, Columbia University. All rights reserved.

"No One Can 'Complete an Education,' " by Margaret Mead. Reprinted by permission of the *Harvard Business Review.* A portion of "Why Is Education Obsolescent?" by Margaret Mead (*HBR,* November–December 1958). Copyright © 1958 by the President and Fellows of Harvard College. All rights reserved.

"Why Only Adults Can Be Educated," by Mortimer J. Adler. From "Adult Education" in *Great Issues in Education* (Great Books Foundation). Copyright © 1956 by Mortimer J. Adler. Reprinted by permission of the author.

"Education for Critical Consciousness," by Paulo Freire. From *Education for Critical Consciousness,* published by Continuum, The Seabury Press. Copyright © 1973 by Paulo Freire. Published with permission of the publisher. All rights reserved.

15

"To Put Meaning into the Whole of Life," by Eduard Lindeman. From *The Meaning of Adult Education*, published by Harvest House. Copyright © 1961 by Harvest House Ltd. Published with permission of the publisher. All rights reserved.

"American Triumphs in Adult Education," by Fred Harrington. Reprinted by permission of the Adult Education Association of the United States of America. Copyright © 1980. All rights reserved.

"The Three Kinds of Lifelong Learners," by Cyril Houle. From *The Inquiring Mind*, published by The University of Wisconsin Press. Copyright © 1961 by The University of Wisconsin Press. Published with permission of the publisher. All rights reserved.

"Andragogy: The New Science of Education," by Malcolm Knowles. From *The Modern Practice of Adult Education* (Revised Edition), published by Follett Publishing Company. Copyright © 1980 by Malcolm Knowles. Reprinted by permission. All rights reserved.

"The Other 80 Percent of Learning," by Allen Tough. Copyright © 1980 by Allen Tough. Reprinted by permission of the author. All rights reserved.

" 'Passages' of Adulthood and Triggers to Learning," by Carol Aslanian and Henry Brickell. Reprinted by permission from *Americans in Transition: Life Changes as Reasons for Adult Learning*, by Carol B. Aslanian and Henry M. Brickell. Copyright © 1980 by College Entrance Examination Board, New York.

"Learning, 'Flow,' and Happiness," by Mihaly Csikszentmihalyi. Copyright © 1981 by Mihaly Csikszentmihalyi. Reprinted by permission of the author and the Syracuse Research Corporation.

"Success Stories of Adult Learning," by Samuel Brightman. Reprinted from *Success Stories of Adult Learning in America* by permission of the National Advisory Council on Adult Education, 1978.

"Education in the Shoe Shop," by Frank Adams. Reprinted by permission of the author. Copyright © 1977 by Frank Adams.

"Now I Am Only Interested in Learning," by Carl Rogers. Copyright © 1961 by Carl Rogers. Reprinted by permission of the author and Wayne State University Press, current publisher and copyright holder of the *Merrill-Palmer Quarterly* effective November 1980. All rights reserved.

"The Shape of Adult Education in the Eighties," by Jerold W. Apps. From *Lifelong Learning: The Adult Years* (June 1980). Copyright © 1980 by the Adult Education Association of the United States of America. Reprinted by permission. All rights reserved.

"Missing Links in the Learning Society," by K. Patricia Cross. Reprinted by permission from an article by K. Patricia Cross in *The College*

Introduction

Ronald Gross

Lifelong learning is *us*. You, the reader of this book, and I, its editor, are both constantly engaged in our own ongoing lifelong learning. Even as we grapple with the new ideas about adult learning presented by contributors to this book, we embody the very process we are seeking to understand. As we sharpen our awareness of the ideals that drive lifelong learning, we refine our image of what we expect of ourselves. As we enlarge our vision to embrace a rich historic tradition and to encompass the worldwide scope of adult education, we place ourselves more confidently in time and space.

This book opens with Plato's parable of the cave, the most haunting image of adult learning in the Western tradition. As we read it, we, too, squat in that shadowy crypt, our eyes fixed on the flickering shadows just as our eyes are so regularly fixed on our television screens. The book ends with a vision of the planetary "invisible college," in which people of goodwill can join by self-declaration and work toward a better world through the power of the human mind. As we read Kenneth Boulding's words, we cannot help but rise to the challenge, to lend our strength to those values that hold out hope for humanity.

And in between these initial and concluding statements, again and again we find our own experiences, our own potentialities, illuminated. Cyril Houle delineates the three kinds of adult learners, and we suddenly understand our own motivations a bit better. Allen Tough shares his discovery that 80 percent of the learning in the lives of adults is self-directed, and suddenly a vast new frontier for adult education services looms on the horizon. John Ohliger warns against the trend toward compelling adults to return to school, and we realize how different is the quality of our own learning when it is coerced instead of voluntary. Margaret Mead argues the need for parents to learn what the new world is like from their children, and we grasp a key to the generation gap in our own families.

19

That self-reflexive quality makes the field of lifelong learning, adult education, continuing education, or whatever we choose to call it, uniquely rewarding. In our thought and practice, we cannot but find constant relevance to ourselves. The adult educator is constantly learning. Not in the sense of going to classes, but in the far more important sense— itself one of the chief lessons of the discipline—of shaping and reshaping oneself by the intelligent use of one's experiences. "We have met the learner"—to paraphrase Pogo—"and she is *us.*"

The ideal of lifelong learning reflects, too, our whole American culture and historical experience. In 1930 John Dewey wrote, "Schools are not the ultimate formative force. Social institutions, the trend of occupations, the pattern of social arrangements, are the finally controlling influences in shaping minds. . . . Effective education, that which really leaves a stamp on character and thought, is obtained when graduates come to take their part in the activities of adult society."

We learn what we live. That is a touchstone of sanity when thinking about the roots of learning and growth. A traditional, sequential education in schools offers one specialized kind of learning, confined to one period of life and one part of the population. But the learning that enables individuals and communities to meet changing conditions and fulfill their potentialities is not stored up during the years of schooling alone. It is, as it has always been, the daily creation of people learning and living together. The further back we peer into our educational history, and the further we look into its future, the clearer we see the force of lifelong learning.

As we cast our eyes backward, it becomes clear that for the pioneers the teacher was the land itself, with its demand for self-reliance and its promise of richness. For later immigrants, learning was concomitant with the political and economic challenges of building whole communities, and later a whole society, from rough beginnings. Voluntary groups, which the French observer Alexis de Tocqueville rightly remarked were so characteristically American, were the adult's school. So also was popular culture, variously represented by early newssheets, the lyceums and chautauquas of the nineteenth century, and the commercial and public television of the twentieth. There was a potent and pervasive tradition of self-education stretching from Benjamin Franklin, Abraham Lincoln, Dorothea Dix, and Harriet Tubman, through Thomas Edison and Henry Ford, down to Eric Hoffer and Malcolm X in our own day.

Above all, the great spur to lifelong learning was the American Dream itself. The driving idea was that in this new world we could fulfill our highest potentialities, become all that we were capable of being. In practice, to be sure, that noble ideal has not been uniformly applied. Throughout our history considerably less than unlimited individual opportunity has been afforded to various minorities, and perhaps most pervasively to black Americans. The ideal nevertheless persists. Thus, in *Frontiers of American Culture,* the eminent historian James Truslow Adams observed after a lifetime of studying our past: "I think that what has perhaps struck me most has been the almost unique mobility of life in America, and, due to its infinite opportunities, the variety of jobs and positions— economic, social, political or other—which any individual may find himself filling in the course of his life. . . . From this has followed the need, above that felt in almost any other country, for constant readjustments, with their educational adjuncts of one sort or another, at almost any age. . . . This appears to have been an essential corollary to the whole nature of American life and the American dream."

But we do not have to peer into the past to see the potency of lifelong learning. If we merely open our eyes, we will see it all around us today.

Even with youth-oriented schools and colleges so dominating our vision of education, the pervasiveness and importance of lifelong learning are readily demonstrable. Consider the vast educational enterprises of business and industry: occupational training, in-service training, occupational upgrading, human resources development, management and executive training. Add to them education in labor unions, such as apprentice programs and training of supervisors and shop stewards, and an enormous armed forces network involving correspondence study, televised courses, and classroom instruction. Include the educational work of churches and synagogues, community centers, civic organizations, voluntary groups, professional organizations (and their conferences and conventions), the national health organizations, museums and galleries, libraries, government agencies, service clubs, and public television. And most significant of all, add the individual learning projects that research reveals most adults engage in but don't consider "education" because they have been schooled to equate learning with taking courses.

Cumulating these diverse learning activities reveals the lineaments of a vast nonsystem of individual and group learning that dwarfs institutionalized schooling. That learning is the kind by which Americans as persons, and our communities and society, really keep changing and expanding to meet the changing challenges of individual and collective life. The quality of learning and of life for us as individuals, and for our nation, is best measured by the quality of these learning opportunities. If they are narrow in breadth and unimaginative in character, our lives will be parochial and unenterprising. If they are varied, handsome, and challenging, so too will be our prospects for growth.

Lifelong learning is indeed *us*. But it is *us* grown more aware of ourselves, our past, our world, our fellow human beings, and our future. It is to this enlargement of ourselves that the mentors in this book beckon us. They have taken the pains to see more clearly, or deeply, or widely, what those of us who are adult educators might become in this field. Among the principle things they tell us:

1. *Lifelong learning is a personal, existential challenge to each of us, not just a rubric for certain educational activities.*

Lifelong learning means self-directed growth in directions of our own choosing. It means understanding ourselves and the world ever more widely and deeply. It means acquiring new skills and powers—the only true wealth, the only wealth we can never lose. To become a lifelong learner is to become more alive. Each day becomes an adventure in discovery, challenging us to add to our experience and knowledge. Rather than a struggle within well-worn ruts, the passing weeks and months become milestones in constant exploration, inquiry, and development. John Gardner puts it eloquently in his depiction of the self-renewing person: "Exploration of the full range of [our] own potentialities is not something that [we] leave to the chances of life. It is something [we] pursue systematically, or at least avidly, to the end of [our] days."

Once we share that vision, we have a touchstone for the spirit that should inform all our endeavors to help adults learn and grow. Whatever courses or programs or conferences we plan, whatever subject or skills we teach, whatever organizational or communications media we use, it is that spirit that we must appeal to, instill, and express. Without it, our offerings become mere administrative shells.

2. *Lifelong learning is a perennial humanistic ideal, not merely a new educational concept.*

To many people in and out of education, lifelong learning is merely educationese for More School. To them, it is a fancy term for adults' returning to college, or taking some noncredit enrichment courses, or honing their professional skills and knowledge. That assumption is false. Whereas the ideal of universal schooling—of "teaching all things to all men"—derives from Comenius, the authentic tradition of lifelong learning stems from quite a different source, as Robert McClintock shows. It derives from the classical concept of self-formation that he calls *study.*

These historical niceties aside, the important point is that the concept behind lifelong learning is central to the Western intellectual tradition. One of its finest expressions in our time is Jacob Bronowski's book and television series *The Ascent of Man.* That concept would still animate much of what is best in our culture, whether or not people were enrolling for GEDs, external degrees, or continuing engineering education. In fact, to the degree that those enterprises are fulfilling their missions, they are undergirded, consciously or not, by that powerful commitment to a "democracy of intellect" combined with excellence based on knowledge that Bronowski exalted.

3. *Lifelong learning takes diverse forms, not one pattern.*

Each time a new program or pattern of adult education seizes on the label "lifelong learning," there is a tendency to equate it with that particular pattern. Even the excellent annual National Adult Education Conference cannot help but suggest to its participants that its deliberations encompass all of adult education in the United States; yet it barely concerns itself with, say, programs in libraries, which Fred Harrington rightly singles out as being among the major American achievements in the field.

The protean forms of lifelong learning can only be suggested, even in this volume, but some are alluded to in contributions ranging from Frank Adams's "Education in the Shoe Shop" to the other areas commended by

Fred Harrington. It is important to affirm such breadth in the range of lifelong learning forms and patterns. Only by keeping in mind their full scope can we remind ourselves, and convince others, of their great significance in American culture.

4. *Lifelong learning is an international movement, not an American invention.*

In other countries lifelong learning is increasingly recognized as a prime concern of those committed to enhancing the role of reason in national life. In nations as diverse as France, Denmark, Yugoslavia, China, and Tanzania, the first principle of educational theory and practice is that what we learn and what we become derive from the press of our entire social and cultural experience.

A proper concern for education, therefore, must far transcend preoccupation with schools and colleges. It must embrace not only continuing education of a formal or an informal kind, but also what the British cultural historian Raymond Williams calls "the whole environment, its institutions and relationships, [which] actively and profoundly teach." "Education permanente" is the label UNESCO has given to this broader set of concerns; it might also be described simply as learning and growth that are lifelong and lifewide, supported by a congenial environment of institutions and laws.

Americans have much to learn from the rest of the world. There are nations that lead us by far in enabling workers and professionals to update and change their skills constantly. Others, in the Third World, transcend us in evoking widespread support for high ideals of service and mutual help. And there are specific institutions, such as the Scandinavian folk schools and the study circles in those same countries, that we might do well to imitate.

Every adult educator should have an international perspective of the field, and there is no document worth closer study, for its importance in the field and to the world's future, than the UNESCO Declaration of Adult Education.

5. *Lifelong learning is both individual and communal, not just one or the other.*

There's a distinct tendency to polarize lifelong learning, thinking of it either as mainly initiated by an individual or as arranged by certain institutions. In truth, it's both. Learning is accomplished by individuals *and* is inherently social and interdependent. Only *we* can learn; no one can do it for us. But we need other people—both forebears and contemporaries—from which to learn most of the things we want and need to know in our lives. Maintaining a healthy balance in our attention to these two sides of the equation is one key to success in adult education.

That principle is best illustrated in "Success Stories of Adult Learning," where we see the interplay between personal motivation and institutional services. These sensitive portrayals bring to life the typical complexity of lifelong learning. Other contributors, such as Malcolm Knowles and even Ben Franklin, underscore the lesson.

In summary, lifelong learning entails a faith in people, not just a professional role. Competence alone is not sufficient in any of the helping professions, as Paul Halmos has shown in *The Faith of the Counselors*. The sine qua non of successful work with human beings is a commitment to them as individuals. In the field of adult education, where the stuff of our work is human potential itself, that is twice true. Competence defined as technique is not sufficient. Caring, commitment, even love must undergird and inform our skills.

Part I

THE GREAT TRADITION

The Ordeal and Ecstasy of Learning   One of the prisoners in an underground cave who have never seen anything more substantial than shadows is unchained and brought out into the blazing sunlight. At first he wants to withdraw from the painful brightness, but eventually he comes to realize that the vision of things as they really are is the only one for a human being. Now he resists returning to the cave and its world of illusion. But just as he had an undeniable right to find the truth, so he has an inescapable duty to go back and help others see through their illusions.

This unforgettable and endlessly suggestive parable is a basic source of the classical philosophy of education. Plato portrays the process of learning as an individual's radical encounter with a truth that exists independently of oneself. The process is, moreover, no mere preparation for a person's role in society. It is a lonely, harrowing experience through which each one frees his or her mind from the prejudices of those nearby and accepts responsibility for helping others achieve the same goal.

Obviously, such a conception of education goes far beyond the potentialities of what we usually think of as formal schooling. For Plato, one of the effects of true education is to make us profoundly dissatisfied with what we have previously been taught. While schools may be necessary to provide the rudiments and tools of learning, it is futile and dangerous to ask them to bring immature pupils to an awareness of the highest truths. Formal schooling should culminate not in a finished body of knowledge but in the mastery of a method for the lifelong pursuit of wisdom.

This selection is excerpted from Book VII of *The Republic,* Benjamin Jowett translation.

The Ordeal and Ecstasy of Learning

Plato

And now, I said, let me show in a parable what education means in human life. Behold! human beings living in an underground den, which has a mouth open towards the light and reaching all along the den; here they have been from their childhood, and have their legs and necks chained so that they cannot move, and can only see before them, being prevented by the chains from turning round their heads. Above and behind them a fire is blazing at a distance, and between the fire and the prisoners there is a raised way; and you will see, if you look, a low wall built along the way, like the screen which marionette players have in front of them, over which they show the puppets.

I see.

And do you see, I said, men passing along the wall carrying all sorts of vessels, and statues and figures of animals made of wood and stone and various materials, which appear over the wall? Some of them are talking, others silent.

You have shown me a strange image, and they are strange prisoners.

Like ourselves, I replied; and they see only their own shadows, or the shadows of one another, which the fire throws on the opposite wall of the cave?

True, he said; how could they see anything but the shadows if they were never allowed to move their heads?

And of the objects which are being carried in like manner they would only see the shadows?

Yes, he said.

And if they were able to converse with one another, would they not suppose that they were naming what was actually before them?

Very true.

And suppose further that the prison had an echo which came from the other side, would they not be sure to fancy when one of the passers-by spoke that the voice which they heard came from the passing shadow?

No question, he replied.

29

To them, I said, the truth would be literally nothing but the shadows of the images.

That is certain.

And now look again, and see what will naturally follow if the prisoners are released and disabused of their error. At first, when any of them is liberated and compelled suddenly to stand up and turn his neck round and walk and look towards the light, he will suffer sharp pains; the glare will distress him, and he will be unable to see the realities of which in his former state he had seen the shadows; and then conceive someone saying to him, that what he saw before was an illusion, but that now, when he is approaching nearer to being and his eye is turned towards more real existence, he has a clearer vision—what will be his reply? And you may further imagine that his instructor is pointing to the objects as they pass and requiring him to name them—will he not be perplexed? Will he not fancy that the shadows which he formerly saw are truer than the objects which are now shown to him?

Far truer.

And if he is compelled to look straight at the light, will he not have a pain in his eyes which will make him turn away to take refuge in the objects of vision which he can see, and which he will conceive to be in reality clearer than the things which are now being shown to him?

True, he said.

And suppose once more, that he is reluctantly dragged up a steep and rugged ascent, and held fast until he is forced into the presence of the sun himself, is he not likely to be pained and irritated? When he approaches the light his eyes will be dazzled, and he will not be able to see anything at all of what are now called realities.

Not all in a moment, he said.

He will require to grow accustomed to the sight of the upper world. And first he will see the shadows best, next the reflections of men and other objects in the water, and then the objects themselves; then he will gaze upon the light of the moon and the stars and the spangled heaven; and he will see the sky and the stars by night better than the sun or the light of the sun by day?

Certainly.

Last of all he will be able to see the sun, and not mere reflections of him in the water, but he will see him in his own proper place, and not in another; and he will contemplate him as he is.

Certainly.

He will then proceed to argue that this is he who gives the season and the years, and is the guardian of all that is in the visible world, and in a certain way the cause of all things which he and his fellows have been accustomed to behold?

Clearly, he said, he would first see the sun and then reason about him.

And when he remembered his old habitation, and the wisdom of the den and his fellow prisoners, do you not suppose that he would felicitate himself on the change, and pity them?

Certainly, he would.

And if they were in the habit of conferring honors among themselves on those who were quickest to observe the passing shadows and to remark which of them went before, and which followed after, and which were together; and who were therefore best able to draw conclusions as to the future, do you think that he would care for such honors and glories, or envy the possessors of them? Would he not say with Homer,

"Better to be the poor servant of a poor master,"

and to endure anything, rather than think as they do and live after their manner?

Yes, he said, I think that he would rather suffer anything than entertain these false notions and live in this miserable manner.

Imagine once more, I said, such a one coming suddenly out of the sun to be replaced in his old situation; would he not be certain to have his eyes full of darkness?

To be sure, he said.

And if there were a contest, and he had to compete in measuring the shadows with the prisoners who had never moved out of the den, while his sight was still weak, and before his eyes had become steady (and the time which would be needed to acquire this new habit of sight might be very considerable), would he not be ridiculous? Men would say of him that up he went and down he came without his eyes; and that it was better not even to think of ascending; and if any one tried to loose another and lead him up to the light, let them only catch the offender, and they would put him to death.

No question, he said.

This entire allegory, I said, you may now append, dear Glaucon, to the previous argument; the prison house is the world of sight, the light of the fire is the sun, and you will not misapprehend me if you interpret the journey upwards to be the ascent of the soul into the intellectual world according to my poor belief, which, at your desire, I have expressed— whether rightly or wrongly God knows. But, whether true or false, my opinion is that in the world of knowledge the idea of good appears last of all, and is seen only with an effort; and, when seen, is also inferred to be the universal author of all things beautiful and right, parent of light and of the lord of light in this visible world, and the immediate source of reason and truth in the intellectual; and that this is the power upon which he who would act rationally either in public or private life must have his eye fixed.

I agree, he said, as far as I am able to understand you.

Moreover, I said, you must not wonder that those who attain to this beatific vision are unwilling to descend to human affairs; for their souls are ever hastening into the upper world where they desire to dwell; which desire of theirs is very natural, if our allegory may be trusted.

Yes, very natural.

And is there anything surprising in one who passes from divine contemplations to the evil state of man, misbehaving himself in a ridiculous manner; if, while his eyes are blinking and before he has become accustomed to the surrounding darkness, he is compelled to fight in courts of law, or in other places, about the images or the shadows of images of justice, and is endeavoring to meet the conceptions of those who have never yet seen absolute justice?

Anything but surprising, he replied.

Any one who has common sense will remember that the bewilderments of the eyes are of two kinds, and arise from two causes, either from coming out of the light or from going into the light, which is true of the mind's eye, quite as much as of the bodily eye; and he who remembers this when he sees any one whose vision is perplexed and weak, will not be too ready to laugh; he will first ask whether that soul of man has come out of the brighter life, and is unable to see because unaccustomed to the dark, or having turned from darkness to the day is dazzled by excess of light. And he will count the one happy in his condition and state of being, and he will pity the other; or, if he have a mind to laugh at the soul which comes from below into the light, there will be more reason in this than in the laugh which greets him who returns from above out of the light into the den.

That, he said, is a very just distinction.

But then, if I am right, certain professors of education must be wrong when they say that they can put a knowledge into the soul which was not there before, like sight into blind eyes.

They undoubtedly say this, he replied.

Whereas, our argument shows that the power and capacity of learning exists in the soul already; and that just as the eye was unable to turn from darkness to light without the whole body, so too the instrument of knowledge can only by the movement of the whole soul be turned from the world of becoming into that of being, and learn by degrees to endure the sight of being, and of the brightest and best of being, or in other words, of the good.

Very true.

And must there not be some art which will effect conversion in the easiest and quickest manner; not implanting the faculty of sight, for that exists already, but has been turned in the wrong direction, and is looking away from the truth?

Yes, he said, such an art may be presumed.

And whereas the other so-called virtues of the soul seem to be akin to bodily qualities, for even when they are not originally innate they can be implanted later by habit and exercise, the virtue of wisdom more than anything else contains a divine element which always remains, and by this conversion is rendered useful and profitable; or, on the other hand, hurtful and useless. Did you never observe the narrow intelligence flashing from the keen eye of a clever rogue—how eager he is, how clearly his paltry soul sees the way to his end; he is the reverse of blind, but his keen eyesight is forced into the service of evil, and he is mischievous in proportion to his cleverness?

Very true, he said.

But what if there had been a circumcision of such natures in the days of their youth; and they had been severed from those sensual pleasures, such as eating and drinking, which, like leaden weights, were attached to them at their birth, and which drag them down and turn the vision of their souls upon the things that are below—if, I say, they had been released from these impediments and turned in the opposite direction, the very same faculty in them would have seen the truth as keenly as they see what their eyes are turned to now.

Very likely.

Yes, I said; and there is another thing which is likely, or rather a necessary inference from what has preceded, that neither the uneducated and uninformed of the truth, nor yet those who never make an end of their education, will be able ministers of State; not the former, because they have no single aim of duty which is the rule of all their actions, private as well as public; nor the latter, because they will not act at all except upon compulsion, fancying that they are already dwelling apart in the islands of the blest.

Very true, he replied.

Then, I said, the business of us who are the founders of the State will be to compel the best minds to attain that knowledge which we have already shown to be the greatest of all—they must continue to ascend until they arrive at the good; but when they have ascended and seen enough we must not allow them to do as they do now.

What do you mean?

I mean that they remain in the upper world: but this must not be allowed; they must be made to descend again among the prisoners in the den, and partake of their labors and honors, whether they are worth having or not.

But is not this unjust? he said; ought we to give them a worse life, when they might have a better?

You have again forgotten, my friend, I said, the intention of the legislator, who did not aim at making any one class in the State happy above the rest; the happiness was to be in the whole State, and he held the citizens together by persuasion and necessity, making them benefactors of the State, and therefore benefactors of one another; to this end he created them, not to please themselves, but to be his instruments in binding up the State.

True, he said, I had forgotten.

Observe, Glaucon, that there will be no injustice in compelling our philosophers to have a care and providence of others; we shall explain to them that in other States, men of their class are not obliged to share in the toils of politics: and this is reasonable, for they grow up at their own sweet will, and the government would rather not have them. Being self-taught, they cannot be expected to show any gratitude for a culture which they have never received. But we have brought you into the world to be rulers of the hive, kings of yourselves and of the other citizens, and have educated you far better and more perfectly than they have been educated, and you are better able to share in the double duty. Wherefore each of you, when his turn comes, must go down to the general underground abode, and get the habit of seeing in the dark. When you have acquired the habit, you will see ten thousand times better than the inhabitants of the den, and you will know what the several images are, and what they represent, because you have seen the beautiful and just and good in their truth.

We Humans Must Create Ourselves Are human beings unique among creatures? If so, in what way?

That question is still hotly debated in our own time, as behaviorists like B. F. Skinner contest with religious fundamentalists. One of the classic texts in this perennial debate is the *Oration on the Dignity of Man,* published in 1496, shortly after the death of its youthful author, Pico della Mirandola. This manifesto of the new humanism proclaimed a concept of human nature that informed the Renaissance and that resonates powerfully in existential and phenomenological philosophies of our own day.

Pico della Mirandola contended that the uniqueness of human beings lies in their capacity to determine their own nature. Rather than having a nature given at birth, like animals or, indeed, angels, human beings have the opportunity—and the inescapable responsibility—to create themselves. "Thou . . . art the molder and maker of thyself; thou mayest sculpt thyself into whatever shape thou dost prefer."

What better motto for the doorway of any adult education meeting place? And what better motto for each of our own private places of reflection?

This selection is excerpted from "A Speech by Giovanni Pico della Mirandola, Prince of Concord, on the Dignity of Man," from *Pico della Mirandola: On the Dignity of Man and Other Works,* published by the Library of Liberal Arts, the Bobbs Merrill Co., Inc., 1965. Translated by Glenn Wallis.

We Humans Must Create Ourselves

Pico della Mirandola

Most venerable fathers, I have read in the records of the Arabians that Abdul the Saracen, on being asked what thing on, so to speak, the world's stage, he viewed as most greatly worthy of wonder, answered that he viewed nothing more wonderful than man. And Mercury's, "a great wonder, Asclepius, is man!" agrees with that opinion.[1] On thinking over the reason for these sayings, I was not satisfied by the many assertions made by many men concerning the outstandingness of human nature: that man is the messenger between creatures, familiar with the upper and king of the lower; by the sharpsightedness of the senses, by the hunting-power of reason, and by the light of intelligence, the interpreter of nature; the part in between the standstill of eternity and the flow of time; and, as the Persians say, the bond tying the world together, nay, the nuptial bond; and, according to David, "a little lower than the angels."[2] These reasons are great but not the chief ones, that is, they are not reasons for a lawful claim to the highest wonder as to a prerogative. Why should we not wonder more at the angels themselves and at the very blessed heavenly choirs?

Finally, it seemed to me that I understood why man is the animal that is most happy, and is therefore worthy of all wonder; and lastly, what the state is that is allotted to man in the succession of things, and that is capable of arousing envy not only in the brutes but also in the stars and even in minds beyond the world. It is wonderful and beyond belief. For this is the reason why man is rightly said and thought to be a great marvel and the animal really worthy of wonder. Now hear what it is, fathers; and with kindly ears and for the sake of your humanity, give me your close attention:

Now the highest Father, God the master-builder, had, by the laws of his secret wisdom, fabricated this house, this world which we see, a very superb temple of divinity. He had adorned the super-celestial region with minds. He had animated the celestial globes with eternal souls; he had filled with a diverse throng of animals the cast-off and residual parts of

37

the lower world. But, with the work finished, the Artisan desired that there be someone to reckon up the reason of such a big work, to love its beauty, and to wonder at its greatness. Accordingly, now that all things had been completed, as Moses and Timaeus testify, He lastly considered creating man.[3] But there was nothing in the archetypes from which He could mold a new sprout, nor anything in His storehouses which He could bestow as a heritage upon a new son, nor was there an empty judiciary seat where this contemplator of the universe could sit. Everything was filled up; all things had been laid out in the highest, the lowest, and the middle orders. But it did not belong to the paternal power to have failed in the final parturition, as though exhausted by childbearing; it did not belong to wisdom, in a case of necessity, to have been tossed back and forth through want of a plan; it did not belong to the loving-kindness which was going to praise divine liberality in others to be forced to condemn itself. Finally, the best of workmen decided that that to which nothing of its very own could be given should be, in composite fashion, whatsoever had belonged individually to each and every thing. Therefore He took up man, a work of indeterminate form; and, placing him at the midpoint of the world, He spoke to him as follows:

"We have given to thee, Adam, no fixed seat, no form of thy very own, no gift peculiarly thine, that thou mayest feel as thine own, have as thine own, possess as thine own the seat, the form, the gifts which thou thyself shalt desire. A limited nature in other creatures is confined within the laws written down by Us. In conformity with thy free judgment, in whose hands I have placed thee, thou art confined by no bounds; and thou wilt fix limits of nature for thyself. I have placed thee at the center of the world, that from there thou mayest more conveniently look around and see whatsoever is in the world. Neither heavenly nor earthly, neither mortal nor immortal have We made thee. Thou, like a judge appointed for being honorable, art the molder and maker of thyself; thou mayest sculpt thyself into whatever shape thou dost prefer. Thou canst grow downward into the lower natures which are brutes. Thou canst again grow upward from thy soul's reason into the higher natures which are divine."

O great liberality of God the Father! O great and wonderful happiness of man! It is given him to have that which he chooses and to be that which he wills. As soon as brutes are born, they bring with them, "from their dam's bag," as Lucilius says, what they are going to possess.[4] Highest spirits have been, either from the beginning or soon after, that which they are going to be throughout everlasting eternity. At man's birth the Father placed in him every sort of seed and sprouts of every kind of life. The seeds that each man cultivates will grow and bear their fruit in him. If he cultivates vegetable seeds, he will become a plant. If the seeds of sensation, he will grow into brute. If rational, he will come out a heavenly animal. If intellectual, he will be an angel, and a son of God. And if he is not contented with the lot of any creature but takes himself up into the center of his own unity, then, made one spirit with God and settled in the solitary darkness of the Father, who is above all things, he will stand ahead of all things. Who does not wonder at this chameleon which we are? Or who at all feels more wonder at anything else whatsoever? It was not unfittingly that Asclepius the Athenian said that man was symbolized by Prometheus in the secret rites, by reason of our nature sloughing its skin and transforming itself; hence metamorphoses were popular among the Jews and the Pythagoreans. For the more secret Hebrew theology at one time reshapes holy Enoch into an angel of divinity, whom they call *malach hashechina*, and at other times reshapes other men into other divinities.[5] According to the Pythagoreans, wicked men are deformed into brutes and, if you believe Empedocles, into plants too.[6] And copying them, Maumeth [Mohammed] often had it on his lips that he who draws back from divine law becomes a brute. And his saying so was reasonable: for it is not the rind which makes the plant, but a dull and non-sentient nature; not the hide which makes a beast of burden, but a brutal and sensual soul; not the spherical body which makes the heavens, but right reason; and not a separateness from the body but a spiritual intelligence which makes an angel. For example, if you see a man given over to his belly and crawling upon the ground, it is a bush not a man that you see. If you see anyone blinded by the illusions of his empty and Calypso-like imagination, seized by the desire of scratching, and delivered over to the senses, it is a brute not a man that you see. If you come upon a philosopher winnowing out all things by right reason, he is a heavenly not an earthly animal. If you come upon a pure contemplator, ignorant of the body, banished to the innermost places of the mind, he is not an earthly, not a heavenly animal; he more superbly is a divinity clothed with human flesh.

Who is there that does not wonder at man? And it is not unreasonable that in the Mosaic and Christian holy writ man is sometimes denoted by the name "all flesh" and at other times by that of "every creature"; and man fashions, fabricates, transforms himself into the shape of all flesh, into the character of every creature.[7] Accordingly, where Evantes the Persian tells of the Chaldaean theology, he writes that man is not any inborn image of himself, but many images coming in from the outside: hence that saying of the Chaldaeans: *enosh hu shinuy vekamah tevaoth baal chayim*, that is, man is an animal of diverse, multiform, and destructible nature.

But why all this? In order for us to understand that, after having been born in this state so that we may be what we will to be, then, since we are held in honor, we ought to take particular care that no one may say against us that we do not know that we are made similar to brutes and mindless beasts of burden.[8] But rather, as Asaph the prophet says: "Ye are all gods, and sons of the most high," unless by abusing the very indulgent liberality of the Father, we make the free choice, which he gave to us, harmful to ourselves instead of helpful toward salvation.[9] Let a certain holy ambition invade the mind, so that we may not be content with mean things but may aspire to the highest things and strive with all our forces to attain them: for if we will to, we can. Let us spurn earthly things; let us struggle toward the heavenly. Let us put in last place whatever is of the world; and let us fly beyond the chambers of the world to the chamber nearest the most lofty divinity. There, as the sacred mysteries reveal, the seraphim, cherubim, and thrones occupy the first places. Ignorant of how to yield to them and unable to endure the second places, let us compete with the angels in dignity and glory. When we have willed it, we shall be not at all below them.

Notes

1. *Asclepius* I. 6 (*Hermetica,* ed. W. Scott, I, 294).
2. Psalms 8:5.
3. Plato, *Timaeus* 4lb ff.
4. Lucilius, *Satyrarum* VI (22), in Nonius Marcellus, *De compendiosa doctrina II* (Lindsay, I, 109).
5. Book of Enoch 40:8.
6. Empedocles, fr. 117 (Diels).
7. Genesis 6:12; Numbers 27:16; Mark 16:15.
8. Psalms 48:21 (King James Version, Psalms 49:20).
9. Psalms 81:6 (King James Version, Psalms 82:6) cs. John 10:34.

The Founding of the Junto   "If American adult educators want to select a hero from among the fathers of the nation," writes C. Hartley Grattan, "their choice must inevitably fall upon Franklin." But one's recollection of Franklin's *Autobiography* tends to fix on the account of his self-cultivation through *reading*. That is important, surely. But equally so was his initiation of *group* ventures, such as the Junto and local libraries. Indeed, the Junto is the forerunner of all those special interest groups (SIGs) that today are standard devices for mutual education within every major field and profession. It also links American adult education to that exciting new import from the Scandinavian countries: the study circles that are pervasive in those nations and that are currently burgeoning throughout the United States, stimulated by a project at the New York State Education Department under the direction of Norman Kurland.

This selection can be found under the title "A Founding Father as Adult Educator," in *American Ideas About Adult Education, 1710-1951,* edited by C. Hartley Grattan and published by Teachers College Press, 1959. It was excerpted in that book from Benjamin Franklin's *Autobiography,* originally published in America in 1818.

The Founding of the Junto

Benjamin Franklin

I should have mentioned before, that, in the autumn of the preceding year, I had form'd most of my ingenious acquaintance into a club of mutual improvement, which we called the JUNTO; we met on Friday evenings. The rules that I drew up required that every member, in turn, should produce one or more queries on any point of Morals, Politics, or Natural Philosophy, to be discuss'd by the company; and once in three months produce and read an essay of his own writing, on any subject he pleased. Our debates were to be under the direction of a president, and to be conducted in the sincere spirit of inquiry after truth, without fondness for dispute, or desire of victory; and, to prevent warmth, all expressions of positiveness in opinions, or direct contradiction, were after some time made contraband, and prohibited under small pecuniary penalties.

About this time, our club meeting, not at a tavern, but in a little room of Mr. Grace's, set apart for that purpose, a proposition was made by me, that, since our books were often referr'd to in our disquisitions upon the queries, it might be convenient to us to have them altogether where we met, that upon occasion they might be consulted; and by thus clubbing our books to a common library, we should, while we lik'd to keep them together, have each of us the advantage of using the books of all the other members, which would be nearly as beneficial as if each owned the whole. It was lik'd and agreed to, and we fill'd one end of the room with such books as we could best spare. The number was not so great as we expected; and tho' they had been of great use, yet some inconveniences occurring for want of due care of them, the collection, after about a year, was separated, and each took his books home again.

And now I set on foot my first project of a public nature, that for a subscription library. I drew up the proposals, got them put into form by our great scrivener, Brockden, and, by the help of my friends in the Junto, procured fifty subscribers of forty shillings each to begin with, and ten shillings a year for fifty years, the term our company was to continue. We afterwards obtain'd a charter, the company being increased to one hundred: this was the mother of all the North American subscription libraries, now so numerous. It is become a great thing itself, and continually increasing. These libraries have improved the general conversation of the Americans, made the common tradesmen and farmers as intelligent as most gentlemen from other countries, and perhaps have contributed in some degree to the stand so generally made throughout the colonies in defense of their privileges.

Reaffirming a Great Tradition   This book lacks the space for a full-scale presentation of the great tradition of humanistic thought that affirms the reality and importance of lifelong learning. But this brilliant essay by Professor Robert McClintock of Teacher's College, Columbia, distills that wisdom and projects it provocatively into the future.

In using the word *study* as his central concept, the author designates that classical conception of how each of us grows and fulfills his or her potentialities through "a life of continuous self-education," "a continuous heightening of consciousness, an unceasing sharpening of judgment," and not through "a training administered by some external teacher, but a self-imposed bringing of one's mental powers to their full potential, as an athlete in training brings his physical powers to a peak." That is what education meant to our intellectual forebears, McClintock insists. When they spoke about education, they meant *that*, not being taught, not attending school or college, not amassing credits and diplomas.

If, as Malcolm Knowles argues, andragogy is what comes *after* the educational era of pedagogy, study is what came *before* our present era dominated by instruction.

This is no mere antiquarian exercise. McClintock spells out some revolutionary implications of seeing study as the center and epitome of education. And recent research by such investigators as Allen Tough has propelled adult education toward a keener appreciation of this classical truth: The source of success in lifelong learning lies within the individual.

This selection is excerpted from "Toward a Place for Study in a World of Instruction," in *Teachers College Record,* December 1971, vol. 73, no.2.

Reaffirming a Great Tradition

Robert McClintock

"Preserve measure, observe the limit, and follow nature." This line from Lucian was one of fifty-seven favored phrases that Montaigne inscribed upon his study wall.[1] All offer terse advice, one man to another, on the discipline of life: resist illusion, aspire to humility, beware vanity, judge cautiously, love mankind but be not its dupe. A series of sayings from sources both familiar and obscure: they are a key to our past, a sign of its character, frailty, and future.

Fifty-seven sayings upon the wall, upon the *study* wall. A skeptical, ironical egoist, Montaigne was but one vital vector in the myriad of human lives. Still, he stands out as a significant person, advantaged to be sure, but accomplished as well; and both his advantages and his accomplishments were what they became because he sustained himself in a life of continuous self-education. The sobering sentences that surrounded Montaigne as he worked helped direct and sustain his formation of self; they reinforced a regimen of self-culture, speaking to him sagely as he cut his quill, shelved a book, stoked his stove, or gazed in silent introspection. Such sayings were the stuff of pedagogical philosophy, classically conceived. Such sayings set forth the ends and means of study, of meditation, inquiry, and self-formation.

Study, inward driven study, was no mere private matter for Montaigne: it is a theme that pervades his essays. For him, education was a continuous heightening of consciousness, an unceasing sharpening of judgment. When he spoke "Of Training," it was not a training administered by some external teacher, but a self-imposed bringing of one's mental powers to their full potential, as an athlete in training brings his physical powers to a peak. He admired Canius Julius, an unfortunate Roman noble wrongly condemned by Caligula. Canius spent his last moments bringing his attention to the full alert so that as the ax cut he could perceive the nature of dying. To celebrate this example, Montaigne quoted Lucan: "That mastery of mind he had in death."[2]

47

Like a number of the ancients, especially the stoical Seneca, Montaigne cautioned against reliance on teachers in the course of education. Passive knowing was less important than the work of finding out, and authoritative instruction simply put the youthful mind to rest. Teaching and learning might impart knowledge, whereas study led to understanding, whereby things known were made one's own and became a part of one's judgment, and "education, labor, and study aim only at forming that." Yes, Montaigne went to school, to the College de Guienne, the best in France, at a precocious six. "At thirteen . . . I had completed my course (as they call it), and, in truth, without any benefit that I can now take into account." Like many students of today and yore, Montaigne shirked his assignments, instead reading avidly Virgil, Terence, Plautus, and other authors that struck his, not his teachers', fancy. When mature, Montaigne remembered the wisdom of one instructor, "who knew enough to connive cleverly at this escapade of mine. . . . Pretending to see nothing, he whetted my appetite, allowing me to devour these books only on the sly and holding me gently at my job on the regular studies."[3] Whether in or out of school, education for Montaigne was a process of self-set study, not of learning the lessons that others prescribed.

Montaigne, moreover, was not alone in preferring a theory of study to a theory of teaching. In his taste for improving mottoes, he was of his time and of his tradition. Erasmus is a case in point. Not a few of Montaigne's fifty-seven sentences had appeared among the 4,251 that Erasmus collected and elucidated in his vast work, the *Adages*, a crescent compendium that he meant to "be neither unprofitable nor unpleasing" for those who would study the ways and the wisdom of the ancients.[4]

Erasmus wrote for men studying. The bulk and the best of his work he designed to provide others in all manner of situations with matter worthy of study. "He whose single aim it is, not to exhibit himself, but to do some good to others, is not concerned so much with the splendour of the matters in which he is engaged, as with their utility; and I shall not refuse any task . . . , if I see that it will conduce to the promotion of honest study."[5]

With this sentiment, Erasmus turned himself into the great printer-pedagogue, the first tycoon of the text. His was a life well-timed; he had the fortune, the genius, to first put a heritage into print, magnificently facilitating the studies of others. Usually ensconced in one or another printing house, where the best libraries were then to be found, Erasmus proved himself the exemplary editor of all time. Little of his work was original, yet his spirit was strong all the same, for it turned the seeds of others into fruit: he transformed the oral medieval tradition, the newly dynamic classical literature, and even the consecrated works of the Church; he adapted all for publication, each as befit the type, revising, translating, reorganizing, elucidating, collating, emending, correcting, perfecting—in sum, preparing the texts for profitable study by a growing reading public.

To begin, *de Copia* was a straightforward text on how to study, not only the teacher's lessons, but more essentially the rhetorical riches to be found in the school of life.[6] Then, second, Erasmus labored unceasingly as an editor of both pagan and Christian classics. As a result, in theology he won fame, not for doctrines duly devised and taught, but for his scholarly editions of the New Testament and the Church fathers, which enlivened history by much facilitating the independent studies of others.[7] Likewise, Erasmus' reputation as a learned humanist primarily rested, not on his own work, but on his editorial industry, for he put into print writings by Ausonius, Cicero, Quintus Curtius, Horace, Livy, Ovid, Persius, Plautus, Pliny, Seneca, Suetonius, Publius Syrus, and Terence; Aesop, Aristotle, Demosthenes, Euripides, Galen, Isocrates, Josephus, Libanius, Lucian, Plutarch, Ptolemy, and Xenophon.[8] To be sure, many of these works found their way into the classroom of the school, but their prime justification was to provide more readers with more literature worthy of personal study.

In writing, too, Erasmus showed clearly his commitment to study and self-formation. His first fame came from the *Enchiridion,* or *The Handbook of the Christian Knight,* which he wrote—with rather medieval moralizing about the war of virtues and vices—to help wayward courtiers win their self-possession. This dagger, as it could be called, he fashioned for a man who "was no one's enemy so much as his own, a man of dissolute life, but in other respects an agreeable companion"; the writer hoped that on some morning after the reader would resolve to "achieve a character acceptable of Christ," and that in the pursuit of this resolve the writer's precepts might prove of use.[9] *The Praise of Folly* and *The Education of a Christian Prince* had similar aims but different methods. In the former, Erasmus used satire and negative models, not to point the way to a character acceptable to Christ, but to explode the manifold self-deceptions by which men smugly shirk the endless difficulties of mastering humble excellence.[10] In the latter, Erasmus built on the Platonic convention, putting before everyman a regimen of political self-formation through the literary artifice of describing an ideal education that might give rise to a perfect prince.[11]

Erasmus shows how an educator who dedicates his labor to the man studying can find variety and vitality within his unitary purpose. The active spirit can learn something from everything. The Erasmian ideal is not that of dead pedantry; it is antithetical to learning by rote. He who would get the most from study must be willing to give unceasing effort, a protean effort that is ever adapted to the matter at hand, savoring a joke with mirth, applying a precept with wisdom, proving a truth with learning. Thus, Erasmus' labor of leisure, the *Colloquies,* had an extraordinary duality of intent—simultaneously to provide adults with recreational reading and schoolboys with grammatical exercises. With the art of the satirical moralist, he recorded scenes from life around him, larding them with models of good Latin, proper manners, and a living wit. He composed these dialogues to repay his open art of study, which included both discipline and delight: "you must discipline your character in order to win self-control and to find delight in things productive of utility rather than [of] pleasure. . . . . For my part, I know no other art of learning than hard work, devotion, and perseverance."[12]

Some may say that this passage admits a rather faint delight and so it might seem to those who torpidly find satisfaction in happenstance pleasures. But the artful hedonist, like most others, closely calculates utilities, and delight *is* most often found in things of use to an active spirit, not in things pleasurable to a voluptuous passivity. Men work hard at play, they persevere at sport, they are devoted to a laugh. Utility has many shapes and the effort to win self-control is exerted differently in different situations. The ways of study are as diverse as the ways of men, for both result, not from conformity to outward percept, but from the aspiration to assert inward control over the moving conjunction between one's self and one's circumstances.

Study—if all follow it to its highest end—may have a single goal, or so we Platonists believe; but the path, the course of study, that leads to the goal will differ for each: thus the study appropriate for the quiet cleric will not suit the proud prince, the worldly merchant, or the sturdy artisan. Study itself is neither a single path nor the final goal; it is the motivating power by which men form and impose their character upon their role in life. Through study each man reaches out to the resources of nature, faith, and reason, to select from them as best seems to suit his situation and to develop powers by which he can turn the accidents of time, place, and station into a work of achieved intention. In this art of study, each component of culture has a part to play, and every component of art, literature, science, and thought can be seen as educational in a rigorous sense. In one of these, which well illustrates my point, Erasmus was a giant.

From Theognis through Valerius Maximus right down to John Bartlett and his compendium of *Familiar Quotations,* there stretches a continuous tradition, a wisdom literature for the busy man of affairs. As the hurried man is a perennial type—one now encounters specimens bedecked in beard, long hair, and beads—he is not about to disappear, and hence he has his claim on culture. Therefore, we may perhaps object to the inelegance of Bartlett's work. Whereas its mechanical listing of sayings, with little concern for context or connection, reduces it to an efficient work of reference, and little more, its great predecessors encouraged haphazard reading, and thus they served both as works of reference and as regaling bedtime books, as improving recreation for any idle moment.[13] But still, in substance and function, Bartlett's *Quotations* is of a piece with Erasmus' *Adages* and *Apothegms.* And we, who are wont to sneer at rushed seers who mine their erudition from Bartlett's pages, might consider Erasmus' preface to his *Apothegms,* for there he offered the pedagogical justification for all such works.

Erasmus dedicated the *Apothegms* to the son of a friendly duke with the hope that the work would prove useful in the education of the duke-to-be. For the learned, Erasmus avowed, the moral writings of Plato, Aristotle, and Cicero were the most instructive, but these repaid only careful, extended study, the kind of study for which busy men had neither the time nor the taste. Was all then lost? Must power be the province of the boor? He thought not. The ancients had another tradition of moral learning, the apothegm, "which in a few words does rather by a color signify than plainly express a sense . . . , and which the longer you do consider it in your mind, the more and more does it still delight you."[14] Such apothegms were the studies suited to buoyant spirits who would learn best with a laugh, a frown, and a pouting smirk. From these studies, from these recreations taken up with ease in unexpected pauses, active people could acquire a vital wisdom with which to manage the affairs of life. The work was an educative treatise, a book to be lived with, mulled, and internalized; Erasmus offered it to the prince and the ubiquitous adolescent, "to all children and young striplings that labor and sue to attain the knowledge of good learning and honest studies."[15]

Whenever education functions primarily as a process of study, adages, sentences, commonplaces, apothegms serve as a staple substance in popular education, in the education of busy people of every type. Here, however, a question may be raised whether in fact this education is a popular education or whether perhaps self-set study is an education designed to perpetuate privilege and to create elites. By its means, the rich may get richer, the powerful more powerful, the cultured more cultured, while the common man gets more common yet. For instance, during the period separating Hesiod's *Works and Days* and Franklin's Preface to *Poor Richard's Almanac*, most collections of wise saws and modern instances were compiled for men in high places, in places at least as high as that of Shakespeare's justice. Pithy wisdom easily catered to the powerful. Thus, during the twelfth-century Renaissance, William of Conches compiled a book of moral extracts for the future Henry II of England.[16] Thus too, Erasmus told how proud Caesar would copy down every wise riposte he heard, and when a specially barbed insult would be directed at him, he would react, not with anger, but with delight, noting down the phrase, eagerly awaiting the moment when he could return it with barb yet further sharpened.[17]

Even in its most open components, the tradition of self-culture has seemed allied to elitism. Hence, we shall have to return to the question whether self-education through personal study is intrinsically an education for the privileged, and incompatible with the democratic ethos of modern life, or whether it merely appeared to have been so because its more eminent exponents happened to have lived in times and places where none imagined that privilege would pass. This problem will be a proper concern while assessing the present-day state of study, but to dwell on it here, while considering the historic character of study, would project an anachronistic concern back into the past.

Study as Education

Whether we like it or not, many former educators considered education to consist of neither teaching nor learning; instead, they found the diverse forms of study to be the driving force in education. We could considerably extend our sense for the diversity of forms that this study could take by dwelling further on the Renaissance. To begin we might read carefully the letter that Pantagruel received from his Rabelaisian father, Gargantua. Then we might assay *The Benefit of a Liberal Education* as Robert Pace perceived it; ascetics could also try *The Spiritual Exercises* suggested by Ignatius Loyola, and the aspiring could emulate the arts and ideals of the courtier, as well as his amusements, that Castiglione portrayed. Aesthetes might observe the profound blend of pagan and Christian iconography that Italian artists worked into scenes seemingly so realistic, while the responsible could practice the political pedagogy propounded by Sir Thomas Elyot's *Book Named the Governor*. Finally, summing it up, we might all savour the bittersweet wisdom that Cervantes hoped his readers would extract from his *Exemplary Novels* and the adventures of *Quixote*.[18] Such a survey, however, would simply display more and more of the innumerable uses to which study would be put; yet men relied on study not only because it suited many uses, but more importantly, because it seemed to them to be in accord with the intrinsic character of human life.

Many held that study was not only a convenient form of education, but that it was the essential basis of all education. This conviction developed as men dwelt on human individuality, autonomy, and creativity. Considering each man in his living particularity, he was more than the sum of the influences playing upon him; rather each made himself individual by responding freely and creatively to his mundane problems, great and small. In this self-formation each man appropriated ideas and skills, tastes and beliefs from the world around him, doing so with a certain selectivity, even on the part of the most humble: this selectivity was the great conundrum to be understood. Did the teacher make the choices that guide the learner? Sometimes, perhaps; but not always, and perhaps not usually: instead there seemed to be an inward, almost inborn power of judgment in every man—as it directed the man would attend. To those who thus recognized each person's autonomy of judgment, education could only incidentally be a process of teaching and learning; more essentially, it had to be a zig-zag process of trial and error, of studious, self-directed effort by which an inchoate, infantile power of judgment slowly gave itself form, character, perhaps even a transcendent purpose. This effort was study in its most general sense.

Socrates was the first educator, of those whose work we know, to have based his practice on the primacy of study, and Plato was the first theorist to have abstracted from that practice a complete theory of education through study. Here the historian meets a subtle problem, the problem inherent in all efforts to teach: he cannot by himself communicate an understanding of the importance of study; he can only remind others of the doctrines, which they must put to the test of their own judgment and experience. So too Plato cautioned his readers against believing in the adequacy of his words; words alone could not teach, although they might prompt recognition and help us discover what deep down we know, provided we are willing to study the matter, to question, inquire, weigh, conclude, and question anew. Plato, the poet, practiced his doctrine: within his writings, therefore, one encounters numerous contradictions that draw the thoughtful reader into the labor of dialectical study. For instance, with respect to the theme of education, Plato wrote striking passages that seem to counsel a most paternal instruction. At the same time, he hinted that these passages were not to be taken too literally, and his invitation still stands—for any who judge that they may profit from the effort—to give it trial and to study the problem themselves. In doing so, they will experience the heuristic pedagogy that is the mission of philosophy.[19]

Historically, what Plato hoped to achieve by prescribing a program of instruction for his guardians matters little. Plato had scant effect on programmatic practice, for practice was shaped instead by Isocrates and the Sophists. What Plato did accomplish, however, was to influence educational theory through a number of his most characteristic doctrines, which all coincided in suggesting that meaningful education could result only from personal study, from inwardly directed inquiry. In his theory, Plato preferred neither general education nor technical training; his doctrines were amenable to both, and to much else, too, provided that in all cases the condition of the student was recognized concretely, and not by means of thoughtless stereotype, and that the initiative of study was always left with the man studying. These stipulations rested on Plato's most important convictions.

First, the Socrates of historic influence, the hero of the early dialogues, depicted himself explicitly as the spiritual midwife, the teacher who could not teach but who could help another give birth to his soul; Plato immortalized this Socrates as the Delphic martyr, the inspiring questioner who provoked others to know that they did not know and thus to join the thoughtful search for self. Second, the doctrine of recollection asserted that words could teach only more words, that all comprehension of things, be they corporal or intelligible, derived not from words but from prior experience with the things and from inward reflection about them; this doctrine was an early, profound, yet unsatisfactory, effort to make sense of the unsolved mystery of creative thinking, thinking by which men really learn.

Third, the fervid god, Eros, denoted the expectant, fecund force that stimulates man's craving urge, drawing men towards all forms of perfection; thus ardent attraction and vaulting aspiration were unconditioned, they existed in the eager eyes of the beholder; this Platonic eroticism, this insatiable, polymorphous teleology, has not been bettered as an explanation of the student's essential power, his selective attention. Fourth, the theory of forms presented a reasoned idea of transcendent perfection; its metaphysical fruits and difficulties have been great, but its pedagogical implications were clear as they took hold in diverse systems: superficial opinion and commonplace discourse were estranged from reality and hence neither could teach; rather men learned from the ideas, from the logos, principle, reason, form, law—natural or divine—for in searching incessantly for the stable idea behind every appearance men would find form in the flux around and within them. Men in search of wisdom would study form in life, form in their lives, converting the chaos to a cosmos; all else was either preparation or slack evasion.

What these convictions implied for educational doctrine Plato best summed up in his allegory of the cave. Vital truths, he stipulated, could not be taught; they could be learned only through the pains of uncertain, unconditioned, open study, for which every man had the capacity but not necessarily the will. "We must conclude that education is not what it is said to be by some, who profess to put knowledge into a soul which does not possess it, as if they could put sight into blind eyes. On the contrary, our own account signifies that the soul of every man does possess the power of learning the truth and the organ to see it with; and that, just as one might have to turn the whole body round in order that the eye should see light instead of darkness, so the entire soul must be turned away from this changing world, until its eye can bear to contemplate reality and that supreme splendour which we have called the Good."[20] Teachers, Plato added, could not fruitfully instruct those who would not teach themselves, who would only respond passively to the most convenient appearance; the most teachers could do was to convert such inert souls to active study. This theory of teaching has sunk deep into our philosophical heritage, but it has not fared well in practice.

After Plato

Before charting the historic swings between Platonic pedagogy and didactic instruction, before, that is, observing the practical frailty of study, let us note two cautions: what follows is a point of view that should not be confused with the past itself, and what follows is meant to celebrate any form of schooling, even pedantic instruction, provided that it is energized by the aspiring student. A world of instruction does not include all efforts at schooling; rather, it includes those that do not believe that the students' active studying is the essential educative power. Schooling that respects the autonomy of study, even though it might deal with study in a quite formal, disciplinary way, should not be confused with a system of instruction, a system of injecting knowledge into inert and empty spirits. Schooling keyed to the self-active student is properly part of the world of study. For this reason the guiding principle in a world of instruction should be understood to be, not schooling, but the delusion that the teacher, on his own initiative, can shape plastic pupils and unilaterally fill their vacant slates with the wisdom of the ages.

Further, in opposing a world of study to a world of instruction, I write primarily as a critic, not as a Rankean historian who aspires to describe the past in all its details as it actually was. At any time, real life is infinitely complicated; it is all things imaginable and cannot be summed up under any single heading. Amidst this complexity, instruction and study at all times co-exist; they will always both be present in varying proportions in all educational phenomena. Consequently, to characterize a particular time and place as either a world of study or one of instruction is to make a defensible judgment about the dominant tone in its educational practice; it is not to make an exclusive description that must hold absolutely with respect to all particulars. And further, the purpose of making such a judgment is not to assert a real, implacable progression in history, as it were, for such progressions are but specters conjured up by scholars turned prophets in order to harry the probity of practice. The purpose of estimating the pedagogical character of various periods is critical; it is to provoke and evoke a sharpened awareness of past, present, and future. By putting the case for a particular characterization as compellingly as possible, one challenges the proponents of contrary views, which may have grown slack for want of opposition, to look at the past anew, to revise or revive their convictions as they then see fit. To put the case for study vis-à-vis an excess of instruction is not to deny categorically the value of instruction, but to try to save it from its own prodigality, for instruction will not suffice to the near exclusion of study.

Those who doubt this proposition might attend to the classical experience. As small cities grew into giant empires, the reliance on instruction waxed. To be sure, here and there the post-Platonic theorists—whether Stoic or Epicurean, skeptic or cynic—preferred to stimulate and assist the inquisitive few, or at most to shock the stolid into self-sustaining doubt. But in far higher numbers, and with greater prestige and influence, the ancient practitioners took up Sophistic rhetoric with didactic diligence. Imperial expansion always creates a heavy demand for paternal schooling; dependably, the gracious government, the magnanimous military, and the many, well-regulated enterprises that sustain their noble efforts all send forth frequent calls for functionaries. Dutifully responding, educators in the Hellenistic and Roman empires created worlds of instruction in which the schoolmen flourished. As never before in the West, they became honored servants of a paternal state, disbursers of coveted skills, the Charons ferrying fated spirits over the Styx of success. "Hellenism," an authority states, "has world-historical significance in the full sense only as an educational power. This was in great part the result of a new valuation and use of training."[21]

In this world of instruction, this scribal culture as H. I. Marrou has termed it, paternal teachers flourished until . . . their profligate pedantries consumed the capital of the pagan spirit, a capital that had been slowly built up by the chancy, passionate labors of great men studying. Greek and Roman authors had movingly hallowed the aspiring spirit. But the imperial scale, especially in late Rome, overwhelmed creative effort; talent became degraded as the ersatz esteem of affluent crowds jumped from one empty idol to the next. With self-important caution, the schools won munificent patronage while they adroitly managed to transmit a sycophantic mediocrity from one generation to another. Among the well-instructed, deep thought earned suspicion; to speak truly was imprudent where so many could flatter with finesse. The house of intellect ceased to be a home; it became a whoring road to preferment or to ruin. The young would mock the endless hypocrisies of this righteous sham, until their turn would come to heed the Imperial call: then they too would don their mask according to their rank. Thus sorely used, the state schools became sites of tumult; scholars gave way to placemen who vied for the patronage of the powerful; sincere instruction gave way to entertainment, an aimless effort to gain and hold the fleet attention of the aimless.[22]

Instruction did not suffice; it left too little room for human doubt, inquiry, uncertainty, the search for self. One by one, more and more, men gave up the sham in this way or that. Hollow figures filled each empty office, and thus the spirit rebelled against the sword. Classical paganism, equipped with an apparatus of self-propagation unmatched until modern times, could not command allegiance. With mounting frequency, in every order of the state, for good reasons and for bad, a miraculous series of personal conversions occurred: ineluctably the triumphant idea of Rome, the universal city, withered and gave way to love for the wretched victim, to belief in the martyred God and in his martyred followers with their subversive strength in weakness, and to hope for a personal salvation through the grace of an unfathomable father, son, and holy ghost.

From the start, Christianity was a religion of considerable complexity; it harbored diverse, divergent tendencies. Be that as it may, at least in that portion of Christianity that became dominant as Western Catholicism, there was considerable respect for the Platonic view of education, for no matter how much ritual might help, in the end—before one's end—the spirit had to move communicants from within. Mechanistic behaviorism could not suffice for teachings meant to redeem the soul. Consequently, the Apostolic Church functioned strangely like an institutionalized Socrates: at its best it did remarkably little instructing and a great deal of reminding. Rome withered, and, together, chance and the Church turned the ancient world of instruction into the medieval and Renaissance world of study.

Augustine set the tone. His *Confessions* reveal the inward struggle of the honest student, the demanding search for a sense of significance, the ever-recurring need for *relevance*.[23] And in *De magistro*, he gave a rationally rigorous Christian statement of the Platonic theory of study. He began with an inquiry into the limits of speech, respect for which gave rise to his carefully limited conception of instruction. Formal teaching must occur through words and other signs; but words do not by themselves give an understanding of their referents, the physical and intellectual things they signify. Rather it is quite the reverse: only with a prior personal comprehension of the thing can we make sense of the sign; hence people learn by judging what others say according to their inner sense of truth. "All those sciences which they profess to teach, and the science of virtue itself and wisdom, teachers explain through words. Then those who are called pupils consider within themselves whether what has been explained has been said truly; looking, of course, to that interior truth, according to the measure of which each is able. Thus they learn. . . ."[24]

And truly, thus they learned. In far off Ireland, in isolated monasteries, a heritage passed from student to student according to an intense, convoluted, runic measure. As monasteries multiplied, their scriptoria slowly enlarged the repertory of texts, which they so carefully *manu*factured so that the precious books might be studied over centuries. Devout artists learned to transmute words into pictures of paint and stone so that more people might measure their meaning according to the interior truth. The urge to study touched not only the devout; Charlemagne called Alcuin to his court so that the worldly might better discipline both their speech and their conduct. Despite setbacks, the urge to study spread to the Ottonian north, to the Norman south, and along the Romanesque routes of pilgrimage; and when the medieval world burst into the Gothic era of dynamic expansion, study flourished in that fast growing institution, the *studium generale,* or as we call it, the university. Here, students gathered from across Europe to listen to the doctors, the learned ones, and to test their wit and knowledge in the clash of disputation.

Make no mistake, this world of study harbored a significant but subordinate place for instruction, which instruction kept well through the Renaissance. Despite the limits that Augustine put on teaching, he did much to make room in the Christian system for the classical curriculum of rhetorical instruction, the circle of studies that was coming to be known as the seven liberal arts. Throughout the Middle Ages, these were celebrated in poetry, iconography, and learned treatises; these were the stuff of the young cleric's early education, his prelude to independent inquiry and self-sustained study. Unfortunately, the elementary arts were a drudge to study; they were at once difficult and dull. Therefore, regardless of the age at which students took up these studies, and it might be at any time from six to twenty-six, a teacher was an important aid, not because he could ease the students' ways with lucid explanations, but because he could pace and regulate their work and, with sermon and ferrule, stiffen their flagging wills to get done with the dreadful task. The teacher was the *magister,* the master, the director of the *ludus,* the place where the body or the mind was exercised. Thus the school, the *ludus literarius,* was a place for literary exercise, and that is precisely what early schooling involved, a set of exercises that helped students acquire command of the elementary arts.

Trivial Teachers

Bluntly put, in the world of study that existed until modern times, teaching was trivial; that is, teaching was trivial in the rigourous sense: it pertained primarily to the trivium, to regulating a student's elementary exercises in grammar, logic, and rhetoric.

Trivial teachers had the self-effacing mission of making themselves unnecessary. The young needed help and discipline in working their way through the first steps of study, in acquiring the basic tools without which all else would be arcane. The teacher, the master of exercises, gave indispensible aid in making that acquisition; but as soon as it was made the student would give up studying the elementary arts and go on to more important matters. Reliance on the brute discipline doled out by the master of exercises was demeaning, and numerous sources show how men believed it to be important to get done with the arts, to end dependence on magisterial instruction so that one could begin to study freely, as curiosity dictated, and so that one could do it with dignity, without the humiliating discipline of the master of exercises.

For instance, Seneca derided those who took pride in being occupied with the liberal studies; one should work instead to be done with them, for no good came of them themselves; rather, they served simply as a preparation for the truly serious matter of self-formation.[25] The same valuation can be found in Augustine's remark that, even though he was able to master the liberal arts without the aid of a teacher, he found little value in them per se.[26] In the Middle Ages John of Salisbury explicitly stated the self-effacing mission of the teacher when he answered the question why some arts were called liberal by observing that "those to whom the system of the Trivium has disclosed the significance of all words, or the rules of the Quadrivium have unveiled the secrets of all nature, do not need the help of a teacher in order to understand the meaning of books and to find the solutions of questions."[27] This same desire to end one's dependence on one's teachers was implicit in the way the Renaissance educator, Batista Guarino, recommended his course of studies: "a master who should carry his scholars through the curriculum which I have now laid down may have confidence that he has given them a training which will enable them, not only to carry forward their own reading without assistance, but also to act efficiently as teachers in their turn."[28] To a remarkable degree the trivial teachers of the Middle Ages and Renaissance agreed with Plato that their job was not "to put knowledge into a soul which does not possess it"; rather, they simply directed, disciplined, and exercised the inborn organ of learning possessed by every man.

As a consequence of this view, educational theorists in the world of study had no difficulty denoting as potential or actual educators all sorts of people who made no claim to imparting knowledge, for these theorists saw that it was not only the schoolmaster who put a man's capacity for learning through a constructive or destructive sequence of exercise. If we were to pursue this observation to the full richness of its implications, we would have to witness the medieval morality plays, study the doctrines of virtues and vices, and follow how they were used to explain the degradation and the elevation of character in works such as Dante's *Divine Comedy*.[29]

But by understanding the teacher as a master of exercises, and not as an imparter of knowledge, old-time theorists were also able to identify a most varied group of potential educators in a more narrow sense. Thus, a number of books called "the schoolmaster" were intended only in part to be used by masters of actual schools; in the other part, the authors were using the schoolmaster as a literary device for explaining the sequence of exercises for those who would oversee students who were to labor on the elementary matters at home or in the apprentice shop. For instance, Roger Ascham did not write *The Schoolmaster* only to improve class-room practices; his book was "specially purposed for the private bringing up of youth in gentlemen and noble men's houses, and commodious also for all such, as have forgot the Latin tongue, and would by themselves, without a schoolmaster, in short time, and with small pains, recover a sufficient hability, to understand, write, and speak Latin."[30] Edmund Coote soon extended this genre to a more popular audience with *The English Schoolmaster*, which was specially purposed for providing the hard-working artisan with a vernacular tool of self-instruction.[31]

As a result of this flexibility, which inhered in the triviality of teaching, schooling keyed to study—schooling based on a system of exercises, not on the impartation of knowledge—could be found occurring most any-where, for most anyone could regulate the regimen. This fact made possi-ble what Lawrence A. Cremin has found for the seventeenth-century American colonies, namely "that schooling went on anywhere and every-where, not only in schoolrooms, but in kitchens, manses, churches, meet-inghouses, sheds erected in fields, and shops erected in towns; that pupils were taught by anyone and everyone, not only by schoolmasters, but by parents, tutors, clergymen, lay readers, precentors, physicians, lawyers, artisans, and shopkeepers; and that most teaching proceeded on an indi-vidual basis, so that whatever lines there were in the metropolis between petty schooling and grammar schooling were virtually absent in the colo-nies: the content and sequence of learning [study] remained fairly well defined, and each student progressed from textbook to textbook at his own pace."[32]

What was well defined, it is important to remember, was not learning, but "learnyng," getting one's basic linguistic skills through a regulated process of study. Old-time books that addressed the schoolmaster con-cerned the art of "keeping school," and they show how deeply "teachyng" designed to regulate "learnyng" was pervaded by respect for study. Such a work is the *Ratio Studiorum* of the Jesuits, which set forth a detailed regimen for conducting schools, higher and lower. Its precepts had been derived from a careful study of successful practices as these had devel-oped in the Renaissance, the Middle Ages, and back even to Quintilian and before; and its precepts were to guide the conduct, not only of the many schools the Jesuits founded, but numerous others, Catholic, Protes-tant, and even secular.[33] Precocious self-starters like Montaigne would repeatedly find these schools to be confining, a check on their power to study; but despite the occasional operative shortcoming, clearly their ra-tionale was the conviction that the students' business was to study: thus Montaigne's teacher could connive with the boy's independent tastes.

Few innovations are to be found in the *Ratio;* it described conven-tional practice with simplicity and clarity; it specified the duties of all without demeaning the intelligence of any. The system of education that the *Ratio* laid down did not function through a process of teaching and learning; its motive force was study, a word that recurs over and over in the text. The duty of students was to "resolve to apply their minds seriously and constantly to their studies . . . ," and the function of the faculty, from the rector through the professors down to the lowly beadle, was to regulate, modulate, sustain, correct, and stimulate the students' studies.[34] Consequently, although the *Ratio* said almost nothing about methods of classroom instruction, of imparting knowledge, it precisely described the programs of disputations, declamations, and other exercises by means of which the faculty could oversee the pupils' progress.

Only the professors of the lower classes were explicitly charged with a responsibility to instruct their students: here again one encounters the old-time triviality of teaching.[35] For the most part, however, regardless of level, the professor's purpose was hortatory and heuristic, rather than didactic: "to move his hearers, both within class and out, as opportunity offers, to a reverence and love of God and of the virtues which are pleasing in His sight, and to pursue all their studies to that end."[36] In the Jesuit system, and in most systems of education well into the Enlightenment, the moving force was the student, and the teacher's function was not to instruct, but to incite, discipline, and modulate that youthful energy.

Here, however, we begin to touch on the historic frailty of equating education with a process of study. As passionate causes wracked human affairs, as they have done from the Reformation onward, men found it hard to maintain restraint; they ceased to be willing merely to help in the self-development of their fellows; they discovered themselves burdened, alas, with paternal responsibility for ensuring that their wards would not falter and miss the mark. Thus the methodological restraint, the respect for study, that characterized the Jesuit *Ratio* did not fully accord with the historic mission of that order, and in practice, over a period of time, its educational methods became less heuristic, more didactic, some would even say rather jesuitical.[37] Pressures—religious, political, social, economic, humanitarian pressures—began to mount upon the schools, and it soon became a mere matter of time before schools would be held accountable for the people they produced.

Signs of transition were frequent during the seventeenth century. An educational lodestone such as Samuel Hartlib drew to himself traditional theorists of the process of study and visionary proponents of our present-day process of teaching and learning. In "Of Education," a letter solicited by Hartlib, John Milton suggested a few innovations in the traditional scholastic program, but those notwithstanding, his views conventionally concerned the ends and methods of study. He prescribed a taxing but familiar circle of studies, and he explained, not how these should be taught, but how the student should work his way through them. Like the Jesuits, the great Puritan assigned the teacher a hortatory, not a didactic task: to incite the students with a passion for study, "to temper them

[with] such lectures and explanations, upon every opportunity, as may lead and draw them in willing obedience, inflamed with the study of learning and the admiration of virtue; stirred up with high hopes of living to be brave men and worthy patriots, dear to God, and famous to all ages."[38] The pressures mounting on the educator to produce stellar students are here reflected in Milton's rhetoric; but his system still assigned initiative, not to the teacher, but to the student: "these are the studies wherein our noble and gentle youth ought to bestow their time, in a disciplinary way, from twelve to one and twenty."[39]

Hartlib must have winced at Milton's derisive reference to Comenius— "to search what many modern *Januas* and *Didactics*, more than ever I shall read, have projected, my inclination leads me not"—for Comenius had first fired Hartlib's pedagogical interest and was then the fashionable fascination of the educational avant-garde.[40] And Comenius—curious Comenius!—best represents the other tendency of the time, the new tendency to create a world of instruction, to respond to the growing pressures with a visionary program, a still visionary program, in which universal schooling would be the cause of universal peace. Ah! To the lecterns, heroic pedagogues! Your hour is come. The future is yours to make. Hear and heed the noble call: *The Great Didactic Setting forth the whole Art of Teaching all Things to all Men, or A certain Inducement to found such Schools in all the Parishes, Towns, and Villages of every Christian Kingdom, that the entire Youth of both Sexes, none being excepted, shall Quickly, Pleasantly, and Thoroughly Become learned in the Sciences, pure in Morals, trained to Piety, and in this manner instructed in all things necessary for the present and for the future life. . . .*[41]

Comenius cared nought for study; teaching and learning were his thing. He said little about the sequence of exercises to be performed by students in acquiring the elementary arts, but instead set forth the techniques and principles by means of which teachers were to impart knowledge, virtue, and faith to empty minds "with such certainty that the desired result must of necessity follow."[42] Teaching ceased to be trivial; it became essential, it became the desideratum, the arbiter of worth, the very source of man's humanity. "He gave no bad definition who said that man was a 'teachable animal.' And indeed it is only by proper education that he can become a man. . . . We see then that all who are born to man's estate have need of instruction, since it is necessary that, being men, they should not be wild beasts, savage brutes, or inert logs. It follows also that one man excels another in exact proportion as he has received more instruction."[43] Here is the basis for our cult of the degree; and Comenius' faith in the power of the school had no bounds: he even suggested that had there been a better school in Paradise, Eve would not have made her sore mistake, for she "would have known that the serpent is unable to speak, and that there must therefore be some deceit."[44]

In his time, Comenius was a futile visionary. There is much in his thought that his later disciples would not care to follow. In lieu of reasoned argument, Comenius frequently relied on rather forced rendering of Biblical precedent. He was a spokesman for neither classical humanism nor the budding tradition of inductive and deductive science; he was content to reason by analogy, no matter how strained, and his thought was influenced by the hermetic tradition and by exotic Renaissance memory systems.[45] Yet sharp judgments are often garbed with bizarre accouterments, and Comenius shrewdly perceived the pedagogical future. All the basic concerns of modern Western education were adumbrated in *The Great Didactic:* there was to be universal, compulsory, extended instruction for both boys and girls in efficient, well-run schools in which teachers, who had been duly trained in a "Didactic College," were to be responsible for teaching sciences, arts, languages, morals, and piety by following an exact order derived from nature and by using tested, efficacious principles. This outline has been given fleshly substance; initiative has everywhere been thoroughly shifted from the student to the teacher; a world of instruction has completely displaced the bygone world of study.

Signs abound of how teaching has won precedence from study. Rarely does one hear that study is the *raison d'être* of an educational institution; teaching and learning is now what it is all about, and with this change, has come a change in the meaning of the venerable word "learning." Once it described what a man acquired as a result of serious study, but now it signifies what one receives as a result of good teaching. The psychology of learning is an important topic in educational research, not because it will help students improve their habits of study, but because it enables instructors to devise better strategies of teaching. Recall how the *Ratio Studiorum*, a teacher's handbook, was all about the regimen of study, and then compare it to *The Teacher's Handbook*, edited by Dwight W. Allen and Eli Seifman. Of its seventy-five chapters, none deal with study, although dependably, the section on "The Instructional Process" opens with chapters on "The Teaching Process" and its responsive correlate "The Learning Process."[46]

Interest in study has largely disappeared. Consult the profile of current educational research: whereas the 1969 ERIC catalogue lists a meager thirty-eight entries for all topics concerning study, it has 277 entries for Teaching Methods alone, and hundreds and hundreds more for other aspects of that sacred occupation.[47] Furthermore, in the same way that the meaning of "learning" has changed, so has that of "study." It has ceased to be a self-directed motivating force, which to be sure, may have needed a master of exercises to help sustain it through the dull preliminaries. No longer the source, study itself has become a consequence of instruction, or such is the premise of those inevitable treatises that expertly explain how to teach pupils how to study. In these, study no longer depends on the student's initiative; no—study, according to a dissertation on *The Problem of Teaching High School Pupils How to Study*, "is a pupil activity of the type required to satisfy the philosophy of education held by the teacher."[48] Ah yes; man is a teachable animal—*animal docilis.*

A World of Instruction

Since the mid-eighteenth century, the Comenian vision has been pro-gressively actualized. A complicated constellation of causes, many of which began working in the Renaissance or before, helped to create the present world of paternal instruction. A hasty rehearsal of the more sali-ent of these will show how our reliance on teaching has behind it a pow-erful impetus.

During the late seventeenth century, European population, especially in the north, declined as the result of the recurrent demographic pres-sures, which were caused by the ineluctable positive checks that Malthus described—poor climate, epidemic, war, and famine. Around 1700, de-mographic advance again got underway, and despite occasional halts and minor regressions, it is still going on.[49] The population of Europe is esti-mated to have been about 110 million in 1720, 210 million in 1820, 500 million in 1930, and 614 million in 1968.[50] A general rise in per capita wealth accompanied the increase in population; and since the demand for formal education is partly a function of the wealth people command, a growing percentage of the growing population in Europe has been seeking formal education. This fast acceleration in the demand for education fostered increased reliance on the pedagogical agency of mass production, the instructional program of the school.

At the same time that the demographic expansion increased the de-mand for education, it made the school a more convenient educational agency and weakened the effectiveness of certain long-standing alterna-tives to the school. Europeans had long before cleared their meager com-plement of the world's land, and consequently the growth of population meant an increase in its density; larger cities, more towns, fewer areas of rural isolation. Population per square mile in Western Europe in 1720 was 92, in 1820, 150, in 1930, 247, and in 1968, 306. The figures for those years for the British Isles were 66, 173, 406, and 488. In the Netherlands, population density was 231 in 1840, 480 in 1914, and almost one thou-sand in 1966.[51] With this growth in density, the day school became a more feasible, efficient, and convenient institution, for even most rural areas were sufficiently well populated to sustain schools without grave prob-lems of transportation. The same increase in population density and growing ease of travel that made the school more feasible had the oppo-site effect on the school's major competitor, apprenticeship, for young people, having put in a year or two learning the skills of their trade, found it increasingly easy to then jump their contracts, à la Rousseau, and to melt into the sea of people, ready to earn a living without having to work off their debts to their teachers.[52]

Over time, these demographic causes greatly increased the reliance on schools as the main agency of education. Other causes contributed to transforming the school from a place of study into a means of instruction. Such was the effect of diverse philosophical and psychological developments. Lockean empiricism, especially as it was developed in France by the sensationalists and ideologues, gave rigor to the view that man was a teachable animal, for it held that ideas and intellectual qualities were not inborn, but that these were etched into the receptive human slate by the hand of experience. With packaged experiences, the school could etch fine minds and upstanding characters.[53] Nor was empiricism the only metaphysic to hold such a view; similar results came from quite different tendencies in German thought. On the one hand, Herbartian realism postulated the conditioned formation of mind as a person's subjective phenomenal awareness was continually disrupted by the interventions of objective realities; the claim that experimental psychology should be the scientific base for instructional technique rests primarily on Herbart's philosophy.[54] On the other hand, absolute idealists such as Fichte avoided postulating the perfect solipsism, towards which they tended, by pointing to the practical effect of language conditioning, observing how each ego became locked into a definite community by the inevitable acquisition of one or another mother tongue, its concomitant culture, its characteristic style of life and thinking; this theory of language conditioning provided the theoretical basis for developing national systems of education, that is, education for and through a nationality.[55]

As these divergent theories of man all coincided in depicting him as highly teachable, a number of divergent historic visions all concurred in requiring that men be taught paternally. In the mid-eighteenth century, spokesmen for the state and its prerogatives began to see that investment in the training of the population was a good way to increase the power of the state. Whatever its result, the intent behind the *Landschulreglement* that Frederick the Great instituted in Prussia in 1763 was to increase the power of the state by improving the productive skills of the people and sharpening the acumen of prospective officers and civil servants. Likewise, *raison d'état* was the rationale for the educational reforms imposed by Joseph II in Austria in the 1780s. In his attempt to institute compulsory, secular education, he stressed an elementary and secondary training that would improve the productivity of the population and carefully limited higher education so as not to produce a flock of underemployed, meddlesome intellectuals.[56]

Others, who advocated pedagogical programs not much different from those of Frederick the Great or Joseph II, did so with quite different motives, yet despite these differences, the motives all led to a paternal pedagogy. One rationale came from the spreading fascination with the possibility of progress: day by day, so it seemed, men were discovering ever better ways to order their affairs, and if some agency such as the school could systematically disseminate this knowledge, men could look forward to steady, unlimited improvement in the quality of life on earth. Such was the vision inspiring educational planners like Condorcet. Another view, closely related to the progressive, might be called the philanthropic; here men like Robert Owen and Johann Pestalozzi looked to schooling, not only as a means of ensuring continuous future improvement, but, further, as a means of correcting the human degradation that presently resulted from economic exploitation and social dislocation. Still another view, which could partake of both the progressive and the philanthropic, was that of the political idealists; thus one found both French revolutionaries and German patriots who resisted Napoleonic domination arguing that the educator must train the perfect citizen of the perfect polity.[57] In these ways, statists, progressives, philanthropists, and political idealists all looked to a system of compulsory instruction and state influence in higher education as an important, positive means of implementing their historic visions. Add to this the fact that most everywhere those who controlled dynamic industrial wealth were easily convinced that educational reform would be to their economic interest, and one should not be surprised that universal, compulsory schooling has indeed become universal.

Once these systems of schooling were set up, secondary causes began to work, making the schools increasingly places for instruction, rather than for study. Whatever the rationale behind it, the principle of compulsory schooling automatically put the student in a subservient relation to his teachers, and it became most difficult to maintain the conviction that the student provides the motive force of the whole process. The principle of compulsion proclaimed to each and every person that there was something essential that he must allow one or another school to do to him between the ages of six and sixteen. Such a proclamation did not encourage initiative on the part of the student, but it did give the professional educator a very strong mandate and considerable responsibility to shape his wards according to one favored pattern or another. Thus, a large teacher corps has come into being in every Western country; it is accorded professional status and is charged with a clear-cut mission: it must produce, and in order to produce, it must assert initiative. Student servility is an integral function of professional accountability in compulsory systems of schooling.

As the principle of compulsion and the drive towards professionalism both decreased the student's initiative and increased the reliance on instruction, so too did the ancillary functions that were added on to the instructional system once it came into being. One such function was the practice of making school attendance and performance the basic means of certifying the competence of people in every Western society. With this practice the student has not only become legally subservient to his teachers for the better part of his early years, he has also become socially and economically dependent on them, and on his ability to perform as they command, for the general outline of his life prospects. As communities come to rely on schools to certify the competencies of their people, they project onto those schools a productive mission to mold mechanically the populace; and students, who have increasingly seen schooling as a huge machine for stamping them with success or failure, have acquiesced, eagerly or hopelessly according to their prospects, and have been content to be taught. Consequently, the social uses to which an apparatus of instruction could be put reinforced the single-minded reliance on instruction within that apparatus. From this stemmed the following paradox: at no time in the West have there been greater resources for self-education available to all than in the twentieth century, yet at no time has there been more extensive reliance on formal instruction for the education of all. . . .

The Future

Certainly the cultural atmosphere crackles with intimations of departures at once imminent and immanent. The bestsellers speak of "future shock" and an intriguing greening of America. But the one is a breathless compilation of every harbinger of change held together with slogans, not ideas, and assured of proving partly prophetic by virtue of repeating uncritically most every prophecy that an energetic journalist can collect.[58] And the other charts a wistful, wonderful revolution of ideas that perhaps may come about, but again, provided only that it can draw sustaining energies from the hard facts of the historic flux.[59] Still it is to these that we must look.

Prophets of environmental crisis point to what may be compelling realities, and if the worst of their projections prove true, the effects on our civic institutions would be immense.[60] In large part, however, ecological imbalances are portents of future changes in the physical environment, and whatever adaptations men will have to make in their mores and institutions will have to be carried out under the aegis of other historic forces that may already be coming into play within the social realm. Education occurs primarily within that realm, in the company of men; nature provides but a backdrop, sometimes fresh, but often grim. Are there historic forces newly operative in the social sphere that have a direct, palpable influence on the education of men, their character formation, their intentional shaping of their personalities?

So far, probably the most important attempt to indicate a basic change in the pattern of character formation in the West is *The Lonely Crowd* by David Riesman, et al. In some ways the book is a period piece; writing in the late forties, its authors took the conformist, who proved so prevalent in the fifties, to be a more enduring type than he now seems to have been. Be that as it may, what is important here is the general structure of the argument, which purported to find a demographic basis for long-term shifts in patterns of character formation. Thus, Riesman connected the historic transition from tradition-directed to inner-directed and finally to other-directed character with the so-called S-curve that population growth has followed in the post-Renaissance West. As Riesman saw it, population in the West passed in the seventeenth century from a long period of general stasis, through a sustained period of rapid growth, and entered in the mid-twentieth century into an indefinite time of incipient decline. He then connected his three basic character types to these demographic conditions: tradition-directed men characterized a static population, inner-directed men dominated a rapidly growing population, and other-directed men would proliferate among an incipiently declining population.[61]

A number of questions might be raised about the empirical accuracy of these correlations. In particular, one might ask whether in fact the point of incipient population decline has been reached in the West; for population has increased about 40 percent in both the United States and Europe since *The Lonely Crowd* appeared. One might also ask why, if these correlations are correct, did the highly tradition-directed character of medieval man flourish during the era of dynamic population growth from 1100 to 1300. But more is amiss than such quibbles would indicate. Accepting the broad outline of Riesman's demographics and valuing his ideal character types as useful, illuminating constructs, one nevertheless finds that no compelling causal connection has been explicated between the demographic situation at one or another time and the purported dominance of the appropriate character type. And when hard reasons were given for expecting other-directed men to typify the present day, the reasons concerned the nature of urban life, the mass media, a consumption economy, peer-group politics, and patterns of schooling and child rearing, all of which are, at most, indirectly demographic.[62]

Yet the intention was a good one; in the demographic situation one finds the basic, gross influences affecting the character formation of every person. To come to terms with these effects, however, one needs a more refined measure than simple changes in overall population. What matters for character formation is not primarily a change in the total number of people, but a change in the number of opportunities each person has for day-to-day contact with others, a change, that is, in his chance for company. A man both acquires and displays character—his beliefs, skills, thoughts, and tastes—through involvements of some sort with other people; hence patterns of character formation can change as options for interpersonal contact change. To be sure, the range of opportunities open to one man for dealing with other men vary in part according to changes in population, or more precisely, to changes in the density of population. But another factor is equally important for determining the chances for intimate relations between man and man; this factor is the ease or difficulty with which men living at a certain time and place can move, travel, and communicate. Today, in some locales the density of rural population has declined from what it was in the Middle Ages; yet the peasant who now may have a telephone, television, and auto has far greater opportunities for becoming involved with other people than did his medieval predecessor, a serf of the manor who could make the day-long trek to the neighboring village only with his lord's permission.

Through most of Western history, each person, be he lowly or exalted, had limited opportunities for day-to-day contact with others. Population was sufficiently sparse and communication sufficiently difficult that each person had to choose his companions from a finite number of possibilities, some tens of thousands, and many sides of his potential character, which he might have liked to cultivate, he had to leave undeveloped for want of anyone to join him in the endeavor. Hence, in the past the demographic trend that was significant for character formation would vary between three basic conditions; the finite number of options for interpersonal contact open to each might be rising, static, or falling, depending on the combined changes in population density and ease of communication. If opportunities for companionship were finite and static for several generations, a tradition-directed type might well become common, for few changes would confront individuals and groups with new experiences and hence custom could be consolidated. During a long period in which men's choices were limited but rising, inner-directed types might flourish, for tangible growth in a man's possibilities would call forth innovations, optimism, an inner confidence that with drive, concentration, and systematic effort an aspiring individual could accomplish significant achievements. Finally, when men found that their opportunities to commune with their fellows were both restricted and falling, they would tend towards pessimism, conflict, and despair, as happened in the Roman twilight and in the years following the Black Death.

During the past century, however, these situations have ceased to be pertinent to character formation throughout most Western societies. And here, cheerless old Henry Adams, with his reflections on "The Rule of Phase Applied to History," gave an important clue that must be added to meditations on demographic S-curves, for in recent decades each man's opportunities for contact with others have gone through a change of phase that is analogous to the change of water from fluid to steam.[63] Consider a crude measure of the number of options that a man has for daily involvement with others; let us call it "the opportunity factor." Thus, $O = D\pi R^2$, the number of people from among whom a particular person can choose his day-to-day companions equals the density of population per square mile times pi times the square of the distance that he or his communication can travel in a day. Let us see what the opportunity factor can tell us about the historic conditions influencing character formation for the average European.

Population density for the whole of Europe was approximately 36 people per square mile in 1750, 49 in 1800, 70 in 1850, 111 in 1900, 149 in 1939, and 172 in 1966.[64] Let us say roughly that the average man could travel eighteen miles per day in 1750; with some improvement of roads and canals we could put the figure at twenty-two miles for 1800; by 1850 with short rail lines beginning to be built the distance might jump to forty miles; with the filling out of the railways and the effective introduction of the telegraph, a man's range in 1900 might have trebled to 120 miles; in 1939, with the telephone and the automobile not yet in full popular use and air travel only in its early stages, the figure should probably be put at no more than 250 miles; but by 1966, despite the devastation of World War II, with cars, telephones, and televisions being articles of mass consumption and jet travel open to most, the average man could easily cover over 1,000 miles in a day.[65]

With these figures we can find the opportunity factor for each period. In 1750, the average European had the physical possibility of choosing his daily contacts from among roughly 36,800 other persons; in effect, therefore, he formed his character within the confines of a substantial provincial town. In the next fifty years his options doubled, becoming some 74,500; thus his personality could then develop in a sphere equivalent perhaps to a thriving provincial capital. During the next half century the increase in opportunity quickened, multiplying almost five times to 352,000; in this way the average person had options equivalent to those then offered by the grim new industrial cities. By 1900 the opportunity factor jumped significantly and multiplied fourteen times to 5,020,000; the average man lived in a realm a bit more populous than London of the day. On the eve of World War II there had been another six-fold expansion to 29,200,000; each man's world was then coextensive with a middling nation. Then, in the shortest period, much of which was occupied with a most destructive war, the range of choice confronting the average European increased more than in any other period, multiplying almost twenty times to 540,000,000; thus each man could choose his companions from roughly the population of Europe, east and west.

Infinite Possibilities

In human terms, this range of possibilities—which, with worldwide jet travel and a global telephone system, is numerically understated—is for all practical purposes infinite. This, then, is the change of phase that has occurred with respect to character formation: whereas in the past the average man had limited opportunities for day-to-day contact with others, he now has infinite options. Although the conditions making this change of phase possible have been developing during the past hundred years, it is mainly since World War II that they have taken full effect as virtually everyone gained easy access to road, rail, and air travel, to telephone, radio, and television. Mankind is fast approaching the unprecedented situation in which anyone, on a day's notice or less, can involve himself directly with anyone else. Thinkers have still to come to terms with the implications of this change for society, economics, politics, and education; and the implications augur well for the future of study.

On the surface, the assertion that personal possibilities have become unlimited seems to ignore obliviously the conditions producing a pervasive fear of the all-surveillant state. Arbitrary political barriers still exist, and the ability to accumulate facts and fictions about every individual has increased portentously. Not only in America does the invasion of privacy and the official abuse of civil rights seem rampant. But perhaps the surest way to cooperate with potential persecutors is to take them too seriously, to recoil, not in the face of repression, but at the thought of repression, allowing the action of the state to have a chilling effect in areas where in fact it has little force. Officials of state turn to surveillance and repression out of weakness, not strength; they seek to dominate, not by virtue of their own great stature, but by casting fearful shadows, by amplifying their ability to destroy this or that individual into an appearance of complete and arbitrary command. To be sure, the centralized, bureaucratic state can gather vast quantities of information, but it can concentrate and act on a human level only on infinitesimal parts of the bulk. And furthermore, in the long run, the most significant consequence for individual autonomy that will result from the change of historic phase may pertain less to privacy and surveillance and more to the nature of social sanctions. It may turn out that big brother will know all about what each does but be powerless to do much about it.

With no implacable limits on the range of personal relations open to most, people have a good chance of finding companions for any imaginable undertaking; and in time, in a rather short time, this latitude may lead to a thorough transformation in the nature of authority. In a world in which each individual can pursue most any personal purpose in most any place that suits him, all on his own initiative, the habit of relying on authoritative institutions, which operate through commands enforced by penalties and inducements, may sharply diminish. With the change of phase in the opportunity factor, people need less and less to rely on formal institutions for a chance to fulfill their personal purposes. And as more and more people become aware of the unlimited choices that they have in their personal lives, sanctions and incentives will become ineffectual means of administering authoritative commands in government, society, business, and education. As everything becomes possible for everyone in their personal lives, only the most extreme sanctions—sanctions that deprive the person of his mobility through extended incarceration or death—have a significant effect on his personal possibilities; and these extreme sanctions must be reserved to check serious crime. But minor sanctions—social disapproval, loss of a job, fines, or even short-term imprisonment—cannot significantly narrow the range of infinite options open to most individuals, nor can minor, perhaps even substantial, incentives meaningfully broaden what is already infinite. Hence, increasingly, attempts to coerce daily behavior will fail, and any and all relationships entered into by consenting adults, provided these do not lead to the serious harm of others, will become both socially and legally acceptable.

Although authority based on sanction is likely to diminish in societies that offer individuals infinite possibilities for involvement with others, authority itself will not disappear, for allocations of effort will still have to be made, but on the basis of a quite different principle. All the iconography of love that has become so popular with the young is indicative of more than a fad, for all around coercive authority is giving way to erotic authority, and many functions that in the past were performed by the use of causal manipulation will occur in the future by virtue of erotic attraction.[66] Erotic authority has always operated among men, but as never before it is likely to become the dominant form of authority. This change is patent in economics where desire has long since displaced need as the arbiter of demand and where sex is the smooth salve of sales. And in most other areas as well, one finds endless signs of the transformation; in politics, art, science, and education, men are more and more acting according to their aspiration, pursuing what seems to them to be good or beautiful or true because they are drawn to it, for nothing compels them to it. As sanction becomes less effective, allurement will take over, not to enforce the same goals that coercion would assert, but to promote its own goals, so that society will not drift without direction. In a world in which men share unlimited personal opportunities, the natural form of authority will be erotic, not only in the crass sense, but in the best Platonic sense, on the basis of which effort will distribute itself as it is drawn to various possibilities according to a many layered teleology.

A society governed by eros will not automatically be a good society, for, like any other principle, eros can go astray. The Manson family, for instance, is among the authentic combinations possible when people have infinite options; but it is neither representative nor inevitable. As with any mode of human order, the quality of life attained depends on the wisdom with which the controlling principles are understood and applied. Because of this imperative, man will not make an erotic society better simply by trying to deny its nature; rather the wise course is to accept and understand its nature and to act in sympathy with its principles so that the best in it will fully develop. The principle of eros is to forego domination, to resist the compulsion to correct petty faults in others, and to concentrate on helping those who attract one's attention to achieve fruition. Many in positions of "authority" have still to start acting in sympathy with this principle, yet it is hard to imagine a reversion to a situation in which they can effectively rely on domination, command, and sanction.

Certainly a retreat to strict standards, social and sexual, to be enforced by parents and the pillars of society, is most improbable. As soon as the child masters the basic means of movement that life now offers, he is largely impervious to parental sanction, and whatever parental authority remains inheres in love, not power. And that bugaboo of reactionaries, "permissive society," is coextensive with the societies that, through a combination of dense population and high mobility, have opened boundless alternatives to their members; consequently the permissiveness results from no mere abdication of authority or slackening of standards: with the mass production of the SEAT 850, it is fast appearing in very fascist, very Catholic Spain. In reality, permissiveness is no mere consequence; permissiveness is the inherent character, the ordering principle, of the social flux that has resulted from the great change of phase in history. To repress permissiveness one would have to do away with the extensive personal mobility that has given rise to the cornucopia of choice confronting each and every person. Such a reaction will not come except through an atomic war, and public leaders had best face the new realities rather than bemoan bygone simplicities.

Here then, in the change of historic phase, is a complicated, tangible, palpitating force within the flux that is incongruent with systems of compulsory education, for these function by means of sanctions that are weakening visibly as children become aware of their limitless options. Hence, the world of instruction may steadily decline in effectiveness. This would not be the doom of education. Like leaders in other public spheres, educators have the option of working in sympathy with eros. As we have seen, for Plato, eros was one of the principles that made study the most human, most natural form of education, even in times when each man's choices were still severely limited. Hence now—when the most effective authority will be erotic, a set of varied attractions through which men will determine their preferences among their measureless prospects—the character of historic movement will conduce to a spread of comprehensive, voluntary study, directed by the student's selective attention and motivated by his personal initiative. For these reasons, the future of our past looks promising; the prospects for study seem good.

But such an analysis is simply an analysis, one man's interpretation of the way things appear to him. Many words, even when spiced with a few facts and figures, can never encapsulate reality; at best they echo it at considerable remove. Truth is neither in the words nor in the theories that they spin out; truth is in the experiences that each of us has, and the value of words and theories is not that they communicate truth, but that if all is aright they may help us grasp and comprehend the truths of our experience. Hence, in speaking about historic forces and the promising prospects for study, one is establishing no inevitabilities, not even probabilities; rather one is working out certain heuristic propositions, which will hopefully help others understand the truths of their experience, for in the light of that truth, their practice will be wiser, surer, and to greater effect. Such is the praxis of the *Geisteswissenschaften,* the sciences of the spirit.

In this temper, one last hypothesis: in making the case for study, one does not denigrate the teacher's profession. To be sure, one has to speak out against exaggerating the power of instruction. But this criticism does not reject teaching; in place of a rejection, it is a quest for the mean, a celebration of the Greek sense for nothing too much, an attempt to balance an inflated version of the teacher's mission with a touch of reality. Yes—let us continue our effort to teach all as best we can, but let us do so with more humility, sobriety, and realism.

Instruction does not make the man. A teacher gains coercive power to control and mold his students only so long as they abdicate their autonomy and dignity. Such an abdication is not a good foundation for an educational system, especially since it is less common and continuous than many would seem to believe. The teacher's authority, be it as a model of excellence or of folly, is a quality his students project erotically upon him. It is an attraction or repulsion that results because students are forever suspending their interest in learning their lessons; instead they abstract, they reflect; they step back mentally and with curiously cocked heads they observe their didactic deliverer, musing with soaring hope, wonder, joy, resignation, boredom, cynicism, amusement, sad tears, despair, or cold resentment—*Ecce homo!*

A teacher may or may not cause learning, but he will always be an

object of study. Hence the pedant so surely plays the fool. But hence too, the man teaching can often occasion achievements that far surpass his personal powers. Great teachers can be found conforming to every type— they are tall and short, shaggy and trim, timid and tough, loquacious and terse, casual and stern, clear and obscure. Great teachers are persons who repay study, and they repay study because they know with Montaigne, "My trade and my art is to live."[67]

Notes

1. "Les sentences peintes dans la 'Librarie' de Montaigne," Montaigne. *Ouevres completes.* Paris: Bibliothèque de la Pléiade, Editions Gallimard, 1962, pp. 1419–1427.

2. Montaigne, "Of Training," in Montaigne. *Selected Essays*, trans. C. Cotton and W. Hazlitt. New York: The Modern Library, 1949, pp. 116–128, esp. 117.

3. Montaigne, "Of the Education of Children." *Ibid.* pp. 14–53, esp. pp. 20–22 and 50–51. For Seneca's skepticism about the importance of teachers, see Seneca. *Ad Lucilium Epistulae Morales,* trans. Richard M. Gummere. 3 volumes. Cambridge, Mass.: Harvard University Press, 1917, Letters XXXIII, XL, LII, LXXXVIII, CXI, and especially LXXXIV, which is a source of Montaigne's essay, "Of the Education of Children."

4. The best source on the *Adages* is Margaret Mann Phillips. *The 'Adages' of Erasmus: A Study with Translations.* Cambridge, England: Cambridge University Press, 1964; Erasmus' description of them is from his dedicatory epistle to Lord Mountjoy for the first edition, June, 1500, in Francis Morgan Nichols, ed. and trans., *The Epistles of Erasmus from his Earliest Letters to his Fifty-First Year.* New York: Russell and Russell, 1962, Vol. I, p. 243.

5. Erasmus to Bude. Brussels, October 28, 1516, in *Ibid.* Vol. II, p. 415.

6. For a good discussion of the method of study embodied in *de Copia,* see R. R. Bolgar. *The Classical Tradition and Its Beneficiaries.* New York: Harper Torchbooks, 1964, pp. 273–5. The text, *de Duplici Copia Verborum ad Rerum,* is in *Opera Omnia in Decem Tomus Distincta.* Hildesheim, W. Germany: Georg Olms Verlagsbuchhandlung, 1961, Vol. I, pp. 4–110. It was basically a work on Latin usage, designed to be used as we might use *Fowler's Modern English Usage,* except that it was meant to improve the user's spoken as well as his written rhetoric. It suggested that the user make and frequently study a personal commonplace book.

7. For Erasmus' work on the New Testament and the Church fathers, see Preserved Smith. *Erasmus: A Study of His Life, Ideals and Place in History.* New York: Dover Publications, 1962, Chapters VII and VIII.

8. *Ibid.,* p. 195.

9. First quotation: Erasmus to Botzhem, 1523, in *Epistles, op. cit.,* n. 4, Vol. I, p. 337. Second: Erasmus. *The Enchiridion of Erasmus,* trans. Raymond Himelick. Bloomington: Indiana University Press, 1963, p. 37.

74   Robert McClintock

10. Erasmus. *The Praise of Folly*, trans. John Wilson, 1668. Ann Arbor: The
    University of Michigan Press, 1958. The satirical tone of *The Praise of
    Folly* provoked criticism from those who thought it was not sufficiently
    improving. Erasmus' defense of the work can be found in his letter to John
    of Louvain, January 2, 1518, *Epistles, op. cit.*, n. 4, Vol. III, pp. 208-210.

11. Erasmus. *The Education of a Christian Prince*, trans. Lester K. Born. New
    York: W. W. Norton and Co., 1968. Born's long introduction is a useful
    discussion of the "mirror of princes" tradition.

12. Erasmus, "The Art of Learning," trans. Craig R. Thompson. *The
    Colloquies of Erasmus.* Chicago: University of Chicago Press, 1965, pp.
    460-1.

13. John Bartlett. *Familiar Quotations*, 13th ed. Boston: Little, Brown and Co.,
    1955.

14. Erasmus, "Preface," trans. Nicholas Udall. *The Apophthegms of Erasmus,*
    1964. Boston, Lincolnshire: Robert Roberts, 1877, p. xxii. *The Apothegms*
    was based on Plutarch, but had so many additions and expansions that it
    was more than a translation.

15. *Ibid.*, p. xiv.

16. Lynn Thorndike. *University Records and Life in the Middle Ages.* New
    York: Columbia University Press, 1944, p. 9, n. 4.

17. Erasmus, "Preface," *Apophthegms, op. cit.* n. 14, pp. xxv-xxvi.

18. See François Rabelais. *The Five Books of Gargantua and Pantagruel*, trans.
    Jacques Le Clercq. New York: The Modern Library, 1944, pp. 190-4;
    Robert Pace. *De Fructu qui ex Doctrina Percipitur*, eds. and trans. Frank
    Manley and Richard S. Sylvester. New York: Frederick Ungar Publishing
    Co., 1967; Joseph Rickaby. *The Spiritual Exercises of St. Ignatius Loyola:
    Spanish and English with a Continuous Commentary.* New York: Benziger
    Brothers, 1923; Baldesar Castiglione. *The Book of the Courtier*, trans.
    Charles S. Singleton. Garden City, New York: Doubleday Anchor Books,
    1959; Sir Thomas Elyot. *The Book Named the Governor.* S. E. Lahmberg,
    ed. New York: Everyman's Library, 1962; Miguel de Cervantes, *Novelas
    ejemplares*, texto intego. Garden City, New York: Doubleday and Co.,
    1962; and Miguel de Cervantes, *Don Quixote*, trans. Ozell and Motteux.
    New York: The Modern Library, 1930. For the iconography of the Italian
    Renaissance, see Erwin Panofsky. *Studies in Iconology: Humanistic Themes
    in the Art of the Renaissance.* New York: Harper Torchbooks, 1962; Jean
    Seznec. *The Survival of the Pagan Gods: The Mythological Tradition and
    Its Place in Renaissance Art*, trans. Barbara F. Sessions. New York: Harper
    Torchbooks, 1961; and Carroll W. Westfall, "Painting and the Liberal Arts:
    Albert's View," *Journal of the History of Ideas*, October-December, 1969,
    Vol. XXX, No. 4, pp. 487-506.

19. See Günther Böhme. *Der pädagogische Beruf der Philosophie.* Munich:
    Ernest Reinhardt Verlag, 1968, for an interesting discussion of the
    philosopher's educational role.

20. Plato. *Republic*, 518 c-d; from *The Republic of Plato*, trans. F. M.
    Cornford. New York: Oxford University Press, 1945, p. 232.

21. Carl Schneider. *Kulturgeschichte des Hellenismus.* Munich: Verlag C. H.
    Beck, 1961, Vol. 1, p. 131.

22. For the world of instruction in the Roman empire, see Tom B. Jones. *The Silver-Plated Age.* Sandoval, N.M.: Coronado Press, 1962; G. W. Bowersock. *Greek Sophists in the Roman Empire.* Oxford: Oxford University Press, 1969; and H. I. Marrou. *A History of Education in Antiquity,* trans. George Lamb. New York: Sheed and Ward, 1956, pp. 306–7, 310–12. For the Hellenistic world, see M. P. Nilsson, *Die hellenistische Schule.* Munich: C. H. Beck Verlag, 1955, which puts excessive stress on the archaeological reconstruction of school buildings, rather than on their function in the culture; and Carl Schneider. *Kulturgeschicte des Hellinismus, op. cit.,* pp. 131–147.

23. Augustine. *The Confessions,* trans. J. G. Pilkington, in Whitney J. Oates, ed. *Basic Writings of St. Augustine.* New York: Random House, 1948, Vol. 1, pp. 1–256.

24. Augustine. *Concerning the Teacher,* trans. George G. Leckie. New York: Appleton-Century-Crofts, Inc., 1938, p. 55.

25. Seneca, *Epistulae Morales, op. cit.,* n. 3, Letter LXXXVIII, Vol. II, pp. 349–377.

26. Augustine. *Confessions, op. cit.,* n. 23, pp. 55–6.

27. John of Salisbury. *The Metalogicon: A Twelfth-Century Defense of the Verbal and Logical Arts of the Trivium,* trans. Daniel D. McGarry. Berkeley: University of California Press, 1962, p. 36.

28. Battista Guarino, "De Ordine Docendi et Studenti," in William Harrison Woodward. *Vittorino da Feltre and Other Humanist Educators.* New York: Teachers College Press, 1963, p. 172.

29. See Sandro Sticca. *The Latin Passion Play: Its Origin and Development.* Albany: State University of New York Press, 1970; Adolf Katzenellenbogen. *Allegories of the Virtues and Vices in Medieval Art,* trans. Alan J. P. Crick. New York: W. W. Norton and Co., 1964; Emile Mâle. *The Gothic Image: Religious Art in France of the Thirteenth Century,* trans. Dora Nussey. New York: Harper Torchbooks, 1958; Dante Alighiere. *The Divine Comedy,* trans. Dorothy L. Sayers. 3 volumes. Baltimore: Penguin Books, 1949 ff.; and for a coming together of many of these strands, see Peter Brieger, Millard Meiss, and Charles S. Singleton. *Illuminated Manuscripts of the Divine Comedy.* 2 vols. Princeton: Princeton University Press, 1969. A fascinating book could be written on character formation in the Middle Ages.

30. Roger Ascham, from the full title of *The Schoolmaster,* in Ascham. *English Works.* W. A. Wright, ed. Cambridge, England: Cambridge University Press, 1903, p. 171.

31. See the brief analysis of *The English Schoolmaster* in Philippe Aries. *Centuries of Childhood: A Social History of Family Life,* trans. Robert Baldick. New York: Vintage Books, 1962, pp. 298–9.

32. Lawrence A. Cremin. *American Education: The Colonial Experience,* 1607–1783. New York: Harper and Row, 1970, pp. 192–3.

33. For a good discussion of pedagogical method in the various seventeenth-century colleges, see George Snyders. *La Pédagogie en France aux XVII et XVIII siècles.* Paris: Presses Universitaires de France, 1965.

34. Edward A. Fitzpatrick, ed. *St. Ignatius and the Ratio Studiorum.* New

York: McGraw-Hill Book Co., 1933, includes a translation of the 1599 version of the *Ratio* by A. R. Ball. For the quotation, see p. 234, for the duties of the faculty, pp. 137–234 *passim.*

35. *Ibid.,* p. 195: "Let the master so instruct the boys who are entrusted to the discipline of our Society, that they will thoroughly learn, along with their letters, the habits worthy of Christians." Aside from this brief mention of instruction, the incessant theme is study.

36. *Ibid.,* p. 150.

37. For an unsympathetic depiction of later Jesuit education by an excellent Spanish novelist, see Ramón Pérez de Ayala. *A.M.D.G.: La vida en un colegio de Jesuitas* in *Obras completas.* Vol. 4. Madrid: Editorial Pueyo, 1931. For an example of the moralizing that penetrated the colleges, albeit not a Jesuit example, read the little book, specially printed for the winners of schoolboy prizes by M. l'Abbe Proyard. *L'Écolier Vertueux ou vie édifiante d'un écolier de l'université de Paris,* 6th ed. Paris: Audot et Compagnie, 1810.

38. Milton, "Of Education," F. A. Patterson, ed. *The Student's Milton.* New York: F. S. Crofts and Co., 1930, p. 728.

39. *Ibid.,* p. 729.

40. *Ibid.,* p. 724.

41. From the title, *The Great Didactic,* trans. M. W. Keating. New York: Russell and Russell, 1967.

42. *Ibid.,* p. 111. In the whole book, a bit over 300 pages long, there is one brief mention of study, per se, with respect to the university, which was to operate on a very high level with only very selected students; *Ibid.,* pp. 281–4. With this exception, instruction, teaching, and learning was Comenius' incessant theme.

43. *Ibid.,* pp. 52 and 56.

44. *Ibid.,* p. 54.

45. Frances A. Yates in *The Art of Memory.* Chicago: The University of Chicago Press, 1966, pp. 377–8, draws this connection. It is developed more fully by Maria Teresa Gentile in her fascinating book *Immagine e parola nella formazione dell'uomo.* Rome: Armando Editore, 1965, pp. 286–319. Comenius' place in the pansophic and encyclopedic movement is examined well by Eugenio Garin. *L'educazione in Europa, 1400–1600,* 2nd ed. Bari: Editori Laterza, 1966.

46. See the table of contents, Dwight W. Allen and Eli Seifman, eds. *The Teacher's Handbook.* Glenview, Ill.: Scott, Foresman and Co., 1971. On the change in the meaning of "learning" see the *Oxford English Dictionary* where the first meaning of to learn, generally meaning to acquire knowledge, emphasizes acquisition through study and experience more than through teaching and has generally older examples. The second meaning, emphasizing to receive instruction, is newer and has particularly clear examples from the late 1700s on.

47. The sub-headings under "study" show that a good part of the 38 do not really concern study in its traditional senses: Study Abroad–2, Study Centers–6, Study Facilities–1, Study Guides–15, Study Habits–5, Study Skills–9.

48. Joseph Seibert Butterweck. *The Problem of Teaching High School Pupils How to Study*. New York: Teachers College Bureau of Publications, 1926, p. 2; C. A. Mace. *The Psychology of Study*. Baltimore: Penguin Books, 1968, is somewhat of an exception in that it is written directly for the student, and it only in part, the lesser part, advises on how to learn simply what the teacher tries to teach; the better part concerns how to study on one's own motivation.

49. For a good, brief discussion of this turning point, see K. F. Helleiner, "The Vital Revolution Reconsidered," in D. V. Glass and D. E. C. Eversley, eds. *Population in History: Essays in Historical Demography*. London: Edward Arnold Publishers, 1965, pp. 79–86.

50. W. Gordon East, "The Historical Background," in George W. Hoffman, ed. *A Geography of Europe*, 3rd ed. New York: The Ronald Press, 1969, p. 83.

51. Figures for Western Europe (France, Low Countries, and Luxembourg) and for the British Isles are from *Ibid.*, p. 83; for the Netherlands, from Guido G. Weigand, "Western Europe," in *Ibid.*, p. 250. For comparison, population density in the United States was 5.5 in 1820, 41.2 in 1930, and 56 in 1968. Colonial population in 1720 is estimated to have been about 466,000 in comparison to the 110,000,000 for Europe.

52. For Rousseau's apprenticeship, see *Les Confessions*, in *Oeuvres complètes*. Paris: Bibliothèque de la Pléiade, 1959, Vol. 1, pp. 30–44.

53. For an excellent study of the ideologues, see Sergio Moravia. *Il tramonto dell'illuminismo: Filosofia e politica nella societa francese, 1770–1810*. Bari: Editori Laterza, 1968, esp. pp. 315–444.

54. On Herbart, see Fritz Seidenfaden. *Die Pädagogik des Jungen Herbart*. Weinheim: Verlag Julius Beltz, 1967; Arthur Bruckmann. *Pädagogik und philosophisches Denken bei J. Fr. Herbart*. Zurich: Morgarten Verlag, 1961; and Alfredo Saloni. *G. F. Herbart: La vita—Lo svolgimento della dottrina pedagogica*, 2 vols. Florence: La Nouva Italia Editrice, 1937.

55. See for the basic conception, Johann Gottlieb Fichte. *Addresses to the German Nation*, trans. R. F. Jones and G. H. Turnbull. Chicago: The Open Court Publishing Co., 1922. Fichte was not the originator of inquiry into the relation between language and the idealistic ego; the history of the subject is dealt with in great detail by Brune Liebrucks. *Sprache und Bewusstein*, 5 vols. Frankfurt: Akademische Verlagsgesellschaft, 1964 ff.

56. See A. V. Judges, "Educational Ideas, Practice and Institutions," in A. Goodwin, ed. *The American and French Revolutions, 1763–1793 (The New Cambridge Modern History*, Vol. VIII). Cambridge, England: Cambridge University Press, 1965, esp. pp. 167–9.

57. For Condorcet and other French examples, see Frank E. Manuel. *The Prophets of Paris*. New York: Harper Torchbooks, 1965; H. C. Barnard. *Education and the French Revolution*. Cambridge, England: Cambridge University Press, 1969; E. Allain. *L'Oeuvre scolaire de la Revolution, 1789–1902*. New York: Burt Franklin, 1969; and Paul Arboursse-Bastide. *La doctrine de l'education universelle dans la philosophie d' Auguste Comte*. Paris: Presses Universitaires de France, 1957. For the Owenites and other English figures, see John F. C. Harrison, ed. *Utopianism and Education: Robert Owen and the Owenites*. New York: Teachers College Press, 1968, and W. A. C. Stewart and W. P. McCann. *The Educational*

Innovators, 1750–1880. New York: St. Martin's Press, 1967. For political idealism in Germany, see the excellent study by Andreas Flitner. *Die politische Erziehung in Deutschland: Geschichte und Problem, 1750–1880.* Tübingen: Max Niemeyer Verlag, 1957.

58. Alvin Toffler. *Future Shock.* New York: Random House, 1970. If one can grit one's teeth and bear with Toffler's incredible abuse of language, the book can serve as an interesting compendium of curious signs of the time.

59. Charles A. Reich. *The Greening of America.* New York: Random House, 1970, *passim,* and esp. Ch. XI, pp. 299–348.

60. For an excellent application of ecological analysis to problems of planning the proper use of the land, see Ian L. McHarg. *Design with Nature.* Garden City, N.Y.: The Natural History Press, 1969. McHarg touches on, but does not fully face, some of the profound questions of public power that will have to be raised as planning becomes more and more ecologically exact.

61. David Riesman, Nathan Glazer, and Ruel Denney. *The Lonely Crowd: A Study of the Changing American Character,* abridged ed. Garden City, N.Y.: Doubleday Anchor Books, 1953, pp. 17–53.

62. *Ibid.,* pp. 100–4, 120–132, 151–186, 196–200, 210–217.

63. Henry Adams, "The Rule of Phase Applied to History," in Henry Adams. *The Degradation of the Democratic Dogma.* New York: Capricorn Books, 1958, pp. 261–305. Cf. Adams. *The Autobiography of Henry Adams.* New York: The Modern Library, 1931, which will become recognized as a classic study of education if we discover the importance of study in education.

64. These figures are from the *Rand McNally Cosmopolitan World Atlas.* New York: Rand McNally and Co., 1968, p. 140.

65. These figures are my own rough estimates, and although as absolute numbers they are rather arbitrary, the progression they define is fairly accurate, I believe.

66. My conception of eros as a form of authority is more deeply influenced by Plato, especially the *Symposium;* Dante throughout *The Divine Comedy;* Goethe, especially in *Wilhelm Meister;* Nietzsche, throughout his work and especially in *Schopenhauer as Educator;* and Ortega, especially in *On Love;* than it is by Herbert Marcuse's *Eros and Civilization: A Philosophical Inquiry into Freud.* New York: Vintage Books, 1961, although I have studied the latter with profit. I am working on an historical inquiry into erotic theories of education which I hope to publish in the near future in a book, *Eros and Education.*

67. Montaigne, "Of Training," *Selected Essays, op. cit.,* n. 2, p. 126.

Part II

LIFELONG LEARNING: A CONTEMPORARY IMPERATIVE

No One Can "Complete an Education" World-renowned anthropologist Margaret Mead changed our way of thinking about education when she introduced the concept of the lateral transmission of knowledge.

She argued that in today's fast-changing world "we are no longer dealing primarily with the *vertical* transmission of the tried and true by the old, mature, and experienced teacher to the young, immature, and inexperienced pupil." Rather, adults must continue to learn from, and teach, other adults. "What is needed and what we are already moving toward is the inclusion of another whole dimension of learning: the *lateral* transmission, to every sentient member of society, of what has just been discovered, invented, created, manufactured, or marketed. This need for lateral transmission exists no less in the physics or genetics laboratory than it does on the assembly line with its working force of experienced and raw workmen."

A unique fact of our time—its pace of change, which Alvin Toffler dubbed "future shock"—is the first of a number of compelling reasons for lifelong learning. People in earlier times faced the task of absorbing an essentially stable body of knowledge. During each person's lifetime, not that much more was added to the store of learning. But nowadays there can be no such thing as "completing" one's education, even if one proceeds to the most advanced degree. Within five or ten years of graduation, 50 percent or more of what one has learned will likely be obsolete.

This selection is excerpted from "Why Is Education Obsolescent?" in the *Harvard Business Review*, November–December 1958.

No One Can
"Complete an Education"

Margaret Mead

When we look realistically at the world in which we are living today and
become aware of what the actual problems of learning are, our conception of education changes radically. Although the educational system remains basically unchanged, we are no longer dealing primarily with the
vertical transmission of the tried and true by the old, mature, and experienced teacher to the young, immature, and inexperienced pupil. This was
the system of education developed in a stable, slowly changing culture. In
a world of rapid change, vertical transmission of knowledge alone no
longer serves the purposes of education.

What is needed and what we are already moving toward is the inclusion of another whole dimension of learning: the *lateral* transmission, to
every sentient member of society, of what has just been discovered, invented, created, manufactured, or marketed. This need for lateral transmission exists no less in the physics or genetics laboratory than it does on
the assembly line with its working force of experienced and raw workmen. The man who teaches another individual the new mathematics or
the use of a newly invented tool is not sharing knowledge he acquired
years ago. He learned what was new yesterday, and his pupil must learn
it today.

The whole teaching-and-learning continuum, which once was tied in an
orderly and productive way to the passing of generations and the growth
of the child into a man—this whole process has exploded in our faces. Yet
even as we try to catch hold of and patch up the pieces, we fail to recognize what has happened. . . .

Thus we avoid facing the most vivid truth of the new age: *no one will
live all his life in the world into which he was born, and no one will die in
the world in which he worked in his maturity.*

For those who work on the growing edge of science, technology, or the
arts, contemporary life changes at even shorter intervals. Often, only a
few months may elapse before something which previously was easily

taken for granted must be unlearned or transformed to fit the new state of knowledge or practice.

In this world, no one can "complete an education." The students we need are not just children who are learning to walk and talk and to read and write plus older students, conceived of as minors, who are either "going on" with or "going back" to specialized education. Rather, we need children *and* adolescents *and* young *and* mature *and* "senior" adults, each of whom is learning at the appropriate pace and with all the special advantages and disadvantages of experience peculiar to his own age.

If we are to incorporate fully each new advance, we need simultaneously: (1) The wide-eyed freshness of the inquiring child. (2) The puzzlement of the near-dunce who, if the system is to work, must still be part of it. (3) The developing capacities of the adolescent for abstract thinking. (4) The interest of the young adult whose motives have been forged in the responsibilities of parenthood and first contacts with a job. (5) The special awareness of the mature man who has tempered experience, skepticism, and the power to implement whatever changes he regards as valuable. (6) The balance of the older man who has lived through cycles of change and can use this wisdom to place what is new.

Each and every one of these is a learner, not of something old and tried—the alphabet or multiplication tables or Latin declensions or French irregular verbs or the rules of rhetoric or the binomial theorem, all the paraphernalia of learning which children with different levels of aspiration must acquire—but of new, hardly tried theories and methods: pattern analysis, general system theory, space lattices, cybernetics, and so on.

Learning of this kind must go on not only at special times and in special places, but all through production and consumption—from the technician who must handle a new machine to the factory supervisor who must introduce its use, the union representative who must interpret it to the men, the foreman who must keep the men working, the salesman who must service a new device or find markets for it, the housewife who must understand how to care for a new material, the mother who must answer the questions of an observant four-year-old.

In this world the age of the teacher is no longer necessarily relevant. For instance, children teach grandparents how to manage TV, young expediters come into the factory along with the new equipment, and young men invent automatic programing for computers over which their seniors struggle because they, too, need it for their research.

This, then, is what we call the *lateral transmission* of knowledge. It is not an outpouring of knowledge from the "wise old teacher" into the minds of young pupils, as in vertical transmission. Rather, it is a sharing of knowledge by the informed with the uninformed, whatever their ages. The primary prerequisite is the desire to know.

Given this situation, which of the institutions that are concerned with the revision of our educational system is to take the initiative: the educational world, the government, the armed services, citizens' voluntary organizations, churches, or industry? Each has a stake in the outcome; each has power to influence what happens; each each has its own peculiar strengths and weaknesses.

Industry, however, has the peculiar advantage of understanding the major evil from which our whole educational system is suffering—*obsolescence.* Modern ideas of obsolescence have come out of studies of industrial processes, and industrialists have made these ideas so much a part of their thinking that making allowance for the costs of obsolescence and supporting continuing research on problems of obsolescence are a normal part of their professional behavior. In any major effort to modernize our educational system, of course, it would be appropriate for all the institutions to have a voice. It would be well, for example: for educators to watch out so that all they know would not be lost in the shuffle; for government to guard the needs of the nation; for church and synagogue to protect the religious values of the past; for the armed services to concentrate on our defense needs; for citizens to organize means of protecting the health, safety, and welfare (present and future) of their own and the community's children.

In these circumstances, would it not be most appropriate for industry to take the lead in highlighting the obsolescence of our present educational system? In the United States, in 1958, approximately 67 percent of the civilian labor force was engaged in some kind of work in industry. Of the advances which account for obsolescence, a very large proportion have come out of industry. But at the same time, much of the thinking that is holding up a real revision of our school system is based on an outmoded public image of industry as a monstrous and wicked institution which, if not restrained, would permit little boys to be sent down into coal mines or to work in conditions in which their lungs would be filled with powdered silicon.

In fact, industry has already taken the lead—within its own walls—in developing a new type of education that includes all levels of competence and training and that freely faces the need for education at the senior levels of management. . . . The thinking that has gone into this contribution, however, has not yet become an articulate, leading part of our rethinking of the educational system as a whole. But if industry, as represented by individual leaders from management and labor in many parts of the country, would come forward with plans which dramatized our dilemma, such plans would be heard.

What might these plans be? First, in regard to work perfomed by young people, industry could say to all those who believe that children should be kept in school primarily so that they will not be on the streets or at work under bad conditions: "We will agree that young people need more supervision than older workers—that someone should know where they are each day, that their health should be protected and checked, and that they should be protected from organized attempts to deprave them. We will undertake to train and supervise the young people who *at this time* cannot gain anything by remaining in school."

But this would not be enough. This offer would need to be accompanied by a second one: "As soon as *any* worker—of any age, at any level—in our plant, office, or laboratory is ready to study again, we will facilitate his, or her, doing so."

This is, admittedly, a large order. But we cannot have one without the other. For as long as we continue to think that free and, when necessary, subsidized education is appropriate *only* when it is *preliminary* to work (though, exceptionally, it may be continued after some inevitable "interruption"), just so long the guardians of character, of political literacy, and of our store of talent that comes from all classes and in many cases shows itself only very slowly, will argue for—and will get—longer and longer years of compulsory education and longer and longer years of free education.

Under these circumstances, the meaning of education and the purpose of schools—especially for young people between the ages of 14 and 20—will only become more confused. On the one hand, the education that is absolutely necessary for those who, at an early age, are ready to go on to become scientists, statesmen, philosophers, and poets will be hamstrung by the presence of those others who, at the same age, do not want schooling; and on the other hand, the lives and characters of the temporary nonlearners will be ruined, and they will be incapacitated as potential later learners.

What we need to do, instead, is to separate primary and secondary education—in an entirely new way:

By *primary education* we would mean the stage of education in which all children are taught what they need to know in order to be fully human in the world in which they are growing up—including the basic skills of reading and writing and a basic knowledge of numbers, money, geography, transportation and communication, the law, and the nations of the world.

By *secondary education* we would mean an education that is based on primary education and that can be obtained *in any amount* and *at any period* during the individual's whole lifetime.

By so doing, we could begin to deal effectively with the vast new demands that are being made on us. The high schools would be relieved of the nonlearners, among whom are found a large number of delinquents. But more important, men and women, instead of preparing for a single career to which—for lack of any alternative—they must stick during their entire active lives, would realize that they might learn something else. The very knowledge that this was so would relieve much of the rigidity that now bedevils management. Women, after their children became older, could be educated for particular new tasks—instead of facing the rejection that today is related to fears about new learning that is acquired in middle age.

Whatever their age, those who were obtaining a secondary education at any level (high school, college, or even beyond) would be in school because they *wanted* to learn and *wanted* to be there—*then*. A comparison of GI and non-GI students has shown how great have been the achievements of students who have chosen to go to school. Furthermore, the student—of whatever age—who was obtaining a secondary education would no longer be defined as someone without adult rights who must accept dependency and meager stipends and have a dedicated delight in poverty.

In an educational system of this kind we could give primary education and protection to actual children as well as protection and sensitive supervision to adolescents. We could back up to the hilt the potentiality of every human being—of whatever age—to learn at any level. And we could do this proudly.

The kind and amount of leadership that industry can best take in making individual plans for sending workers—*on pay*—to get more education, and the kind and amount of leadership that can best come from tax-supported activities is a problem that will have to be threshed out. In the United States, we usually depend upon private initiative to make the first experiments before tax-supported agencies pick up the check. So, too, we shall have to work out the problem of providing special work situations for adolescents and on this basis make our decisions as to whether tax-supported institutions—rather than individual industries—should become chiefly responsible for the employment of adolescents.

But we also need to recognize articulately that there are other routes to competence than the one route provided by the conventional school. Experimental co-operative-work plans in the public schools need to be supplemented by experiments in industry. . . .

The right to obtain a secondary education when and where the individual could use it would include not only the right of access to existing conventional types of schools but also the right of access to types of work training not yet or only now being developed—new kinds of apprenticeship and also new kinds of work teams.

In thinking about an effective educational system we should recognize that the adolescent's need and right to work is as great as (perhaps greater than) his immediate need and right to study. And we must recognize that the adult's need and right to study more is as great as (perhaps greater than) his need and right to hold the same job until he is 65 years old.

Among the nations whose industrial capacities make them our competitors, the United States has a comparatively small total population. The more completely we are able to educate each individual man and woman, the greater will be our productive capacity. But we cannot accomplish the essential educational task merely by keeping children and young adults—whom we treat like children—in school longer. We can do it by creating an educational system in which all individuals will be assured of the secondary and higher education they want and can use any time throughout their lives.

Why Only Adults Can Be Educated   True education—as contrasted with schooling—is impossible during one's childhood and youth, contends America's leading classical philosopher, Mortimer Adler. Only adults, with their maturity, experience, and superior capacity to think, can grapple with the most complex ideas and achieve the deepest understandings characteristic of advanced learning.

That is not a thesis likely to be embraced with alacrity by most American professional educators. But it has deep roots in the Western humanistic tradition, as the selections from Plato and McClintock have suggested. Adler's ideas are worth pondering because they offer a rationale for adult education that transcends contemporary imperatives. Lifelong learning, from this perspective, is the oldest idea of education we have.

Interestingly, Adler also adduces out of this tradition some of the basic principles of adult education espoused by leading professionals in the field, such as Malcolm Knowles—most notably the essential *voluntariness* and *equality* of the enterprise.

This selection was originally published under the title "Adult Education" in *Great Issues in Education,* published by the Great Books Foundation in 1956.

Why Only Adults Can Be Educated

Mortimer Adler

I am going to talk to you about education, but the word "education" has come to have so restricted a connotation that you may be misled by this. When you think of education, you tend to think of the development of your children, not of your own development; of learning in school, not outside of school. As a result, the phrase "adult education" is generally misunderstood. Because we think of education as something done primarily with the young and in school, "adult education" comes to be a queer kind of thing, something which you usually think of, if you think of it at all, as for the *other* person, not yourself.

In years of thinking and working in the field of education, the insight that I am going to try to communicate to you is one which is basic to the whole theory of education. It not only changes our conception of what should go on in the schools, and what should be done with children, but it also changes our conception of what each adult must do for himself to sustain his own life of learning.

I can hardly remember what I used to think when I had the mistaken notion that the schools were the most important part of the educational process; for now I think exactly the reverse. I am now convinced that it is adult education which is the substantial and major part of the educational process—the part for which all the rest is at best—and it is at its best only when it is—a preparation.

Words are mischievous and treacherous. Those of us who are engaged in adult education have been thinking for some time of how to avoid using the words "adult education," because in the minds of the general public they have such an unfortunate connotation. If, by issuing an edict, I could get everybody to use words the way I would like them to, I would try to set up the following usage: use "schooling" to signify the development and training of the young; and "education" (without the word "adult" attached to it) to signify the learning done by mature men and women. Then we could say that after schooling, education, not adult education, begins.

That is the main point. From long experience I am sadly aware of the misconceptions in the minds of almost everybody which prevent this basic proposition from being understood. Let me try to indicate the major misconceptions that must be rectified.

Most of us, and most professional educators, hold a false view of schooling. It consists in the notion that it is the aim or purpose of the schools—and I use the word "schools" to include all levels of institutional education from the kindergarten to the college and university—to turn out *educated* men and women, their education *completed* or *finished* when they are awarded a degree or diploma. Nothing could be more absurd or preposterous. This means that young people—children of twenty or twenty-two—are to be regarded as *educated men and women.* We all know, and no one can deny, that no child—in school or at the moment of graduation—is an educated person. Yet this is the apparent aim of the whole school system—to give a complete education. At least this is the conception which governs the construction of the curriculum, and the conduct or administration of the school system, and it is the conception of most parents who send their children to schools and colleges.

That this error about education being completed in school is widespread, is shown by the fact that most of us also hold a false view of (I must use these words I do not like, but I will use them in quotation marks) "adult education." I held it myself for many years. We think of adult education as something for the underprivileged. Some poor people were deprived in youth of schooling by economic circumstance or hardships. Perhaps they were foreigners who came to this country under difficult circumstances. Deprived of the normal amount of schooling, these people in later life, while they are working all day to support a family, go to night school to make up for their lack of schooling in youth. Night schooling or remedial schooling—to compensate for lack of sufficient schooling in youth—is, for a great many people, the essence of adult education. When they think of it in this way, they—the majority who are more fortunate—conclude that adult education is not for them, but only for the unfortunate few who lacked sufficient schooling in youth.

Another false and very misleading notion about adult education is that it is something you can take or leave, because it really is an avocation, a hobby that occupies a little of your spare time, something a little better than canasta or television, but not much. On this level, adult education consists of classes in basket weaving, or folk dancing, or clay modeling—things of that sort. Even lectures about current events are of that sort.

These are all wrong notions—wrong notions of the meaning of what schooling is or should be, and wrong notions of what fundamental education for adults should be. Perhaps the easiest way for me to correct these errors, and state the contrary truth, is to tell you what every schoolboy does not know. Every schoolboy or girl, particularly at the moment of graduation from school, does not know how much he does not know—and how much he has to learn. This is perfectly natural, and the children are not to be blamed for it. This is one of the blindnesses of youth. But there is hardly an intelligent adult—a college graduate two or three years out of college—who will not readily and happily confess frankly that he is not an educated person, that there is much more for him to learn, and that he does not know it all. If we should find a college graduate three years out of college who does not know he needs an education, charity would recommend that we speak no more of him.

When the college graduate, two, three, or five years out of college, recognizes the fact that he was not educated, or that his education or training was far from completed in all the years of schooling, he usually has one or another incorrect explanation of the fact. If he is a gentle and generous person, he is likely to say, "The fault was mine. I went to a good school. The curriculum was good. I had a fine set of teachers. The library facilities and all the other conditions in my formal schooling were excellent; but I wasted my time. I played cards or took the girls out, or went in for extracurricular activities, or something else interfered with study. If only I had studied, I would now be an educated person."

This, I assure you, is quite wrong. But, at the opposite extreme, there is the person who is equally wrong. He is less generous. He puts the blame on somebody else. He says, "It was the school's fault. The teachers were no good; it was a bad curriculum; in general the facilities were poor. If all these had been better, I would now be educated."

This opposite extreme is equally incorrect. The truth can be expressed only by what may seem to you for a moment to be an extreme or outrageous statement. But I must make it.

Consider the brightest boy or girl at the best imaginable college—much better than any which now exists—with the most competent faculty and with a perfect course of study. Imagine this brightest student in the best of all possible colleges, spending four years industriously, faithfully, and efficiently applying his or her mind to study. I say to you that, at the end of four years, this student, awarded a degree with the highest honors, *is not an educated man or woman*. And cannot be, for the simple reason that the obstacle to becoming educated in school is an inherent and insurmountable one, namely, youth.

The young cannot be educated. Youth is the obstacle. Why is this so? We know the answer almost as soon as we ask the question.

What do we mean by young people? What are children? In asking this question, I use the word "children" for all human beings still under institutional care. I do not care what their chronological age is, whether it is fifteen or eighteen or twenty-two. If they are still within the walls of a school, college, or university, they are children. They are living a protected, and in many ways an artificial, life.

I repeat, what does it mean to be a child? What is our conception of being a child? It is obviously a conception of human life at a stage when it is right to be irresponsible to a certain degree. Childhood is a period of irresponsibility. In addition to being irresponsible, the child or young person, precisely because he is protected or safeguarded, is greatly deficient in experience. Most or all of the things that make us adults or mature occur after we leave school. The business of getting married, of having children, of having our parents become ill, or dependent on us, or die, the death of our friends, our business and social responsibilities— these are the things that age us. And aging is a part of what makes us mature. We cannot be mature without being aged through pain and suffering and grief. This kind of suffering children are spared, but they pay a price for being spared it. They remain immature, irresponsible, and unserious, in the basic sense of that word.

Let me indicate this in still another way. In recent years, teachers in colleges and universities have had the experience of having, in the same classroom, the returned G.I., continuing his education on the G.I. Bill of Rights, and ordinary boys and girls right out of high school. The difference between those two groups of students in the same classroom is like the difference between black and white. The actual ages are not too far apart—sometimes the G.I. is hardly more than a year or two older than the boy sitting next to him. But the one is a man and the other is a child. And the difference between a man and a child is a difference wrought by experience, pain and suffering, by hard knocks. It cannot be produced by schooling.

It follows, then, that precisely because they are immature, properly irresponsible, not serious, and lack a great deal of experience, children in school are not *educable*. I do not mean they are not *trainable*. In fact, they are much more trainable than we are. As we get older, our nervous system becomes much less plastic. It is much harder for us to learn languages, much harder for us to learn shorthand, for example, or ice skating. The child, in all matters of simple habit formation, is much more trainable than the adult, but the adult is much more educable, because education is not primarily a matter of training or habit formation. Though these are preparations for it, education in its essence is the cultivation of the human mind. Education consists in the growth of understanding, insight, and ultimately some wisdom. These growths require mature soil. Only in mature soil, soil rich with experience—the soul in the mature person—can ideas really take root.

When I say adults are more educable than children, I am really saying that adults can *think better* than children. I hope you all believe that this is so, because if you do not, then adults ought to stay away from the polls and send their children there instead. But if you really believe—as I certainly do without embarrassment or hesitation—that you can think better than a child, then you must also realize that you are more educable than a child. Basic learning—the acquisition of ideas, insight, understanding— depends on being able to think. If adults can think better than children, they can also learn better—learn better in the fundamental sense of cultivating their minds.

You may suppose that this is a novel educational insight, this insistence that education belongs to the mature, and schooling, at the level of training and habit formation, to the young. But, except for our own century, all the great periods of Western culture have recognized and acted on the simple basic truth I have stated as my central thesis. If we go back to the Greeks, for example, I think I can show you in the works of the two great thinkers of antiquity, Plato and Aristotle, the presence of this fundamental insight.

The *Republic* of Plato outlines the ideal education of the best men to govern the ideal state. The course of study is as follows. Listen to its time schedule. From the beginning until the student reaches the age of twenty, the curriculum is confined to music and gymnastics. Here music stands for the cultivation of the sensibilities and imagination; and gymnastics stands for the acquisition of all the basic bodily coordinations. Between the ages of twenty and thirty there occurs training in the liberal arts, particularly the arts of mathematics (arithmetic, geometry, astronomy, and music), and the basic arts of grammar, rhetoric, and logic. Then, at the age of thirty, the young person goes out into the world. He leaves the academy and undertakes civic duties or public responsibilities, thus becoming a little more mature. He returns to the academy at thirty-five, for the study of philosophy, or the contemplation of ideas. And this continues until the age of fifty, when his formal education is completed. Here is a time schedule which recognizes how slowly the processes of education take place and how maturity is required before the understanding of ideas can occur.

There is another indication of this in the opening chapters of Aristotle's *Ethics.* He points out that you can train the characters of young men, you can form the moral virtues in them by reward and punishment, but, he says, you cannot teach them ethical principles. You cannot teach them ethical theory because they are immature. Lacking moral and political experience, being more or less under the influence of wayward passions, they cannot possibly understand moral and political principles, nor are they in a position to make sound judgments on moral questions. Think of how we violate this insight in our schools today. One of the major subjects for the young, soon after kindergarten, is social studies. Aristotle would not have thought it possible to teach these to young children because to understand the theory of society requires mature experience and judgment.

Perhaps I can communicate my basic insight by a reference to my own biography. When I went to Columbia College, and read the great books under an extraordinarily fine teacher, John Erskine, I read them very studiously. I thought I knew what they were about. I thought I understood them perfectly. To show you how young I was, let me tell you two things about myself. I recall quite clearly what my reaction was to Plato and Aristotle the first time I read the passages I have just reported to you. I was quite sure Plato was wrong that one could not understand ideas until after thirty-five or forty. He must be wrong, because there I was, at twenty, doing it. And Aristotle must be wrong that ethics could not be taught to young men. There I was, a young man who thoroughly understood the principles of Aristotle's *Ethics.*

I now know how silly I was at the age of twenty. I was fortunate enough to have to read again and again in the course of the next twenty-five years the same books I read in college. This experience of reading these books over and over again, during years when I was growing up a little, taught me how much such growth, through experience and living, is required for the understanding of the great books. I have often looked at old lecture notes, or at notes written some years earlier in preparation for leading Great Books discussions. I realize then how far I have come. It is not that I have grown more intelligent, but simply that my capacity for understanding has changed, deepened a little, perhaps, as a result of the intervening experience.

Now suppose that everything I have said is so. Suppose you agree with me that schooling should consist largely in the training of good habits in the young, and that education is principally learning by adults who are mature human beings.

What are the consequences of this proposition? I think that they are very radical indeed, so radical that it would take almost an educational revolution to put them into effect. If it is true that education is primarily a matter for adults, then what we do when we send our children to school, how we understand why we are sending them there, what we do about ourselves after school, and how we understand the necessity for us to continue learning—all these things will follow. If what I am saying is the case, then adult education, or education for adults, is necessary for all adults, not just for those who suffered deprivation in youth through lack of this or that part of formal schooling. It is no longer a matter of what is necessary for the other fellow; it becomes a matter which each of us must face for himself.

Let me now divide the consequences of this proposition into two parts: first, the consequences for the school system; and second, for adults.

I should like, first, to make a few remarks as background for the consideration of the reforms which should take place in the school system. I assume, without any argument at all, that we are committed to a democratic society, a democratic government, and democratic institutions. And I assume without argument that you understand this to mean acceptance of the basic truth about human equality, which expresses itself in the political principle of universal suffrage. What distinguishes democracy from all other forms of government is the extension of the franchise to all citizens, men and women, without regard to race, creed, or color. The only just limitations on universal suffrage involve the exclusion of infants and children, the mentally incompetent, and criminals who have forfeited their political rights by acts of moral turpitude. No one else is justly excluded according to a democratic conception of government. The educational consequence of this political principle is that all children must go to school. Education must be universal and compulsory because, in a democracy, all children must be trained for citizenship. This means, I say, building enough schools and finding enough teachers to take care of the whole population of future citizens in our democratic society.

You may say that we have almost succeeded in doing this in this country. It is true that we have, in the course of the last fifty years, recognized the educational obligations of a democratic society. We have built a tremendous number of schools and trained a vast horde of teachers. We have poured great funds of taxpayers' money into school budgets. This is satisfactory as far as it goes, but it does not go nearly far enough. If any of you have children in school, or know anything about what is going on in most of the schools today, public or private, you will know that most of the children are not being democratically educated. Most of the children—I think I can even safely say more than 75 percent—are, in fact, being given almost no education at all. They are being given vocational training. Vocational training is training for work or for the life of the slave. It is not the education of the future citizen, of the free man who has leisure to use. Liberal education, as distinguished from vocational training, is education for freedom, and this means that it is education for the responsibilities of citizenship and for the good use of leisure.

Again I am using a word [leisure] that is generally misunderstood in this country, if not everywhere, in modern times. Just as the phrase "adult education" is an unfortunate phrase because most people think that education is something that is done with children in school; so the word "leisure" is an unfortunate word, certainly for most Americans, because by "leisure" most of us mean spare time—the time one has to kill, the time one has to use up somehow because it is left over from the time needed for work and sleep. Leisure time, as most Americans think of it, is playtime or pastime, time to fritter away, to occupy with a variety of time-killing or time-consuming, *unimportant* activities. *In terms of this conception of leisure, liberal education has no meaning at all. You might as well close all the schools down.*

Let me give you another conception of leisure. Human life is divided into four parts, not three. Let me deal with work first. Work is that part of life which consists of the activities all of us must perform, if we have any self-respect, in order to earn and deserve our sustenance. Sleep is that part of life which is spent in recuperating from the fatigues of work. No one deserves to sleep who does not work. Sleep is for the sake of work. Play or recreation or amusement is on the same level as sleep. It is not the same as sleep, but it is not much better than sleep.

Let us think for a moment of the word "recreation." Recreational activities would seem to be for the sake of *re-creating* our energies, getting over fatigue, washing away the weariness that comes from labor. So, like sleep, recreational activities also are for the sake of work.

This leaves a set of activities through which we can discharge our obligation to acquire every human excellence which can grace a human person. These—and they are not play in any sense—are the activities of leisure. They are intrinsically good activities, for the sake of which everything else is done—for the sake of which we earn a living. Education is not for the sake of earning a living. American parents and teachers have for many years thought otherwise, unfortunately. Most American parents send their children to school in order to help them get ahead in the world—by beating their neighbors. They think school is the place to learn how to make a better living—"better" only in the sense of more money. This is not the meaning of school or of education. No one has to go to school in order to earn a living. Our grandfathers did not. Perhaps we need schools to train men for the learned professions, but not for the ordinary jobs of an industrial society. The basic tasks of an industrial society can be learned on the job. There is no need for vocational training in the schools.

We need to go to school, not in order to learn how to earn a living, but in order to learn how to use the life for which we are going to earn a living—to learn how to occupy ourselves humanly, to live our leisure hours well and not play them all away, or seek to amuse ourselves to the point of distraction or boredom. We need to learn how to do well what we are called upon to do as moral and political agents, and to do well what we must do for the cultivation of our own minds.

These are the aims of liberal education. Liberal education must be begun in school. If you understand what democracy is and what leisure is, and that to be a free man is to be a man of leisure as well as a citizen, then you will realize that all children not only should go to school, but should also be given a liberal education there. I would go so far as to say that *all* vocational training should be removed from the schools. I would even go further and say that by *liberal education for all the children* I mean education for all up to what is now regarded as the Bachelor of Arts degree.

When I say this, I have the image before me of large audiences of school teachers I have addressed. On their faces I see horror. They tell me, as they have told me, that it is easy for me to say these fine things. I have never faced the ordinary school classroom, with the ordinary assortment of children, of whom I am saying that all of them should go on to college and receive the degree of Bachelor of Arts, signifying the beginning of liberal education. If I had their experience, I would find, as they have found, it difficult, almost impossible, to accomplish even the beginning of what I mean by liberal education with a majority of children.

It was all right, they say, to try to give liberal education a hundred years ago when we had a much smaller and a much more select school population. But now that we have democratically taken all the children into school, it is no longer possible to give that same kind of education. I reply that as we make the transition from our colonial society, which was aristocratic, to our present society, which is democratic, we must undertake to give the same kind of education that was given then in the eighteenth century to the small governing class (the Thomas Jeffersons, the Alexander Hamiltons, the John Adamses, the men who wrote the Constitution and the Declaration) now in the twentieth century to the large governing class (all the citizens of the United States today). Nothing else will do. Nothing else is democratic.

I admit that in one respect the teachers are right. Children are containers of different sizes. They do not all have the same capacity. But the question is not one of the *amount* of education to be given each child, for no child can receive more than his capacity permits. The question has to do with the *kind* of education to be given each child, according to his capacity.

Let me illustrate this with a simple metaphor. Let the child of low intelligence and weak natural endowments be represented by a pint container; and the child of extremely high endowments and intelligence, by a gallon container. According to the democratic concept of education, you must put into the pint container whatever kind of liquid you put into the gallon container, even though only one pint can go here and a gallon there. It will not do to put cream into the gallon container and, say, water—dirty water, at that—into the pint container. Vocational education is the dirty water we are now pouring into our pint containers. Liberal education is the cream we are giving the few.

I think that school teachers, parents, and the country in general, have been misled on this point because the problem is so difficult to solve. The teachers took the wrong turn, though the easier one, when they were first faced with the problem at the turn of the century. They discovered that they did not know *how* to put cream into the pint container. Instead of doing what was required of them—taking the time to face and solve this very difficult problem of finding pedagogical techniques, methods, or means for putting cream into every container, large or small, they backed away, and accepted vocational training for the great majority of children as much the easier thing to do. This profound mistake we must now correct. We must give liberal training, training in the liberal arts, to all the children who are going to inherit the rights of citizenship and the leisure time of free men in their adult years.

What do I mean when I speak of liberal *training* for children? I do not mean a great deal of learning because I do not think that liberal *education* can be accomplished in school. I do not contemplate the production of educated men and women at the age of sixteen. I recommend only these two things. First, our children should be disciplined in the liberal arts, which means the ability to read and write and speak and think as well as they can. Second, our children should experience some intellectual stimulation and be enticed by learning itself. I would hope that somehow the feast of knowledge and the excitement of ideas would be made attractive to them, so that when they left school, they would want to go on learning. In school they must be given, not learning, for that cannot be done, but the *skills* of learning and the wish to learn, so in adult life they will want to go on learning and will have the skills to use in the process.

So much for the Bachelor of Arts degree. This is what the degree meant in the thirteenth century when it was first instituted. In the thirteenth century the baccalaureate did not signify an educated man. On the contrary, the meaning of the word itself is "first degree" or initiation, and the certificate indicated that a young person was now ready to start learning. He could now be admitted to the university to study law, or medicine, or theology. He was certified as a trained student, not as an educated person. It is this kind of liberal schooling we must again restore.

Let me turn now to the consequences of this basic educational proposition for you as adults. Here, too, the consequences are serious. If my understanding of the relation of schooling to education is right, then education is necessary for all adults—just as much for those who have gone through colleges and universities as for those who have not gone beyond elementary school. The person who has had more schooling has some advantage in the long process of learning, but actually all adults, as they begin their adult life, are on much the same footing as far as the goals of education are concerned. In order to explain this to you, let me be sure you understand the difference between education—that is, adult education—and schooling.

There are three remarkable differences between the education which takes place in adult life and the kind of thing that goes on in the schools at any level.

In the first place, adult education must be voluntary. You cannot compel adults to undergo a course of study or a process of learning because, if you have to compel them, that means they are not adults. It is proper to compel children to go to school or to compel their parents to send them. The common good of the republic and the individual good of the human beings who are its citizens require it. Adults are responsible for their own welfare and they participate in their own government. Therefore they must engage in education voluntarily, not under compulsion.

The second characteristic of education in adult life is equality among all those involved. Let me explain. In the schools you have teachers and pupils, and the relation between teacher and pupil is one of inequality—not simply because the teacher knows more than the pupil (let us assume that is the case), but because the teacher is mature, a grown-up man or woman, whereas the pupil is a child. And I hope you all agree with me that grownups are better human beings than children. For if you do not, then there is no point ever in saying, "Oh, grow up," as if you were admonishing somebody to improve.

You may not agree with me because you suffer from the widespread American illusion that the best thing in the world to be is a child. *Nothing could be further from the truth.* A child is the most imperfect of all human beings. Our job is to make him an adult. Except for those progressive schools where teachers mistakenly try to become equal with their pupils by getting on the floor with them, and by asking their opinions about everything, the classroom situation is one in which the teacher is superior.

Now in adult learning situations, we do not have teachers in this sense, or if we have, as we do in the Great Books classes, discussion leaders as well as participants in discussion, we do not admit inequality. The leader may know a little more about the book under discussion than the other persons participating in the class, but that is not the point. The point is that he is one mature human being talking with others, and that is a relation of equality. It is quite different from what goes on in the schools, or should. Most Americans think of adult education as schooling, and therefore misunderstand it. They think it puts them back into a position of inferiority. They think it consists in going to school, sitting under a professor, listening to a lecture. That is not adult education; that is a perversion of it. That is putting schooling into adult life where it does not belong. Adult education, or basic education for adults, involves a relation of equality among all the persons participating.

The third characteristic of education for adults is the most important. Basic education in adult life, which succeeds all the years of schooling, is and must be *interminable*—without end, without limit. Any part of schooling involves a fixed number of years. In this country we have eight years of elementary school, four years of high school or secondary school, four years of college, three years of medical or law or engineering school. This is quite proper, for these spans of time, these terms of years, are intended to provide time for a course of study embodying a subject matter or discipline to be acquired by the student. It is proper that he be certified when and if, upon examination, he shows himself competent. It is proper for a person to say, "I completed my legal education in three years," or "I have completed my four year college program." But think of an adult human being saying, "I have been going on with my learning for the last five years, from thirty to thirty-five, and now I have *completed my adult education.*" No more preposterous words can be uttered. For if anyone were to say, at the age of thirty-five, "I have now completed my adult education," all you could respond is, "Are you ready to die?" What. are you going to do with the rest of your life, if you have completed your *adult education* at the age of thirty-five. As you listen to these words, you know how silly they are, because you know now that adult education does not consist of a course of study or a subject matter to be mastered in a fixed number of years, something to take an examination on and pass, and then be finished with it forever. That is not the point. Adult education, once begun, is interminable. Nothing but a serious illness relieves any adult of his responsibility to continue learning year after year, every part of every year, until the end of his life.

Even though you recognize that what I am saying *must* be so because it is absurd to say, short of death, "I've finished my adult education," you may not fully understand why it is absurd. I think I can show you why. There are two reasons: one in the nature of the human mind itself, and one which derives from the goal of learning. Let me take the second first.

What is the real end of learning? What is the ultimate goal toward which every part of schooling or education is directed? I think you all know the word that describes it. It is wisdom. We would all like to be a little wiser than we are—to have a little more understanding, a little more insight, a little more comprehension of the human situation, of the conditions of our lives, of the world in which we live; to know better the difference between good and evil. But how long does it take to become wise? The answer is, a lifetime. Certainly we all know that we cannot become wise in youth. Nothing would be more preposterous than the supposition that a boy or girl graduating from college could be wise. Nor can you ever have enough wisdom, or too much. No matter how wise we become little by little in the course of a lifetime, we are always less than perfectly wise, nor are we ever as wise as we can be. Hence, if wisdom is the ultimate goal of the whole process of learning, then that process must go on for a lifetime. For any of us to attain even the little wisdom we can acquire in the course of our whole life, there is no stopping short. We can never become wise enough to say, "Now I can stop learning or thinking." Wisdom is hard come by and is slowly won. That is one reason for the interminability of adult education.

The other reason for the interminability of adult education lies in the nature of the mind itself. The human mind is not a muscle. It is not an organic thing, in the sense of an ordinary bodily organ. But it is a living thing. And like any other living thing, there are certain indispensable conditions of its vitality. Think of the body, for instance; think of muscles and body tissues in general. Everyone knows what basic things must be done with and for the human body to keep it healthy, alive, and in repair. You must first of all feed it regularly. No one supposes you can feed the body today or this week, and keep it alive and healthy next week or month or year. In addition, you must exercise it regularly. Everybody knows how a body unexercised, a body that is forced to lie in bed day after day, atrophies. Strength is sapped, muscles grow weak, almost collapse.

What is true of the body is true of the mind. The care and feeding of the mind is just as important as the care and feeding of the body. The mind unfed weakens just as the body does. The mind not sustained by the continual intake of something that is capable of filling it well or nourishing it, shrinks and shrivels. And the mind unexercised, like a muscle unused, atrophies, grows weak, becomes almost paralyzed. Hence, just as we know that we cannot support the life of the *body* this week on the basis of last week's *feeding*, so we ought to realize that we cannot support the life of the *mind* this week on last week's *reading*, much less last year's reading, or the reading done in college.

The process of keeping the mind alive and growing is as perpetual and continual a process as that of keeping the human body alive. But whereas there are limits to the body's growth, the mind, unlike the body, can grow every year of our lives. Until there is a real physical breakdown, real decrepitude, the human mind can grow. The only condition of its growth is that it be fed and exercised. Yet these are the very conditions most of us do not provide for our minds.

Let me add just one more thing that may help to clarify the point. Recently, giving a lecture in Chicago, I had occasion to point out most graphically the need for the actual continuation of learning year after year. I was giving a lecture on a fairly difficult philosophical subject, one about which I had written a book in 1940, and in 1941 a very elaborate essay. And here in 1951, in order to give a lecture on this subject, I had to spend a whole week reading my own book and article, and trying to understand what I thought in 1940 and 1941. I am sure that in 1940 and 1941 I had these thoughts, this analysis, this reasoning, at my fingertips. And in 1951 I had to work a week to recapture them.

This proves that no learning stays with you unless it is used. In the intervening years I had done little thinking on that particular subject, and, consequently, ten years later, I could not pull the ideas out of my mind, as if they had been put into a safe deposit vault or a storehouse, ready to be pulled out. The mind is simply not like that. The only ideas we have at our disposal are the ideas we are living with right now. The thoughts we do not revive by thinking them over again, the ideas we do not resuscitate, die very quickly. By some effort we can breathe life into them, and we must breathe life into them, if they are once more to be lively ideas for us, not dead ones.

Anyone who supposes that he has a set of ideas left over from college days which he can carry around with him the rest of his life, to pull out of a drawer when he wants to use them, is supposing something that simply is not the case. Any ideas we want to think with, we must re-think. We must give life to them by the use we make of them.

What follows from all this for the education of adults? *Every adult who has had the best liberal training we can give in school years needs education which will continue throughout all the years of adult life.* This is a large order, large in two senses: if we really mean *every* adult citizen, that is a large number; and if we really mean *all* the years of adult life, that is many years. The whole school system, from kindergarten through college, only occupies sixteen years; and yet, if you began the education of adults at twenty-two or twenty-five, that would involve thirty or forty years more of learning.

That is a large order. How can we solve a problem of such magnitude? We cannot solve it unless we have some conception of what adults must do in order to sustain their minds, keep them alive, keep them growing, not just for four years, but for ten, twenty, thirty, forty.

The program must be something that treats adults as adults, not as children in school; something they can do voluntarily; something that fits them as adults or mature persons. With all these requirements in mind, I mention the Great Books program as fully and properly fitting all the circumstances of the case. Let me explain why this is so.

First of all, the great books are great because they are inexhaustible. Unlike most of the things we read and could not possibly stand reading a second time, because it would bore us stiff to do so, the great books are indefinitely rereadable. My own experience in rereading them, many of them ten or fifteen times, only to find them each new and more significant than before, is sufficient evidence for me that they are inexhaustible. Because the great books can be read over and over again, this relatively small body of literature is large enough to sustain a lifetime of learning.

Secondly, the great books are intended for the adult mind. They were not written as textbooks for children. The great books are for adults in the sense that theirs is the level at which adults operate and think. (I do not mean that we should not—in fact, I firmly believe that, for the liberal training of children in school, we should—start young people reading the great books in high school or in college. Not because they can understand them at that age; but because, beyond the obvious fact that students must be taught to read and these are good books for the purpose, they must be read several times to be read well, and it is a good idea to accomplish a first reading as early as possible.)

In the third place, the great books deal with the basic problems, both theoretical and practical, of yesterday and today and tomorrow, the basic issues that always have and always will confront mankind. The ideas they contain are the ideas all of us have to think about. The great books represent the fund of human wisdom, at least so far as our culture is concerned, and it is this reservoir that we must draw upon to sustain our learning for a lifetime.

Suppose there were a college or university in which the faculty was thus composed: Herodotus and Thucydides taught the history of Greece, and Gibbon lectured on the fall of Rome. Plato and St. Thomas gave a course in metaphysics together; Francis Bacon and John Stuart Mill discussed the logic of science; Aristotle, Spinoza, and Immanuel Kant shared the platform on moral problems; Machiavelli, Thomas Hobbes, and John Locke talked about politics.

You could take a series of courses in mathematics from Euclid, Descartes, Riemann, and Cantor, with Bertrand Russell and A. N. Whitehead added at the end. You could listen to St. Augustine and William James talk about the nature of man and the human mind, with perhaps Jacques Maritain to comment on the lectures.

In economics, the lectures were by Adam Smith, Ricardo, Karl Marx, and Marshall. Boas discussed the human race and its races, Thorstein Veblen and John Dewey the economic and political problems of American democracy, and Lenin lectured on communism.

There might even be lectures on art by Leonardo da Vinci, and a lecture on Leonardo by Freud. A much larger faculty than this is imaginable, but this will suffice.

Would anyone want to go to any other university, if he could get into this one? There need be no limitation of numbers. The price of admission—the only entrance requirement—is the ability and willingness to read. This school exists for everybody who is willing and able to learn from first-rate teachers, though they be dead in the sense of not jolting us out of our lethargy by their living presence. They are not dead in any other sense. If contemporary America dismisses them as dead, then, as a well-known writer recently said, we are repeating the folly of the ancient Athenians who supposed that Socrates died when he drank the hemlock.

Education for Critical Consciousness   The most radical theory and practice in adult education today derive largely from the work of Paulo Freire. School reformer Jonathan Kozol has described Freire's strategies as the "brilliant methodology of a highly charged and politically provocative character." And social critic Ivan Illich has said, "This is truly revolutionary pedagogy."

Freire developed his ideas through work in adult literacy programs in Brazil and agricultural extension in Chile, but in truth the whole world, and especially the vast Third World, is his classroom. Years before he was "invited" by the Brazilian government to leave his homeland (because his programs promised to truly liberate the peasants from their oppression), Freire had devoted his life to the advancement of the world's poor peoples. During his exile he moved first to the United States, then to the World Council of Churches in Geneva. After an amnesty for exiles declared by the Brazilian government in 1980, he returned to São Paulo.

Freire's "pedagogy of the oppressed" derives from the conviction that all human beings, no matter how "ignorant" they may be, can look critically at their world in a "dialogical" encounter with others and that, provided with the proper tools for such an encounter, they can begin to perceive their personal and social reality and deal creatively with it.

This selection is excerpted from the chapter "Education and Conscientização" in the book *Education for Critical Consciousness,* published by Crossroad/Continuum in 1973. It was originally published in Spanish in 1965.

Education for Critical Consciousness

Paulo Freire

For more than fifteen years I had been accumulating experiences in the field of adult education, in urban and rural proletarian and subproletarian areas. Urban dwellers showed a surprising interest in education, associated directly to the transitivity of their consciousness; the inverse was true in rural areas. (Today, in some areas, that situation is already changing.) I had experimented with—and abandoned—various methods and processes of communication. Never, however, had I abandoned the conviction that only by working with the people could I achieve anything authentic on their behalf. Never had I believed that the democratization of culture meant either its vulgarization or simply passing on to the people prescriptions formulated in the teacher's office. I agreed with Mannheim that "as democratic processes become widespread, it becomes more and more difficult to permit the masses to remain in a state of ignorance."[1] Mannheim would not restrict his definition of ignorance to illiteracy, but would include the masses' lack of experience at participating and intervening in the historical process.

Experiences as the Coordinator of the Adult Education Project of the Movement of Popular Culture in Recife led to the maturing of my early educational convictions. Through this project, we launched a new institution of popular culture, a "culture circle," since among us a school was a traditionally passive concept. Instead of a teacher, we had a coordinator; instead of lectures, dialogue; instead of pupils, group participants; instead of alienating syllabi, compact programs that were "broken down" and "codified" into learning units.

In the culture circles, we attempted through group debate either to clarify situations or to seek action arising from that clarification. The topics for these debates were offered us by the groups themselves. Nationalism, profit remittances abroad, the political evolution of Brazil, development, illiteracy, the vote for illiterates, democracy, were some of the themes which were repeated from group to group. These subjects and others were schematized as far as possible and presented to the groups with visual aids, in the form of dialogue. We were amazed by the results.

After six months of experience with the culture circles, we asked ourselves if it would not be possible to do something in the field of adult literacy which would give us similar results to those we were achieving in the analysis of aspects of Brazilian reality. We started with some data and added more, aided by the Service of Cultural Extension of the University of Recife, which I directed at the time and under whose auspices the experiment was conducted.

The first literacy attempt took place in Recife, with a group of five illiterates, of which two dropped out on the second or third day. The participants, who had migrated from rural areas, revealed a certain fatalism and apathy in regard to their problems. They were totally illiterate. At the twentieth meeting, we gave progress tests. To achieve greater flexibility, we used an epidiascope. We projected a slide on which two kitchen containers appeared. "Sugar" was written on one, "poison" on the other. And underneath, the caption: "Which of the two would you use in your orangeade?" We asked the group to try to read the question and to give the answer orally. They answered, laughing, after several seconds, "Sugar." We followed the same procedure with other tests, such as recognizing bus lines and public buildings. During the twenty-first hour of study, one of the participants wrote, confidently, "I am amazed at myself."

From the beginning, we rejected the hypothesis of a purely mechanistic literacy program and considered the problem of teaching adults how to read in relation to the awakening of their consciousness. We wished to design a project in which we would attempt to move from naïveté to a critical attitude at the same time we taught reading. We wanted a literacy program which would be an introduction to the democratization of culture, a program with men as its Subjects rather than as patient recipients,[2] a program which itself would be an act of creation, capable of releasing other creative acts, one in which students would develop the impatience and vivacity which characterize search and invention.

We began with the conviction that the role of man was not only to be in the world, but to engage in relations with the world—that through acts of creation and re-creation, man makes cultural reality and thereby adds to the natural world, which he did not make. We were certain that man's relation to reality, expressed as a Subject to an object, results in knowledge, which man could express through language.

This relation, as is already clear, is carried out by men whether or not they are literate. It is sufficient to be a person to perceive the data of reality, to be capable of knowing, even if this knowledge is mere opinion. There is no such thing as absolute ignorance or absolute wisdom.[3] But men do not perceive those data in a pure form. As they apprehend a phenomenon or a problem, they also apprehend its causal links. The more accurately men grasp true causality, the more critical their understanding of reality will be. Their understanding will be magical to the degree that they fail to grasp causality. Further, critical consciousness always submits that causality to analysis; what is true today may not be so tomorrow. Naïve consciousness sees causality as a static, established fact, and thus is deceived in its perception.

Critical consciousness represents "things and facts as they exist empirically, in their causal and circumstantial correlations . . . naïve consciousness considers itself superior to facts, in control of facts, and thus free to understand them as it pleases."[4]

Magic consciousness, in contrast, simply apprehends facts and attributes to them a superior power by which it is controlled and to which it must therefore submit. Magic consciousness is characterized by fatalism, which leads men to fold their arms, resigned to the impossibility of resisting the power of facts.

Critical consciousness is integrated with reality; naïve consciousness superimposes itself on reality; and fanatical consciousness, whose pathological naïveté leads to the irrational, adapts to reality.

It so happens that to every understanding, sooner or later an action corresponds. Once man perceives a challenge, understands it, and recognizes the possibilities of response, he acts. The nature of that action corresponds to the nature of his understanding. Critical understanding leads to critical action; magic understanding to magic response.

We wanted to offer the people the means by which they could supersede their magic or naïve perception of reality by one that was predominantly critical, so that they could assume positions appropriate to the dynamic climate of the transition. This meant that we must take the people at the point of emergence and, by helping them move from naïve to critical transitivity, facilitate their intervention in the historical process.

But how could this be done?

The answer seemed to lie:

a. in an active, *dialogical,* critical and criticism-stimulating *method*;
b. in changing the *program* content of education;
c. in the use of *techniques* like thematic "breakdown" and "codification"[5]

Our method, then, was to be based on dialogue, which is a horizontal relationship between persons.

DIALOGUE

A with B = communication

        intercommunication

Relation of "empathy" between two "poles" who are engaged in a joint search.

MATRIX: Loving, humble, hopeful, trusting, critical.

Born of a critical matrix, dialogue creates a critical attitude (Jaspers). It is nourished by love, humility, hope, faith, and trust. When the two "poles" of the dialogue are thus linked by love, hope, and mutual trust, they can join in a critical search for something. Only dialogue truly communicates.

> Dialogue is the only way, not only in the vital questions of the political order, but in all the expressions of our being. Only by virtue of faith, however, does dialogue have power and meaning: by faith in man and his possibilities, by the faith that I can only become truly myself when other men also become themselves.[6]

And so we set dialogue in opposition with the anti-dialogue which was so much a part of our historical-cultural formation, and so present in the climate of transition.

ANTI-DIALOGUE

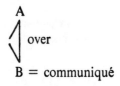

B = communiqué

Relation of "empathy" is broken.
MATRIX: Loveless, arrogant, hopeless, mistrustful, acritical.

It involves vertical relationships between persons. It lacks love, is therefore acritical, and cannot create a critical attitude. It is self-sufficient and hopelessly arrogant. In anti-dialogue the relation of empathy between the "poles" is broken. Thus, anti-dialogue does not communicate, but rather issues communiqués.[7]

Whoever enters into dialogue does so with someone about something; and that something ought to constitute the new content of our proposed education. We felt that even before teaching the illiterate to read, we could help him to overcome his magic or naïve understanding and to develop an increasingly critical understanding. Toward this end, the first dimension of our new program content would be the anthropological concept of culture—that is, the distinction between the world of nature and the world of culture; the active role of men *in* and *with* their reality; the role of mediation which nature plays in relationships and communication among men; culture as the addition made by men to a world they did not make; culture as the result of men's labor, of their efforts to create and re-create; the transcendental meaning of human relationships; the humanist dimension of culture; culture as a systematic acquisition of human experience (but as creative assimilation, not as information-storing); the democratization of culture; the learning of reading and writing as a key to the world of written communication. In short, the role of man as Subject in the world and with the world.

From that point of departure, the illiterate would begin to effect a change in his former attitudes, by discovering himself to be a maker of the world of culture, by discovering that he, as well as the literate person, has a creative and re-creative impulse. He would discover that culture is just as much a clay doll made by artists who are his peers as it is the work of a great sculptor, a great painter, a great mystic, or a great philosopher; that culture is the poetry of lettered poets and also the poetry of his own popular songs—that culture is all human creation.

To introduce the concept of culture, first we "broke down" this concept into its fundamental aspects. Then, on the basis of this breakdown, we "codified" (i.e., represented visually) ten existential situations. . . . Each representation contained a number of elements to be "decoded" by the group participants, with the help of the coordinator. Francisco Brenand, one of the greatest contemporary Brazilian artists, painted these codifications, perfectly integrating education and art.

It is remarkable to see with what enthusiasm these illiterates engage in debate and with what curiosity they respond to questions implicit in the codifications. In the words of Odilon Ribeiro Coutinho, these "detemporalized men begin to integrate themselves in time." As the dialogue intensifies, a "current" is established among the participants, dynamic to the degree that the content of the codifications corresponds to the existential reality of the groups.

Many participants during these debates affirm happily and self-confidently that they are not being shown "anything new, just remembering." "I make shoes," said one, "and now I see that I am worth as much as the Ph.D. who writes books."

"Tomorrow," said a street-sweeper in Brasília, "I'm going to go to work with my head high." He had discovered the value of his person. "I know now that I am cultured," an elderly peasant said emphatically. And when he was asked how it was that now he knew himself to be cultured, he answered with the same emphasis, "Because I work, and working, I transform the world."[8]

Once the group has perceived the distinction between the two worlds—nature and culture—and recognized man's role in each, the coordinator presents situations focusing on or expanding other aspects of culture.

The participants go on to discuss culture as a systematic acquisition of human experience, and to discover that in a lettered culture this acquisition is not limited to oral transmission, as is the case in unlettered cultures which lack graphic signs. They conclude by debating the democratization of culture, which opens the perspective of acquiring literacy.

All these discussions are critical, stimulating, and highly motivating. The illiterate perceives critically that it is necessary to learn to read and write, and prepares himself to become the agent of this learning.

To acquire literacy is more than to psychologically and mechanically dominate reading and writing techniques. It is to dominate these techniques in terms of consciousness; to understand what one reads and to write what one understands; it is to *communicate* graphically. Acquiring literacy does not involve memorizing sentences, words, or syllables—lifeless objects unconnected to an existential universe—but rather an attitude of creation and re-creation, a self-transformation producing a stance of intervention in one's context.

Thus the educator's role is fundamentally to enter into dialogue with the illiterate about concrete situations and simply to offer him the instruments with which he can teach himself to read and write. This teaching cannot be done from the top down, but only from the inside out, by the illiterate himself, with the collaboration of the educator. That is why we searched for a method which would be the instrument of the learner as well as of the educator, and which, in the lucid observation of a young Brazilian sociologist,[9] "would identify learning *content* with the learning *process.*"

Hence, our mistrust in primers,[10] which set up a certain grouping of graphic signs as a gift and cast the illiterate in the role of the *object* rather than the *Subject* of his learning. Primers, even when they try to avoid this pitfall, end by *donating* to the illiterate words and sentences which really should result from his own creative effort. We opted instead for the use of "generative words," those whose syllabic elements offer, through re-combination, the creation of new words. Teaching men how to read and write a syllabic language like Portuguese means showing them how to grasp critically the way its words are formed, so that they themselves can carry out the creative play of combinations. Fifteen or eighteen words seemed sufficient to present the basic phonemes of the Portuguese language.

The program is elaborated in several phases:

Phase 1   Researching the vocabulary of the groups with which one is working. This research is carried out during informal encounters with the inhabitants of the area. One selects not only the words most weighted with existential meaning (and thus the greatest emotional content), but also typical sayings, as well as words and expressions linked to the experience of the groups in which the researcher participates. These interviews reveal longings, frustrations, disbeliefs, hopes, and an impetus to participate. During this initial phase the team of educators form rewarding relationships and discover often unsuspected exuberance and beauty in the people's language.

The archives of the Service of Cultural Extension of the University of Recife contain vocabulary studies of rural and urban areas in the Northeast and in southern Brazil full of such examples as the following:

"The month of January in Angicos," said a man from the backlands of Rio Grande do Norte, "is a hard one to live through, because January is a tough guy who makes us suffer." (*Janeiro em Angicos é duro de se viver, porque janeiro é cabra danado para judiar de nós.*)

"I want to learn to read and write," said an illiterate from Recife, "so that I can stop being the shadow of other people."

A man from Florianópolis: "The people have an answer."

Another, in an injured tone: "I am not angry (*não tenho paixão)* at being poor, but at not knowing how to read."

"I have the school of the world," said an illiterate from the southern part of the country, which led Professor Jomard de Brito to ask in an essay, "What can one presume to 'teach' an adult who affirms 'I have the school of the world'?"[11]

"I want to learn to read and to write so I can change the world," said an illiterate from São Paulo, for whom *to know* quite correctly meant *to intervene* in his reality.

"The people put a screw in their heads," said another in somewhat esoteric language. And when he was asked what he meant, he replied in terms revealing the phenomenon of popular emergence: "That is what explains that you, Professor, have come to talk with me, the people."

Such affirmations merit interpretation by specialists, to produce a more efficient instrument for the educator's action.[12] The generative words to be used in the program should emerge from this field vocabulary research, not from the educator's personal inspiration, no matter how proficiently he might construct a list.

Phase 2 Selection of the generative words from the vocabulary which was studied. The following criteria should govern their selection:

a. phonemic richness;

b. phonetic difficulty (the words chosen should correspond to the phonetic difficulties of the language, placed in a sequence moving gradually from words of less to those of greater difficulty);

c. pragmatic tone, which implies a greater engagement of a word in a given social, cultural and political reality

Professor Jarbas Maciel has commented that "these criteria are contained in the semeiotic criterion: the best generative word is that which combines the greatest possible 'percentage' of the syntactic criteria (phonemic richness, degree of complex phonetic difficulty, 'manipulability' of the groups of signs, the syllables, etc.), the semantic criteria (greater or lesser 'intensity' of the link between the word and the thing it designates), the greater or lesser correspondence between the word and the pragmatic thing designated, the greater or lesser quality of *conscientização* which the word potentially carries, or the grouping of sociocultural reactions which the word generates in the person or group using it."[13]

Phase 3 The creation of the "codifications": the representation of typical existential situations of the group with which one is working. These representations function as challenges, as coded situation-problems containing elements to be decoded by the groups with the collaboration of the coordinator. Discussion of these codifications will lead the groups toward a more critical consciousness at the same time that they begin to learn to read and write. The codifications represent familiar local situations—which, however, open perspectives for the analysis of regional and national problems. The generative words are set into the codifications, graduated according to their phonetic difficulty. One generative word may embody the entire situation, or it may refer to only one of the elements of the situation.

Phase 4 The elaboration of agendas, which should serve as mere aids to the coordinators, never as rigid schedules to be obeyed.

Phase 5 The preparation of cards with the breakdown of the phonemic families which correspond to the generative words.

A major problem in setting up the program is instructing the teams of coordinators. Teaching the purely technical aspect of the procedure is not difficult; the difficulty lies rather in the creation of a new attitude—that of dialogue, so absent in our own upbringing and education. The coordinators must be converted to dialogue in order to carry out education rather than domestication. Dialogue is an I-Thou relationship, and thus necessarily a relationship between two Subjects. Each time the "thou" is changed into an object, an "it," dialogue is subverted and education is changed to deformation. The period of instruction must be followed by dialogical supervision, to avoid the temptation of anti-dialogue on the part of the coordinators.

Once the material has been prepared in the form of slides, filmstrips, or posters, once the teams of coordinators and supervisors have been instructed in all aspects of the method and have been given their agendas, the program itself can begin. It functions in the following manner:

The codified situation is projected, together with the first generative word, which graphically respresents the oral expression of the object perceived. Debate about its implications follows.

Only after the group, with the collaboration of the coordinator, has exhausted the analysis (decoding) of the situation, does the coordinator call attention to the generative word, encouraging the participants to visualize (not memorize) it. Once the word has been visualized, and the semantic link established between the word and the object to which it refers, the word is presented alone on another slide (or poster or photogram) without the object it names. Then the same word is separated into syllables, which the illiterate usually identifies as "pieces." Once the "pieces" are recognized, the coordinator presents visually the phonemic families which compose the word, first in isolation and then together, to arrive at the recognition of the vowels. The card presenting the phonemic families has been called the "discovery card."[14] Using this card to reach a synthesis, men discover the mechanism of word formation through phonemic combinations in a syllabic language like Portuguese. By appropriating this mechanism critically (not learning it by rote), they themselves can begin to produce a system of graphic signs. They can begin, with surprising ease, to create words with the phonemic combinations offered by the breakdown of a trisyllabic word, on the first day of the program.[15]

For example, let us take the word *tijolo* (brick) as the first generative word, placed in a "situation" of construction work. After discussing the situation in all its possible aspects, the semantic link between the word and the object it names is established. Once the word has been noted within the situation, it is presented without the object: *tijolo*.

Afterwards: *ti-jo-lo.* By moving immediately to present the "pieces" visually, we initiate the recognition of phonemic families. Beginning with the first syllable, *ti,* the group is motivated to learn the whole phonemic family resulting from the combination of the initial consonant with the other vowels. The group then learns the second family through the visual presentation of *jo,* and finally arrives at the third family.

When the phonemic family is projected, the group at first recognizes only the syllable of the word which has been shown:

(ta-te-*ti*-to-tu), (ja-je-ji-*jo*-ju), (la-le-li-*lo*-lu)

When the participants recognize *ti,* from the generative word *tijolo,* it is proposed that they compare it with the other syllables; whereupon they discover that while all the syllables begin the same, they end differently. Thus, they cannot all be called *ti.*

The same procedure is followed with the syllables *jo* and *lo* and their families. After learning each phonemic family, the group practices reading the new syllables.

The most important moment arises when the three families are presented together:

THE DISCOVERY CARD

ta-te-ti-to-tu
ja-je-ji-jo-ju
la-le-li-lo-lu

After one horizontal and one vertical reading to grasp the vocal sounds, the group (*not* the coordinator) begins to carry out oral synthesis. One by one, they all begin to "make" words with the combinations available:[16]

tatu (armadillo), *luta* (struggle), *lajota* (small flagstone), *loja* (store), *jato* (jet), *juta* (jute), *lote* (lot), *lula* (squid), *tela* (screen), etc.

There are even some participants who take a vowel from one of the syllables, link it to another syllable, and add a third, thus forming a word. For example, they take the *i* from li, join it to *le* and add *te: leite* (milk).

There are others, like an illiterate from Brasília, who on the first night he began his literacy program said, "*tu já lê*" ("you already read").[17]

The oral exercises involve not only learning, but recognition (without which there is no true learning). Once these are completed, the participants begin—on that same first evening—to write. On the following day they bring from home as many words as they were able to make with the combinations of the phonemes they learned. It doesn't matter if they bring combinations which are not actual words—what does matter is the discovery of the mechanism of phonemic combinations.

The group itself, with the help of the educator (*not* the educator with the help of the group), should test the words thus created. A group in the state of Rio Grande do Norte called those combinations which were actual words "thinking words" and those which were not, "dead words."

Not infrequently, after assimilating the phonemic mechanism by using the "discovery card," participants would write words with complex phonemes (*tra, nha,* etc.), which had not yet been presented to them. In one of the Culture Circles in Angicos, Rio Grande do Norte, on the fifth day of discussion, in which simple phonemes were being shown, one of the participants went to the blackboard to write (as he said) "a thinking word." He wrote: *"o povo vai resouver os poblemas do Brasil votando conciente"* [18] ("the people will solve the problems of Brazil by informed voting"). In such cases, the group discussed the text, debating its significance in the context of their reality.

How can one explain the fact that a man who was illiterate several days earlier could write words with complex phonemes before he had even studied them? Once he had dominated the mechanism of phonemic combinations, he attempted—and managed—to express himself graphically, in the way he spoke.[19]

I wish to emphasize that in educating adults, to avoid a rote, mechanical process one must make it possible for them to achieve critical consciousness so that they can teach themselves to read and write.

As an active educational method helps a person to become consciously aware of his context and his condition as a human being as Subject, it will become an instrument of choice. At that point he will become politicized. When an ex-illiterate of Angicos, speaking before President João Goulart and the presidential staff,[20] declared that he was no longer part of the *mass,* but one of the *people,* he had done more than utter a mere phrase; he had made a conscious option. He had chosen decisional participation, which belongs to the people, and had renounced the emotional resignation of the masses. He had become political.

The National Literacy Program of the Ministry of Education and Culture, which I coordinated, planned to extend and strengthen this education work throughout Brazil. Obviously we could not confine that work to a literacy program, even one which was critical rather than mechanical. With the same spirit of a pedagogy of communication, we were therefore planning a post-literacy stage which would vary only as to curriculum. If the National Literacy Program had not been terminated by the military coup, in 1964 there would have been more than 20,000 culture circles functioning throughout the country. In these, we planned to investigate the themes of the Brazilian people. These themes would be analyzed by specialists and broken down into learning units, as we had done with the concept of culture and with the coded situations linked to the generative words. We would prepare filmstrips with these breakdowns as well as simplified texts with references to the original texts. By gathering this thematic material, we could have offered a substantial post-literacy program. Further, by making a catalog of thematic breakdowns and bibliographic references available to high schools and colleges, we could widen the sphere of the program and help identify our schools with our reality.

At the same time, we began to prepare material with which we could carry out concretely an education that would encourage what Aldous

Huxley has called the "art of dissociating ideas"[21] as an antidote to the domesticating power of propaganda.[22] We planned filmstrips, for use in the literacy phase, presenting propaganda—from advertising commercials to ideological indoctrination—as a "problem-situation" for discussion. For example, as men through discussion begin to perceive the deceit in a cigarette advertisement featuring a beautiful, smiling woman in a bikini (i.e., the fact that she, her smile, her beauty, and her bikini have nothing at all to do with the cigarette), they begin to discover the difference between education and propaganda. At the same time, they are preparing themselves to discuss and perceive the same deceit in ideological or political propaganda;[23] they are arming themselves to "dissociate ideas." In fact, this has always seemed to me to be the way to defend democracy, not a way to subvert it.

One subverts democracy (even though one does this in the name of democracy) by making it irrational; by making it rigid in order "to defend it against totalitarian rigidity"; by making it hateful, when it can only develop in a context of love and respect for persons; by closing it, when it only lives in openness; by nourishing it with fear when it must be courageous; by making it an instrument of the powerful in the oppression of the weak; by militarizing it against the people; by alienating a nation in the name of democracy.

One defends democracy by leading it to the state Mannheim calls "militant democracy"—a democracy which does not fear the people, which suppresses privilege, which can plan without becoming rigid, which defends itself without hate, which is nourished by a critical spirit rather than irrationality.

Notes

1. Karl Mannheim, *Freedom, Power, and Democratic Planning* (New York, 1950).

2. In most reading programs, the students must endure an abysm between their own experience and the contents offered for them to learn. It requires patience indeed, after the hardships of a day's work (or of a day without work), to tolerate lessons dealing with "wing." "Johnny saw the wing." "The wing is on the bird." Lessons talking of Graces and grapes to men who never knew a Grace and never ate a grape. "Grace saw the grape."

3. No one ignores everything, just as no one knows everything. The dominating consciousness absolutizes ignorance in order to manipulate the so-called "uncultured." If some men are "totally ignorant," they will be incapable of managing themselves, and will need the orientation, the "direction," the "leadership" of those who consider themselves to be "cultured" and "superior."

4. Álvaro Vieira Pinto, *Consciência e Realidade Nacional* (Rio de Janeiro, 1961).

5. "Breakdown": a splitting of themes into their fundamental nuclei. See *Pedagogy of the Oppressed*, p. 113ff. "Codification": the representation of a theme in the form of an existential situation. See *Pedagogy*, pp. 106–107 and pp. 114–115. (Translator's Note.)

6. Karl Jaspers, *op. cit.*

7. See Jaspers, *op. cit.*

8. Similar responses were evoked by the programs carried out in Chile.

9. Celso Beisegel, in an unpublished work.

10. I am not opposed to reading texts, which are in fact indispensable to developing the visual-graphic channel of communication and which in great part should be elaborated by the participants themselves. I should add that our experience is based on the use of multiple channels of communication.

11. "Educação de Adultos e Unificação de Cultura," Estudos Universitários, *Revista de Cultura*, Universidade de Recife, 2–4, 1963.

12. Luís Costa Lima, Professor of Literary Theory, has analyzed many of these texts by illiterate authors.

13. "A Fundamentação Teórica do Sistema Paulo Freire de Educação," Estudos Universitários, *Revista de Cultura*, Universidade de Recife, No. IV, 1963.

14. Aurenice Cardoso, "Conscientização e Alfabetização—Visão Prática do Sistema Paulo Freire de Educação de Adultos," Estudos Universitários, *Revista de Cultura*, Universidade de Recife, No. II, 1963.

15. Generally, in a period of six weeks to two months, we could leave a group of twenty-five persons reading newspapers, writing notes and simple letters, and discussing problems of local and national interest.
    Each culture circle was equipped with a Polish-made projector, imported at the cost of about $13.00. Since we had not yet set up our own laboratory, a filmstrip cost us about $7–$8. We also used an inexpensive blackboard. The slides were projected on the wall of the house where the culture circle met or, where this was difficult, on the reverse side (painted white) of the blackboard.
    The Education Ministry imported 35,000 of the projectors, which after the military coup of 1964 were presented on television as "highly subversive."

16. In a television interview, Gílson Amado observed lucidly, "They can do this, because there is no such thing as oral illiteracy."

17. In correct Portuguese, *tu já lês.*

18. *Resouver* is a corruption of *resolver; poblemas* a corruption of *problemas;* the letter *s* is lacking from the syllable *cons.*

19. Interestingly enough, as a rule the illiterates wrote confidently and legibly, largely overcoming the natural indecisiveness of beginners. Elza Freire thinks this may be due to the fact that these persons, beginning with the discussion of the anthropological concept of culture, discovered themselves to be more fully human, thereby acquiring an increasing emotional confidence in their learning which was reflected in their motor activity.

20. I wish to acknowledge the support given our efforts by President Goulart, by Ministers of Education Paulo de Tarso and Júlio Sambaquy, and by the

Rector of the University of Recife, Professor João Alfredo da Costa Lima.

21. *Ends and Means* (New York and London, 1937), p. 252.

22. I have never forgotten the publicity (done cleverly, considering our acritical mental habits) for a certain Brazilian public figure. The bust of the candidate was displayed with arrows pointing to his head, his eyes, his mouth, and his hands. Next to the arrows appeared the legend:

> You don't need to think, he thinks for you!
> You don't need to see, he sees for you!
> You don't need to talk, he talks for you!
> You don't need to act, he acts for you!

23. In the campaigns carried out against me, I have been called "ignorant" and "illiterate," "the author of a method so innocuous that it did not even manage to teach him how to read and write." It was said that I was not "the inventor" of dialogue (as if I had ever made such an irresponsible affirmation). It was said that I had done "nothing original," and that I had "plagiarized European or North-American educators," as well as the author of a Brazilian primer. (On the subject of originality, I have always agreed with Dewey, for whom originality does not lie in the "extraordinary and fanciful," but "in putting everyday things to uses which had not occurred to others." *Democracy and Education*, New York, 1916, p. 187.)

None of these accusations has ever wounded me. What does leave me perplexed is to hear or read that I intended to "Bolchevize the country" with my method. In fact, my actual crime was that I treated literacy as more than a mechanical problem, and linked it to conscientização, which was "dangerous." It was that I viewed education as an effort to liberate men, not as yet another instrument to dominate them.

To Put Meaning into the Whole of Life "The chief danger which confronts adult education lies in the possibility that we may 'Americanize' it before we understand its meaning." These prophetic words were written in 1926 by Eduard Lindeman, often called the father of adult education in the United States.

A longtime teacher at the New York School of Social Work, Lindeman was known throughout North America as a lecturer and workshop leader for a generation of adult educators. But before winning his place as a distinguished academic, Lindeman had been very much a part of the "real world." Until the age of twenty-one, he had virtually no formal schooling, having earned his way in the world from the age of nine. He learned the shipbuilding trade, participated in strikes, and traveled widely. "The desire to somehow free education from stifling ritual, formalism and institutionalization was probably born in those frantic hours spent over books which mystified and confused my mind." How many adult educators might echo that confession!

Lindeman drew much of his inspiration and insight into what true adult education must be from the Danish experiments with folk high schools (Volkshochschulen), in which working people studied not to advance occupationally but simply to make life deeper, better, and more meaningful.

This selection appeared in the book *The Meaning of Adult Education,* published by the New Republic in 1926.

To Put Meaning into the Whole of Life

Eduard C. Lindeman

Education conceived as preparation for life locks the learning process within a vicious circle. Youth educated in terms of adult ideas and taught to think of learning as a process which ends when real life begins will make no better use of intelligence than the elders who prescribe the system. Brief and rebellious moments occur when youth sees this fallacy clearly, but alas, the pressure of adult civilization is too great; in the end young people fit into the pattern, succumb to the tradition of their elders—indeed, become elderly-minded before their time. Education within the vicious circle becomes not a joyous enterprise but rather something to be endured because it leads to a satisfying end. But there can be no genuine joy in the end if means are irritating, painful. Generally therefore those who have "completed" a standardized regimen of education promptly turn their faces in the opposite direction. Humor, but more of pathos lurks in the caricature of the college graduate standing in cap and gown, diploma in hand, shouting: "Educated, b'gosh!" Henceforth, while devoting himself to life, he will think of education as a necessary annoyance for succeeding youths. For him, this life for which he has suffered the affliction of learning will come to be a series of dull, uninteresting, degrading capitulations to the stereotyped pattern of his "set." Within a single decade he will be out of touch with the world of intelligence, or what is worse, he will still be using the intellectual coins of his college days; he will find difficulty in reading serious books; he will have become inured to the jargon of his particular profession and will affect derision for all "highbrows"; he will, in short, have become a typical adult who holds the bag of education—the game of learning having long since slipped by him.

Obviously, extension of the quantity of educational facilities cannot break the circle. Once the belief was current that if only education were free to all intelligence would become the proper tool for managing the affairs of the world. We have gone even further and have made certain levels of education compulsory. But the result has been disappointing; we have succeeded merely in formalizing, mechanizing, educational processes. The spirit and meaning of education cannot be enhanced by addition, by the easy method of giving the same dose to more individuals. If learning is to be revivified, quickened so as to become once more an adventure, we shall have need of new concepts, new motives, new methods; we shall need to experiment with the qualitative aspects of education.

A fresh hope is astir. From many quarters comes the call to a new kind of education with its initial assumption affirming that *education is life*— not a mere preparation for an unknown kind of future living. Consequently all static concepts of education which relegate the learning process to the period of youth are abandoned. The whole of life is learning, therefore education can have no endings. This new venture is called *adult education*—not because it is confined to adults but because adulthood, maturity, defines its limits. The concept is inclusive. The fact that manual workers of Great Britain and farmers of Denmark have conducted the initial experiments which now inspire us does not imply that adult education is designed solely for these classes. No one, probably, needs adult education so much as the college graduate for it is he who makes the most doubtful assumptions concerning the function of learning.

Secondly, education conceived as a process coterminous with life revolves about *non-vocational* ideals. In this world of specialists everyone will of necessity learn to do his work, and if education of any variety can assist in this and in the further end of helping the worker to see the meaning of his labor, it will be education of a high order. But adult education more accurately defined begins where vocational education leaves off. Its purpose is to put meaning into the whole of life. Workers, those who perform essential services, will naturally discover more values in continuing education than will those for whom all knowledge is merely decorative or conversational. The possibilities of enriching the activities of labor itself grow less for all workers who manipulate automatic machines. If the good life, the life interfused with meaning and with joy, is to come to these, opportunities for expressing more of the total personality than is called forth by machines will be needed. Their lives will be quickened into creative activities in proportion as they learn to make fruitful use of leisure.

Thirdly, the approach to adult education will be via the route of *situations*, not subjects. Our academic system has grown in reverse order: subjects and teachers constitute the starting-point, students are secondary. In conventional education the student is required to adjust himself to an established curriculum; in adult education the curriculum is built around the student's needs and interests. Every adult person finds himself in specific situations with respect to his work, his recreation, his family-life, his community-life, et cetera—situations which call for adjustments. Adult education begins at this point. Subject-matter is brought into the situation, is put to work, when needed. Texts and teachers play a new and secondary rôle in this type of education; they must give way to the primary importance of the learner. . . . The situation-approach to education means that the learning process is at the outset given a setting of reality. Intelligence performs its function in relation to actualities, not abstractions.

In the fourth place, the resource of highest value in adult education is the *learner's experience*. If education is life, then life is also education. Too much of learning consists of vicarious substitution of some one else's experience and knowledge. Psychology is teaching us, however, that we learn what we do, and that therefore all genuine education will keep doing and thinking together. Life becomes rational, meaningful, as we learn to be intelligent about the things we do and the things that happen to us. If we lived sensibly, we should all discover that the attractions of experience increase as we grow older. Correspondingly, we should find cumulative joys in searching out the reasonable meaning of the events in which we play parts. In teaching children it may be necessary to anticipate objective experience by uses of imagination but adult experience is already there waiting to be appropriated. Experience is the adult learner's living textbook.

Authoritative teaching, examinations which preclude original thinking, rigid pedagogical formulae—all of these have no place in adult education. "Friends educating each other," says Yeaxlee; and perhaps Walt Whitman saw accurately with his fervent democratic vision what the new educational experiment implied when he wrote: "learn from the simple— teach the wise." Small groups of aspiring adults who desire to keep their minds fresh and vigorous; who begin to learn by confronting pertinent situations; who dig down into the reservoirs of their experience before resorting to texts and secondary facts; who are led in the discussion by teachers who are also searchers after wisdom and not oracles: this constitutes the setting for adult education, the modern quest for life's meaning.

But where does one search for life's meaning? If adult education is not to fall into the pitfalls which have vulgarized public education, caution must be exercised in striving for answers to this query. For example, once the assumption is made that human nature is uniform, common and static—that all human beings will find meaning in identical goals, ends or aims—the standardizing process begins: teachers are trained according to orthodox and regulated methods; they teach prescribed subjects to large classes of children who must all pass the same examination; in short, if we accept the standard of uniformity, it follows that we expect, e.g., mathematics, to mean as much to one student as to another. Teaching methods which proceed from this assumption must necessarily become autocratic; if we assume that all values and meanings apply equally to all persons, we may then justify ourselves in using a forcing-method of teaching. On the other hand, if we take for granted that human nature is varied, changing and fluid, we will know that life's meanings are conditioned by the individual. We will then entertain a new respect for personality.

Since the individual personality is not before us we are driven to generalization. In what areas do most people appear to find life's meaning? We have only one pragmatic guide: meaning must reside in the things for which people strive, the goals which they set for themselves, their wants, needs, desires and wishes. Even here our criterion is applicable only to those whose lives are already dedicated to aspirations and ambitions which belong to the higher levels of human achievement. The adult able to break the habits of slovenly mentality and willing to devote himself seriously to study when study no longer holds forth the lure of pecuniary gain is, one must admit, a personality in whom many negative aims and desires have already been eliminated. Under examination, and viewed from the standpoint of adult education, such personalities seem to want among other things, intelligence, power, self-expression, freedom, creativity, appreciation, enjoyment, fellowship. Or, stated in terms of the Greek ideal, they are searchers after the good life. They want to count for something; they want their experiences to be vivid and meaningful; they want their talents to be utilized; they want to know beauty and joy; and they want all of these realizations of their total personalities to be shared in communities of fellowship. Briefly they want to improve themselves; this is their realistic and primary aim. But they want also to change the social order so that vital personalities will be creating a new environment in which their aspirations may be properly expressed.

American Triumphs in Adult Education   We are heirs to a great tradition of accomplishment, and it is well to remind ourselves regularly that the United States led the world, in some important respects, in adult education. Commissioned to give the first in a series of Kellogg Lectures at the National Adult Education Conference in 1980, Fred Harrington, former president of the University of Wisconsin and author of *The Future of Adult Education,* summarized the milestones in our national progress toward a learning society. Among them are the Americanization of immigrants, the public library movement, Cooperative Extension, continuing professional education, and distance education—each of which the author describes and comments on, and each of which is a continuing strong current within the field.

Harrington's celebration of our tradition and his vision of our future are especially useful because they come from a distinguished leader of higher education. One hopes that more and more university presidents of Harrington's stature will come to see the central and crucial role of adult education, as he does here.

This selection is excerpted and adapted from an address entitled, "Adult Education and the Nation's Problems," given at the 1980 National Adult Education Conference, St. Louis, Missouri.

American Triumphs in Adult Education

Fred Harrington

Many of the great successes in the history of American education have been in the adult learning area. And, almost without exception, these successes show adult educators recognizing problems and working toward solutions.

Some examples:

1. The Americanization of immigrants, the absorption of newcomers into the American culture, is one of the most dramatic stories in American history. And a large role was played by underpaid teachers who taught night classes for adults in our urban schools. The work continues today, with a greater appreciation for the values of cultures not our own. Behind it all is the conviction that immigrants must be responsible citizens and must not remain an unskilled, subordinate mass.

2. The public library movement, largely an adult affair, was launched with the help of philanthropists like Andrew Carnegie. The public library is now a recognized responsibility of local government. It stands as a constant reminder that lifelong learning is possible in every corner of the land. Of late, libraries have become increasingly effective, working with other agencies on broad cultural fronts, serving the practical needs of adults, and building public interest in the issues of the day.

3. Cooperative (agricultural) Extension is globally admired as a triumphant adult education enterprise. A key to its success is the financial backing it has received from the United States government for three-quarters of a century (which is, incidentally, the only example of adequate federal government support for an adult education enterprise). Equally important in this success story is the campus connection. Cooperative Extension transfers university knowledge to the farmer and applies research results in organized problem-solving campaigns. Granted, there are faults (benefits go mainly to the well-to-do). Yet we have here a useful adult education model—useful for its financial structure (shared federal, state, and local funding) and for the way it directly links the education of adults with the solving of problems.

4. Continuing professional education is far and away the fastest growing element in adult education at the present time. Business, government, and institutions of higher education are all incredibly active in this area, which is deplored by some because continuing professional education benefits the already established more than the less fortunate (successful professionals and their employers can afford the stiff fees). There are objections, too, that most CPE centers on technical information rather than on social responsibility. But the knowledge revolution has made continual upgrading essential if professionals are to keep current. And CPE courses, when properly handled, can improve the ability of professionals to deal with the nation's serious problems and can increase their desire to become involved.

5. Distance education. Correspondence courses and off-campus classes have been available for a century; but recent years have brought a great upsurge in activity, with traditional forms supplemented by radio and television, telephone hookups, recordings, courses by newspaper, and off-campus assignments. Adults have been the chief beneficiaries, and they have been helped also by the expansion of credit by examination and credit for experience. I am impressed by the University of Mid-America and its Open University plans; by what is being done by the State University of New York, the Appalachian community colleges, the University of Maryland, and several southern states; by the growing interest of business, foundations, and government in this approach; by the leadership of the Carnegie Corporation and the tremendous Annenberg gift to public television. Numbers remain small, but distance education does give a second chance to adults who have been passed by in the educational parade. Hence, it supplements the opportunities for adults available on campus, in night school, and in regular sessions. And the potential is enormous.

Given these achievements, it is surprising and tragic that adult education has enjoyed little of the enormous prestige that has long been attached to education in the United States. Sadder still that adult education has been on a starvation budget for these many years.

The reasons are clear enough, though not particularly persuasive. Many educators cling to the belief (or myth, really) that learning is for the young, that one "completes" education on graduating from school or college. There is a tendency, too, to sneer at part-time students and at off-campus, nontraditional, and noncredit work—all adult education staples. And to say that grownups can afford to pay (often they cannot) and that adult learners, teachers of adults, and their offerings are inferior in quality. "Adult education!" one campus dean said to me. "That means second-rate courses taught by second-rate teachers to second-rate students."

Happily, there are signs of a new day coming. The quickening pace of technological change has driven home to doubters the need to choose between continuing education and professional obsolescence. Simultaneously, the crushing burden of contemporary social and economic problems has increased interest in the search for solutions, and that almost always leads to adult study and retraining programs. Besides, the shrinking of the pool of younger Americans has forced educators to look for business elsewhere—and where can one look except at disadvantaged youth and the adult population?

While all this has been stirring, adult educators have improved their visibility. Adult education has become an accepted field for college-level teaching and for serious research and specialization. What is more, those professionally involved in adult education have stepped up their public relations and political activity, are speaking out much more than before, and are demanding to be heard. With some effect, we hear many voices saying that the adult revolution is just around the corner or is already here.

Unfortunately, this visibility and partial recognition have come in a period of financial stringency and just when all of education is under attack as seldom before. Consequently, those who are promoting adult learning have had to share with other educators budget cuts and feelings of uncertainty.

In a way, the situation is worse for adult educators than for the rest because they entered this belt-tightening era short of funds and with no great reservoir of public sympathy. And, seeing adult education gaining popularity, they had rising expectations that were not accompanied by rising income.

What do we do about it?

Well, there is no reason for despair. Adult educators are accustomed to adversity; they have had tough going in the past when others were faring well. So the best approach is to realize that attitudes toward the education of adults have in fact changed, which means that the signs are right for the long future. Support will surely come now that the value of lifelong learning is established, now that adult education is accepted as an indispensable element in problem solving.

But that does not mean that adult educators should sit still and await the happy day. Rather it means it is a time to act, to improve organization and to press, within the educational establishment and outside it; a time to insist on proper recognition and status; a time to strengthen the training of adult educators and to push for more and better research about adult learning; a time to play politics, to impress private donors and foundations, the business community, journalists, officeholders, and the general public with the value of adult education.

It should be a pleasure to present the message now that more are listening. And the message is much as before, with some changes in emphasis in keeping with the crises of the times:

First, adult education will, as before, work for the full development of individual Americans, recognizing that in these days of doubt and disillusion, the quest for personal satisfaction must include developing a sense of social responsibility and a willingness to join in attacking the sources of the nation's ills.

Second, through continuing professional education and in other ways, adult educators must concentrate on preparing men and women to deal with the great problems before us: poverty, prejudice, and pollution; energy and the environment; housing, health, and inflation; urban and rural decay; waste of human resources; crime, violence, and inequality; and global unrest. Nor is it enough to provide training; those who educate adults must be willing to participate themselves in action programs and in applying knowledge to the solution of problems.

Third, since education tends to help the haves more than the have-nots, it is imperative that adult educators try to understand and assist and work with the disadvantaged: women; the poor; the sick and the handicapped; senior citizens; blacks, Hispanics, and other minorities; the unemployed and the underemployed; the victims of discrimination; the neglected and forgotten. Adult education is the second-chance field, the field dedicated to improving the human condition. Adult education is a gateway to success, and success for the nation cannot be assured if so many are left behind.

These interrelated points constitute a big (but not too big) assignment. For, after all, adult educators were successful on many fronts when they were generally regarded as second-class citizens. Now that their worth is being recognized (though not yet enough), they should be able to accomplish a great deal.

Part III

UNDERSTANDING ADULT LEARNING

The Three Kinds of Lifelong Learners   The influence of Cyril Houle has been steady and stimulating for the field of adult education for more than twenty years. Through his unflagging research and publications, his advanced teaching and training of researchers at the University of Chicago, and his current work as senior program consultant to the W. K. Kellogg Foundation, Dr. Houle has been an unremitting force for intelligence and venturesomeness in the field.

One of his path-breaking books was a short volume of fewer than a hundred pages, *The Inquiring Mind: A Study of the Adult Who Continues to Learn.* Although based on in-depth interviews with a mere twenty-two individuals who were unusually active adult learners, the book nevertheless had a deep impact on research in the field. It was the first substantial effort to understand adult education through the study of the *individual learner* in his or her own right, rather than merely as a client of one or another organized program or institution, which had been the focus of all previous work in the field. Houle discerned within his subjects' responses a number of themes that have become germinal in the thinking of adult educators, such as the "stimulators," who seem to have an unusual significance in creating among others the desire to learn, and the "enclaves" of learning-oriented people.

In this selection from that book, Houle makes an invaluable distinction among three kinds of continuing learners: the goal-oriented, the activity-oriented, and the learning-oriented. His vivid descriptions of each will apply to virtually any adult education course, offering, program, or clientele.

This selection was excerpted from the chapter entitled, "Two Educations," in *The Inquiring Mind* by Cyril O. Houle, published by the University of Wisconsin Press in 1961.

The Three Kinds of Lifelong Learners

Cyril Houle

My effort in this study . . . has been to examine the lives of a group of adults who are members of our own society. These men and women share a common characteristic: they are so conspicuously engaged in various forms of continuing learning that they could be readily identified for me by their personal friends or by the counselors and directors of adult educational institutions. Otherwise they vary widely in age, sex, race, national origin, social status, religion, marital condition, and level of formal education. All of them live in urban areas, though not necessarily in large cities. University faculty members and people working for degrees were excluded since they make up two groups for whom continuing education is a special way of life.

All of these people were asked by someone in whom they had confidence to participate in an interview; when they agreed, they were provided with a statement describing the nature of continuing education and indicating the general kinds of questions which the interviewer would ask. This statement and the interview schedule itself (both of which had been pre-tested by all of the usual means) included nineteen major questions, all of them worded with an effort to avoid bias. These questions were not asked in any established order and, indeed, each person interviewed was encouraged to talk freely and frankly; often, in the course of a single long monologue, he would answer several questions. The interviews were tape-recorded and later transcribed.

Originally it was planned to collect about twenty case studies but the number was increased to twenty-two in order to be sure that variations in all the characteristics mentioned above were included. This group of cases is in no sense to be considered a statistical sample; it is much too small for that, and there is no way to be certain as yet of the dimensions of the total population which should be represented. Occasionally some clusterings of response appeared to be significant; they will be reported at the appropriate places but with no thought that they are typical of all continuing learners.

133

Preliminary interviews and discussions had revealed that many people have fairly definite ideas about continuing learners, particularly about why they are the way they are. Some observers lay stress on early family influence, others on the inspiration provided by great teachers, and still others on intelligence or other personal characteristics. As for myself, I had no conscious hypotheses. Many hours spent in counseling adults in search of education have made it easy for me to think of countless exceptions to any simple explanation which others might propose. The interviews were so designed, however, as to encourage the exploration of all of the themes suggested in the preparatory discussions. In a sense I was searching for hypotheses in this small group of case studies, each of which was subjected to detailed analysis. More important, I hoped that these people and their activities could somehow be fitted together into patterns that would throw light on the meaning of continuing education. . . .

Taken as a whole, the . . . people, however diverse their backgrounds in other ways, did turn out to be basically similar. They are perceived by others as being deeply engaged in learning and this perception proved to be valid, for they themselves regard continuing education as an important part of their lives even though they differ from each other in their ways of considering it. While there were gradations within the group in the amount, the kind, and the purposes, of their study, everyone interviewed would be near the upper end of any scale which measured the extent of people's participation in educational activities. Moverover, they had the same basic ways of thinking about the process in which they were engaged. They all had goals which they wished to achieve, they all found the process of learning enjoyable or significant, and they all felt that learning was worthwhile for its own sake.

But while they were basically similar they did vary in terms of the major conception they held about the purposes and values of continuing education. As I pondered the cases, considering each one as a whole, it gradually became clear (after many an earlier effort at analysis had led nowhere) that within the group there were in essence three subgroups. The first, or as they will be called, the *goal-oriented*, are those who use education as a means of accomplishing fairly clear-cut objectives. The second, the *activity-oriented*, are those who take part because they find in the circumstances of the learning a meaning which has no necessary connection, and often no connection at all, with the content or the announced purposes of the activity. The third, the *learning-oriented*, seek knowledge for its own sake. These are not pure types; the best way to represent them pictorially would be by three circles which overlap at their edges. But the central emphasis of each subgroup is clearly discernible.

The goal-oriented are the easiest to understand, chiefly because their views accord so well with the usual beliefs about education. "We no more live to know, than we live to eat," said John Ruskin,[1] and most people, if they gave the matter any thought, would agree with him. Knowledge is to be put to use, and, if it is not, why bother to pursue it?

One person who holds such a view is a solid, heavy-set man of fifty, with an air of both substance and vigor. His face is rather pleasantly like that of a bulldog. He started out as an unskilled laborer in the factory of a large corporation, has now risen through several levels of supervisory responsibility, and will almost certainly rise further. He has made his way, he feels, by adult education, earning first a high school diploma and then a Bachelor's degree in commerce by this means. He did not take this credit work merely for the symbols of accomplishment it would provide but because he felt he needed to have "the material that you get in high school and college." He also felt that he lacked self-confidence and therefore he took several courses in public speaking, in order "to learn how to think on my feet." He has "put in for" all of the optional courses in management that his company provides.

But the desire to get ahead on his job has not been the only reason for his interest in continuing education. He and his wife had a problem with one of their children and, on the advice of the school psychologist, they belonged, for a while, to a discussion group made up of parents of children with similar problems. He himself, in his mid-forties, had some of the feelings of tension which are so characteristic of that period and took part in a group therapy course. He was elected to the school board in the small suburban town in which he lives, and it seemed sensible to him to join the state association of school board members, to read its literature, and to take part in its meetings. In this same community, there is enthusiastic support "among all the right people" for a concert series in the high school auditorium and he feels he must attend, partly because he is on the school board. After suffering intense boredom for a while, he "sneaked downtown and took some music appreciation courses," and what used to be a duty is now beginning to seem almost a pleasure.

When he describes other people engaged in continuing education, this man is aware that not all of them view it as he does. But he is chiefly sensitive to and sympathetic with other goal-oriented individuals who, like himself, have clear-cut aims they wish to achieve: "One of my present bosses is a real good example of a desirable kind of self-educating man. He started for our company as a worker when the company was just starting. I think he probably finished high school, but not more than that. I don't know if he even finished high school. He is now the plant superintendent. He has attended many classes at night school. He's done a lot of reading and is really a learned man, now. He speaks very well, he can write very effectively, and he is obviously a very mature, cultivated man. This is the kind of thing you like to see as a result of self-education, and he did it on his own, too, because he did all of this through going to night school classes and reading."

The continuing education of the goal-oriented is in episodes, each of which begins with the realization of a need or the identification of an interest. There is no even, steady, continuous flow to the learning of such people, though it is an ever-recurring characteristic of their lives. Nor do they restrict their activities to any one institution or method of learning. The need or interest appears and they satisfy it by taking a course, or joining a group, or reading a book, or going on a trip. To be sure, the awareness of the need or interest is sometimes aroused because a learning resource becomes available. Fairly often with this group, as with the others, a circular received in the mail will announce a book or an activity, and this event will suddenly crystallize a sense of need which has been only vaguely felt before. But the purpose is always what initiates the educational effort, and the means are selected on the basis of whether or not they will achieve that purpose. For example, a few of the goal-oriented read a great deal, not freely or widely but always along lines of well-defined interests or in connection with courses or organizational work. The following observation is typical: "I do a fair amount of reading related to my work. Now this is in the area of magazines and professional journals. This would include magazines in the field of industrial safety, industrial health, fire protection, and, in addition to that, I do a fair amount of reading in the various areas of business management. I'm a member of the Society for the Advancement of Management."

The activity-oriented take part in learning primarily for reasons unrelated to the purposes or content of the activities in which they engage. Those included in this subgroup have many different kinds of reasons for being continuing learners, only a few of which will be illustrated here.

Loneliness leads many people to education. This viewpoint was expressed in its purest form by one rather intense woman:

> I wish you people in adult education would stop selling tuitions and start selling cordiality or something, or sort of give a little. I think the people that come really want that as much as learning. Forget about the learning part. They are going to learn anyway. That's what they are paying their money for. There is so much that is drab in this world. The real joy of participation, that's the only thing that I think is overlooked in adult education, and I think that's what adults want. They may not recognize that that's what they want, but put it to the test and see. I think that's as important as learning. It's that ingredient that you don't buy over the counter. The real joy of participation.

The adult educational institution, like the church, is an open and socially accepted place for meeting people and making friends. It has, as it were, a kind of preventive psychiatric role. In a mass society many individuals feel lost. They have little or no intimate fellowship and they miss the sense of belonging to a small natural group in which they are important and respected. Therefore they go in search of a social milieu, and the adult educational institution is one of the places where they look for it. In those evening schools which register their students by having them go to the classrooms on opening night, one will often find people moving along from door to door, peering in to see what kinds of folk are already assembled, and choosing finally to enter that class which seems to have the most potentially agreeable group, regardless of the purpose, the content, or the method of the course.

Some people are attracted to adult educational activities because they hope to find a husband or wife. Counselors, ministers, advice-to-the-love-lorn columnists, and others have been suggesting to people for some years now that adult educational classes are good places for finding suitable marriage partners. Among the cases studied, there were two such people—one man, one woman!—who turned to adult education for this reason, though others also had it as a more or less conscious secondary purpose. The problem in almost every case which I have witnessed, in this study and in other situations, goes much deeper than a wish to choose or to be chosen. The problem lies fundamentally in an individual's realization that he or she has somehow not made a proper adjustment to the normal patterns of behavior in a heterosexual society. Such an adjustment is never easy and it is sometimes impossible; that is why the quest for a husband or wife may lead to lengthy and intensive participation in educational activities. Sometimes the remedy is sought directly in courses which are essentially group therapy or have the alluring word "psychology" or "psychiatry" in their titles; to some men and women, however, such courses are too embarrassing or threatening, so that they join more innocuous classes in which members of the opposite sex are to be found, hoping to learn how to adjust to them. As one acute woman, who had had many courses at the YMCA, observed: "I think the initials YM entice a lot of women here."

Still others are primarily seeking to escape from a basic personal problem or an unhappy relationship. A wretched marriage, a demanding elderly parent, a job which is routine and distasteful: these and other misfortunes can father the wish to escape for a time into an activity which is positive, which provides a contrast to the rest of life, and which can be readily explained.

Another kind of person who falls within this subgroup would be the man or woman who takes courses simply for the credits themselves or for the diplomas, certificates, or degrees which may eventually be won by piling up the proper number and kinds of credits. Such people care little (often nothing) for the subject-matter itself and, at the end of a term, they may be found in a long line at the bookstore selling back the volumes which they had been required to buy and for which they now feel no further need. Some credit-seekers (I hope most of them) really want to know the content of the courses they take and therefore are goal-oriented; but most teachers who have taught credit courses for adults have found in their classes individuals who indicated, usually politely but always unmistakably, that it was only the activity and what its completion could bring that mattered to them.

A few people are continuing learners because they believe that they are in this way carrying on a tradition of their family or their culture. The late George Apley collected Chinese bronzes (in the process trying to inform himself fully about them) but not because he liked them. "As a matter of fact," he noted, "I think many of my best ones are overdecorated and look inappropriate in the Hillcrest library. I have made this collection out of duty rather than out of predilection, from the conviction that everyone in a certain position owes it to the community to collect something."[2] One man interviewed for this study said of his family, "We are forward-moving people. Growth and progress have always been in my background." Here before my eyes was one of Mr. David Riesman's tradition-directed men, perhaps laying an unusual stress on this part of his heritage because (as the rest of the interview showed) it was the only remnant of his tradition left to him.

Finally, there are some individuals who have been engaged in education so long and to such an extent that it has become an essentially meaningless activity. One of the men interviewed was such a person. For more than twenty-five years, he has taken every course available to him, sometimes gorging himself with as many as five or six at once, in a wholly meaningless profusion, with no pattern, coherence, or apparent effect. His latest job, in a lifetime of casual employment, is as a salesman in a hardware store which specializes in radio and electronic equipment. About this job, he says, "Like in any profession you've got to start little and then as you go up you may want to go into part commercial and part industrial and part—like manufacturing radios and television sets and maybe owning stations and maybe—I know there's one man whose name is Sarnoff who made his appearance as a poor boy just like me and he went to New York and he's a millionaire now. If I had stayed at Hart, Schaffner, and Marx, and that's almost 24 years ago, I might have been somebody now. You know, when a man works steadily for like 22 or 24 years, I might have been a big-time executive now. If I live to be 55 or 70 or 80 years old, maybe I'll have something then." To hear such a recital as this is to be reminded of the litany which George recited to Lennie in *Of Mice and Men:* "Guys like us, that work on ranches, are the loneliest guys in the world. They got no family. They don't belong no place. They come to a ranch an' work up a stake, and then they go inta town and blow their stake, and the first thing you know they're . . . on some other ranch. They ain't got nothing to look ahead to. . . . With us it ain't like that. We got a future. . . . Someday—we're gonna get the jack together and we're gonna have a little house and a couple of acres an' a cow and some pigs . . . an' live off the fatta the lan'."[3]

All of the activity-oriented people interviewed in this study were course-takers and group-joiners. They might stay within a single institution or they might go to a number of different places, but it was social contact that they sought and their selection of any activity was essentially based on the amount and kind of human relationships it would yield. Most of them said—and it was believable—that they did almost no reading. If the number of cases was enlarged, however, we might find that the desire for social contact is not common to all of the activity-oriented. As we have seen, some people escape from solitude into a classroom; there must be others who retreat from busyness into the quiet of the library or the museum.

For the learning-oriented, education might almost be called a constant rather than a continuing activity. This subgroup differs from the other two much more markedly than either of them does from the other. Each particular educational experience of the learning-oriented is an activity with a goal, but the continuity and range of such experiences make the total pattern of participation far more than the sum of its parts. To draw a parallel, a man reading a novel may be inferred to have a purpose in mind for reading it, but if he reads five novels a week, year after year, his habitual behavior as a novel-reader is more notable than the act of reading any individual novel. So it is with the learning-oriented; what they do has a continuity, a flow, and a spread which establish the basic nature of their participation in continuing education. For the most part, they are avid readers and have been since childhood; they join groups and classes and organizations for educational reasons; they select the serious programs on television and radio; when they travel, as one woman put it, they "make a production out of it," being sure to prepare adequately to appreciate what they see; and they choose jobs and make other decisions in life in terms of the potential for growth which they offer.

The fundamental purpose which lies back of all this activity is, quite simply, the desire to know. Juvenal identified *cacoëthes scribendi*, the itch to write. These people have *cacoëthes studendi*, the itch to learn.

Such a man was Alfred, the ninth-century ruler of England, one of those gifted but unfortunate people about whom the impression has somehow been created that the life of each consisted of a single anecdote. Whatever Alfred's faults as a cake-watcher, he was the very model of a learning-oriented man, as his biography by his tutor, Asser, shows. The modern translator of Asser sums up the character of Alfred in this way:

> . . . while he is no bookworm, he is fully alive to the importance of training the mind no less than the body; he is profoundly convinced of the value of education both for the ruler and the ruled. Every minute that he can spare is devoted to the improvement of his mind . . . he long sought help and opportunity in vain. His intense desire for learning had been thwarted in his early youth, and as he grew to manhood the peril of the state deprived him of the needed leisure. Even when opportunity was at last granted to him, he had not merely to contend with past neglect but also to create the means which should make intellectual advance a possibility. But he does this and more. His naturally quick intelligence was displayed in all his work, and it enabled him to make good the deficiencies in his education. His indomitable will helped him to overcome all other obstacles, permitting neither the lack of early training, nor the many other cares of his position . . . to deter him from the successful pursuit of his object.[4]

Another such person is a thirty-eight-year-old man who is a skilled laborer in an automobile assembly plant. He is married and has four children. He was born of lower-class parents but now is probably in the lower-middle class. He was not able to finish high school, though he would have liked to do so, because the family did not have enough money to permit him to stay. He is a man of muscular physique, who wears glasses and has a crew cut. His manner is dynamic in the extreme and he is often forcefully, though not unpleasantly, dogmatic about his opinions. Here are the salient facts about him assembled from various parts of the interview:

> My relationship with my parents was very close and warm. My father had a third-grade education and my mother an eighth-grade education. My father is open-faced, highly gregarious, extremely interested in other people. A non-intellectual type, who reads a great deal, but reads in terms of newspaper material and this type of analysis, who is highly interested in the world and the problems of the world. My mother is not quite as interested as my father is in all the problems of the world. She is not quite as gregarious as he is. We had a really happy home. I wouldn't say we were really unhappy at the time we were there. I never was unhappy. Everything went along pleasantly and smoothly. You know sometimes economically things weren't so good, but that never disturbed me much. I never went hungry. I always had clothes. Whenever I was sick, I went to the doctor. I would say we managed fairly well.
>
> I don't know why I was always interested in learning. I can remember when I was a kid, my sister always commented on it. I used to play with her and the other kids, baseball and everything, and then I said, "I'm tired of it. I want to go home and read." I remember I had some relatives that lived in Detroit, Michigan; one of the greatest pleasures in my life was to go and visit them. They had two boys, my first cousins. I had a wonderful time there. Even there I would go to the library and read. We'd go out and play tennis or go to the school ground and play. We used to have an old drum and I'd roll on the drum like a clown in the circus. But I always managed to read something somewhere.
>
> I started using the library early. Had to roller skate twenty blocks there and back. I remember I had my bed; I'd read at night. I'd have the book under my bed. I was raised right behind the elevated tracks. Sometimes the screech of the trains would wake me up. I'd read until I couldn't fight off sleep any more. Then I'd wake up at dawn and reach under the bed and get the book and read again. I always went everywhere with a book, always, my whole life. When my mother used to ask me to go on errands, go to the grocery store and so forth, I am sure I was brutal. "I'm too busy reading; don't bother me"; and she never pressed the point. She allowed me to read, in other words. I used to come to eat and probably dawdle over my food for an hour but I'd be reading while doing it and she never stopped me from doing it. Of course, since I became married I stopped reading at the table. Wife objects.

Reading is still his major activity and he manages to do an incredible amount of it. He is very active in his union educational program, both organizing courses and taking them himself. He has enrolled in a number of university week-end and vacation courses for union members. He joins and participates in organizations which will add to his knowledge; at present he is most active as a committee member for a local YMCA. He listens to FM radio, chiefly as background to his other activities, but he pays close attention to some of the talks and the dramatic presentations. He is equally discriminating about television and his own choices of programs are scheduled in the family's plans for the week.

He has a fairly normal social pattern, though he recognizes that he is "a character." Some of the other men at work call him an egghead, and his wife wishes he would spend a little more time working on the apartment. He regards himself quite clearly as a continuing learner and feels that he is different from others on that score. "I know a very few people who continually try to go to school. Most of the people I know, although they don't say so, seem to think that the studying you do is for a very specific purpose that you can see, and feel, and touch. That is, if you don't see, and feel, and touch, and feel a dollar come out of it, well you just don't do it. What's the meaning of it?"

His own interests are very different from those of such people. "All my mature life I have attempted to study three general areas of thought. And the reason I pursue these, I would guess, is because I thought they were the most meaningful and to give me insight. They are history, economics, and philosophy. These three areas I have continued to read in rather indiscriminately always. I am always interested in every little facet among these three fields and in other areas only in the sense that they are subsidiary to and feed into these three areas. I am not interested in science as such, except as it contributes to my thinking about the world."

Why is he the way he is? "I don't know. All I can say is, negatively, there was no one to discourage me and positively I always enjoyed it. The more I fed my appetite, the greater my appetite became." *Cacoëthes studendi.*

This case might be a good one with which to conclude, stressing, as it does, a number of values which many members of a university audience (being, for the most part, learning-oriented themselves) would almost certainly like to emphasize. But no one of the three orientations is, after all, innately better than the others, and to bring matters back to a more proper balance it may be well here at the end to re-state a point made at the beginning of the analysis of the interviews. All of the people in the sample are basically similar; they are all continuing learners. They have goals; they enjoy participation; and they like to learn. Their differences are matters of emphasis. Most of them fit clearly into one or another of the three groups but none is completely contained thereby. A few people stand so near the boundary between groups that there might be difference of opinion as to where they should properly be classified, but a longer or more skillfully conducted interview might well have removed the indecision about where each belonged.

This classification does not necessarily hold true for those who participate less extensively than the people studied; long experience in continuing education may be needed to build up firm conceptions about it. Nor can the grouping be extended to educational activities themselves; a particular course, for example, may attract representatives of all three groups, each attending for his own distinctive reason. A class in English composition may appeal to an activity-oriented person because it offers him credit, to a goal-oriented person because he needs to know how to express himself to get ahead on his job, and to a learning-oriented person because he is concerned with making himself more skilled in one of the liberal arts, not for its value in reaching other ends but because it is good in and of itself.

If adult learners really fall into these three groups, this fact will be useful in understanding and guiding adult education. But we must not be rigid in forcing people into such categories, for the aims of education are as broad as the range of human perfectibility permits. Adulthood offers to the average individual fifty years in which to learn how to solve his own problems as well as to explore the wonderfully inexhaustible realms of knowledge. The young exult in the power and precision of their bodies. They love the swift race; the well-played game; the sense of coördinated strength, of smoothness, skill, and alertness; and the rugged capacity to pursue hard effort and withstand severe trials. In adulthood, the mind reaches its peak. The man or woman is far more able than the youth to know, to understand, to explore, to appreciate, to discern subtle relationships, to judge, and to look behind the surface of things to their deeper meaning. The strength of the mind and the strength of the body should both be enjoyed, each in its own proper season, and the denial of the mind is as great a tragedy as the denial of the body. There is so much to know and so little time in which to learn it that not even the longest lifetime is enough.

Notes

1. *The Stones of Venice,* Everyman Edition, Vol. III (New York: E. P. Dutton, 1907), p. 46.
2. John P. Marquand, *The Late George Apley* (New York: The Modern Library, 1936), p. 163.
3. John Steinbeck, *Of Mice and Men* (New York: The Modern Library, 1937), pp. 28–29.
4. Asser, *Life of King Alfred,* translated with introduction and notes by L. C. Jane (London: Chatto and Windus, 1908), p. xliii.

Andragogy: The New Science of Education The single most influential concept in contemporary American adult education is Malcolm Knowles's "andragogy." Longtime Distinguished Professor of Adult and Community College Education at North Carolina State University, from which he is now retired (though still immensely active as a lecturer and consultant), and one-time executive director of the Adult Education Association of the U.S.A., Knowles is credited with providing the field with the concept that has proved both inspiring in theory and useful in practice.

Here are just some of the pervasive practices in present-day adult education that owe much of their acceptance to Knowles's powerful concept.

• treating students and clients like dignified, competent human beings
• providing a climate and environment more congenial to adults than a schoolroom atmosphere
• basing the offerings on the expressed needs of students
• organizing presentations and courses to involve students actively in their own learning
• having students learn about one another's strengths and resources so they can use one another as learning resources

Significantly, Knowles's concept of andragogy has been increasingly influential in the education of children and youth. "Originally I defined andragogy as the art and science of helping adults learn, in contrast to pedagogy as the art and science of teaching children," Knowles says. "Then an increasing number of teachers in elementary and secondary schools (and a few in colleges) began reporting to me that they were experimenting with applying the concepts of andragogy to the education of youth and finding that in certain situations they were producing superior learning."

Knowles first used the term *andragogy* in an article in *Adult Leadership* in 1968. It was subsequently elaborated upon in the first and subsequent editions of his *Modern Practice of Adult Education*. This selection is from the revised 1980 edition of that book, published by Follett Publishing Company, Chicago.

144

Andragogy: The New Science of Education

Malcolm Knowles

In the Beginning Was Pedagogy

Until recently there was only one model of assumptions about learning and the characteristics of learners on which educators could base their curricula and teaching practices. It evolved in the monastic schools of Europe between the seventh and twelfth centuries and came to dominate secular schools when they were organized in the twelfth century and universities when they began emerging, first in Bologna and Paris, toward the close of the twelfth century. This was the model of *pedagogy*—a term derived from the Greek words *paid* (meaning "child") and *agogus* (meaning "leading"). So "pedagogy" means, literally, the art and science of teaching children.

The pedagogical assumptions about learning and learners were, therefore, based initially on observations by the monks in teaching very young children relatively simple skills—originally mostly reading and writing. With the spread of elementary schools throughout Europe and North America—and much of the rest of the world, especially by missionaries—in the eighteenth and nineteenth centuries this model was adopted and reinforced. And when educational psychologists started scientifically studying learning around the turn of the twentieth century they further contributed to the enthronement of the pedagogical model by limiting their research mostly to the reactions of children and animals to didactic teaching. In fact, as we shall see later, we didn't get much knowledge about *learning* (in contrast to reactions to teaching) until studies on adult learning began to appear after World War II.

When adult education began to be organized systematically during the 1920s, teachers of adults began experiencing several problems with the pedagogical model.

One problem was that pedagogy was premised on a conception of the purpose of education—namely, the transmittal of knowledge and skills that had stood the test of time—that adult learners seemed to sense was insufficient. Accordingly, their teachers found them to be resistant fre-

145

quently to the strategies that pedagogy prescribed, including fact-laden lectures, assigned readings, drill, quizzes, rote memorizing, and examinations. Adults appeared to want something more than this, and drop-out rates were high.

Although the teachers were not aware of it, one of the great philosophers of this century, Alfred North Whitehead, was suggesting what was wrong. In an obscure footnote he pointed out that it was appropriate to define education as a process of transmittal of what is known only when the time-span of major cultural change was greater than the life-span of individuals. Under this condition, what people learn in their youth will remain valid and useful for the rest of their lives. But, Whitehead emphasized, "We are living in the first period in human history for which this assumption is false . . . today this time-span is considerably shorter than that of human life, and accordingly our training must prepare individuals to face a novelty of conditions."[1] An attempt is made in Exhibit 3 to portray Whitehead's concept graphically.

Exhibit 3

The Relationship of the Time-Span of Social Change to Individual Life-Span

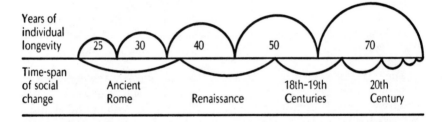

Years of individual longevity	25	30	40	50	70
Time-span of social change	Ancient Rome	Renaissance	18th–19th Centuries	20th Century	

Note that up to the early part of the twentieth century the time-span of major cultural change (e.g., massive inputs of new knowledge, technological innovation, vocational displacement, population mobility, change in political and economic systems, etc.) extended over several generations, whereas in the twentieth century several cultural revolutions have already occurred and the pace is accelerating. Under this new condition, knowledge gained at any point of time is largely obsolete within a matter of years; and skills that made people productive in their twenties become out-of-date in their thirties. So it is no longer functional to define education as a process of transmitting what is known; it must now be defined as a lifelong process of continuing inquiry. And so the most important learning of all—for both children and adults—is learning how to learn, the skills of self-directed inquiry.

Another problem the teachers of adults experienced with the pedagogical model was that many of the assumptions about the characteristics of learners did not seem to fit their adult students. And so they began experimenting with different assumptions and found out that they often produced better results.

Then Came Andragogy

Between 1929 and 1948 the *Journal of Adult Education*, published by the American Association for Adult Education, carried articles by successful teachers of adults[2] describing ways in which they were treating adults that deviated from the pedagogical model. Frequently the authors of these articles expressed a sense of guilt for violating academic standards (such as substituting interviews for quizzes). Obviously, they were feeling guilty because they had no theory to support their practices; they were simply being pragmatic and following their intuitions.

During the 1950s there began appearing books which analyzed these teachers' reports and extracted principles that were common to them— my first book, *Informal Adult Education*, published in 1950, was just such a listing of principles, but it made no attempt to envelop them in a unifying theory.

Then, in the 1960s, we began getting findings from scientifically designed research that focused on the internal processes of adult learning. The seminal study that launched this direction of movement was Cyril O. Houle's *The Inquiring Mind*, published by the University of Wisconsin Press in 1961. Houle found, through in-depth interviews with twenty-two "continuing learners," that his subjects fell into three subgroups:

> The first, . . . the *goal-oriented*, are those who use education as a means of accomplishing fairly clear-cut objectives. The second, the *activity-oriented*, are those who take part because they find in the circumstances of the learning a meaning which has no necessary connection, and often no connection at all, with the content or the announced purposes of the activity. The third, the *learning-oriented*, seek knowledge for its own sake. These are not pure types; the best way to represent them pictorially would be by three circles which overlap [at] their edges. But the central emphasis of each subgroup is clearly discernible.[3]

One of Houle's students, Allen Tough, extended this line of investigation from his position on the faculty of the Ontario Institute for Studies in Education later in the same decade. Tough's research question was, paraphrased: "How do adults learn naturally—when they are not being taught." His first findings, reported in two reports, *Learning Without a Teacher* (1967) and *The Adult's Learning Projects* (1971), showed that 1) almost all adults engage in from one to twenty major learning projects each year—with the average number being around eight; 2) only about 10 percent of the learning projects were associated with educational institutions; 3) there is a fairly universal "natural" process of learning—adults who undertake to learn something on their own go through a similar sequence of steps; 4) adults almost always turn to somebody for help at one or more points in this sequence; 5) usually they go to "helpers" who have not been trained as teachers, but frequently when they go to teachers the teachers interfere with their learning by substituting their own pedagogical sequence of steps rather than flowing with the learners' natural sequence.

A great deal of other knowledge about adult learning was accumulating during the sixties from related disciplines—clinical psychology, developmental psychology (especially the new group of life-span developmental psychologists), gerontology, sociology, and anthropology—both in North America and Europe. By and large, this research-based knowledge supported the intuitions of the earlier teachers, and theorists began fitting the knowledge drawn from both sources into a comprehensive, coherent theory of adult learning.

Early in this process European adult educators felt the need for a label for this new theoretical model that would enable them to talk about it in parallel with pedagogy. They coined the label "andragogy," which is based on the Greek word *anēr* (with the stem *andr-*), meaning "man, not boy" or adult. I first learned of the new label from a Yugoslavian adult educator in the mid-sixties and used it in an article in *Adult Leadership* in 1968. Since that time it has appeared with increasing frequency in the literature around the world, and presumably will be listed in the standard dictionaries before long.[4]

Originally I defined andragogy as the art and science of helping adults learn, in contrast to pedagogy as the art and science of teaching children. Then an increasing number of teachers in elementary and secondary schools (and a few in colleges) began reporting to me that they were experimenting with applying the concepts of andragogy to the education of youth and finding that in certain situations they were producing superior learning. So I am at the point now of seeing that andragogy is simply another model of assumptions about learners to be used alongside the pedagogical model of assumptions, thereby providing two alternative models for testing out the assumptions as to their "fit" with particular situations. Furthermore, the models are probably most useful when seen not as dichotomous but rather as two ends of a spectrum, with a realistic assumption in a given situation falling in between the two ends. For example, taking the assumption regarding dependency versus self-directedness, a six-year-old may be highly self-directing in learning the rules of a game but quite dependent in learning to use a calculator; on the other hand, a forty-year-old may be very dependent in learning to program a computer but completely self-directing in learning to repair a piece of furniture. As I see it, whenever a pedagogical assumption is the realistic one, then pedagogical strategies are appropriate, regardless of the age of the learner—and vice versa. But I would like to make one caveat: an ideological pedagogue—one who has a deep loyalty and commitment to the pedagogical model—may be tempted to underrate the extent to which an andragogical assumption may be realistic and may, for example, want to keep a learner dependent long after the learner has become able to be self-directing.

Assumptions of Pedagogy and Andragogy

Exhibit 4 portrays how I see the difference in assumptions between the two models:

Exhibit 4

**A Comparison of the Assumptions
of Pedagogy and Andragogy**

Regarding:	Pedagogy	Andragogy
Concept of the learner	The role of the learner is, by definition, a dependent one. The teacher is expected by society to take full responsibility for determining what is to be learned, when it is to be learned, how it is to be learned, and if it has been learned.	It is a normal aspect of the process of maturation for a person to move from dependency toward increasing self-directedness, but at different rates for different people and in different dimensions of life. Teachers have a responsibility to encourage and nurture this movement. Adults have a deep psychological need to be generally self-directing, although they may be dependent in particular temporary situations.
Role of learners' experience	The experience learners bring to a learning situation is of little worth. It may be used as a starting point, but the experience from which learners will gain the most is that of the teacher, the textbook writer, the audiovisual aid producer, and other experts. Accordingly, the primary techniques in education are transmittal techniques—lecture, assigned reading, AV presentations.	As people grow and develop they accumulate an increasing reservoir of experience that becomes an increasingly rich resource for learning—for themselves and for others. Furthermore, people attach more meaning to learnings they gain from experience than those they acquire passively. Accordingly, the primary techniques in education are experiential techniques—laboratory experiments, discussion, problem-solving cases, simulation exercises, field experience, and the like.

Regarding:	Pedagogy	Andragogy
Readiness to learn	People are ready to learn whatever society (especially the school) says they ought to learn, provided the pressures on them (like fear of failure) are great enough. Most people of the same age are ready to learn the same things. Therefore, learning should be organized into a fairly standardized curriculum, with a uniform step-by-step progression for all learners.	People become ready to learn something when they experience a need to learn it in order to cope more satisfyingly with real-life tasks or problems. The educator has a responsibility to create conditions and provide tools and procedures for helping learners discover their "needs to know." And learning programs should be organized around life-application categories and sequenced according to the learners' readiness to learn.
Orientation to learning	Learners see education as a process of acquiring subject-matter content, most of which they understand will be useful only at a later time in life. Accordingly, the curriculum should be organized into subject-matter units (e.g., courses) which follow the logic of the subject (e.g., from ancient to modern history, from simple to complex mathematics or science). People are subject-centered in their orientation to learning.	Learners see education as a process of developing increased competence to achieve their full potential in life. They want to be able to apply whatever knowledge and skill they gain today to living more effectively tomorrow. Accordingly, learning experiences should be organized around competency-development categories. People are performance-centered in their orientation to learning.

To summarize, andragogy is premised on at least these four crucial assumptions about the characteristics of learners that are different from the asumptions on which traditional pedagogy is premised.These assumptions are that as individuals mature: 1) their self-concept moves from one of being a dependent personality toward being a self-directed human being; 2) they accumulate a growing reservoir of experience that becomes an increasingly rich resource for learning; 3) their readiness to learn becomes oriented increasingly to the developmental tasks of their social roles; and 4) their time perspective changes from one of postponed application of knowledge to immediacy of application, and accordingly, their orientation toward learning shifts from one of subject-centeredness to one of performance-centeredness.

Notes

1. Alfred N. Whitehead, "Introduction," Wallace B. Donham, *Business Adrift* (New York: McGraw-Hill Book Co., 1931), pp. viii–xix.

2. "Successful teachers of adults" is operationally defined as teachers who can retain their students; note that this is not a criterion of success for teachers of children under compulsory attendance.

3. Cyril O. Houle, *The Inquiring Mind* (Madison, Wis.: University of Wisconsin Press, 1961), pp. 15–16.

4. For a detailed description of the evolution of the term "andragogy," see my *The Adult Learner: A Neglected Species* (Houston: Gulf Publishing Co., 2nd ed., 1978), pp. 48–51.

The Other 80 Percent of Learning   The most provocative single piece of adult education research in the last ten years has been Allen Tough's investigation of the extent and variety of self-planned learning. The major portion of the intentional learning that each of us experiences, it turns out, is not the result of teaching. Rather, we essentially educate ourselves—regularly, continually, and quite effectively. This "other 80 percent of adult learning" has profound implications for the theory and practice of lifelong learning.

Initially greeted with skepticism by the higher education establishment, Tough's research, conducted at the Ontario Institute for Studies in Education (OISE), has gradually become part of the conceptual repertoire of most sophisticated practitioners. Replications of his research both in the United States and in a wide variety of other countries, including underdeveloped ones, have yielded comparable results. In fact, many later investigators have found an even higher percentage of self-directed learning than did Tough.

This selection is excerpted and adapted from a 1977 presentation to national leaders of the lifelong learning movement in Washington, D.C., sponsored by the Postsecondary Education Convening Authority (PECA).

The Other 80 Percent
of Learning

Allen Tough

I have always earned my living as a classroom teacher. First I was a high school teacher. More recently, in graduate school, I teach people from the ages of twenty-two to fifty-two. So I am very solidly grounded in classroom and institutional education. At the same time, in my research I have become interested in the total range of adult learning. I said to myself, "Why don't we look at *all* the kinds of things that adults are trying to learn, at *all* the methods they are using, and not just at what they are doing in our classrooms and in our institutions?"

What I have to share is the picture that has emerged as I and others have gone and simply talked to adults in all walks of life, asking them what they have been learning in the last year, how they have gone about it, and how much time they have been spending on it. What emerges is a picture that is dramatically different from any other picture of adult learning that has been in circulation. And I think the picture has rather dramatic implications for the services that we should be providing for adult learners.

First of all, I had to decide just what exactly I was going to ask people to tell me about, the phenomenon I wanted them to talk about. The thing that interested me most was highly deliberate efforts to learn something. So what I focused on were major learning efforts, or learning projects.

1. A *learning project* is a highly deliberate effort to gain and retain certain definite knowledge and skill. The series of learning sessions (episodes in which the person's *primary intention* was to learn) must add up to at least seven hours.

I was interested only if the person knew what he or she wanted to learn and went ahead and did so in quite a deliberate way. And all these little bits of efforts to learn something had to add up to a total of 7 hours. Now, in fact, it was fairly rare that we had to use that minimum cutoff because it turned out that the average learning effort by an adult is closer to 100 hours. Average learning efforts hover around 80, 90, 100, 110 hours. So they really are *major* learning efforts. We didn't have to use the 7-hour minimum particularly often.

2. Populations surveyed were adult high school diploma students, clerks, college administrators, extension agents, factory workers, general populations in geographical areas (Tennessee, Nebraska, and the United States nationwide), library users, literacy-class members, managers, ministers, mothers, older adults, pharmacists, politicians, professional men, salesmen (IBM), schoolteachers, unemployed people, union members, university professors, and youth (ages ten and sixteen). Locations of surveys were Canada (ten studies), Ghana, Jamaica, New Zealand, and the United States (fourteen studies).

The people came from all walks of life. (For example, a study was done in New Jersey to look at the learning efforts of 100 unemployed individuals.) Yet the same pattern emerges no matter what country you are looking at and no matter what group you interview. There are differences, obviously, but in general the picture remains confirmed as we move over these different groups.

As teachers, students, faculty members, and others in the United States have repeated what we did in Toronto, they get the same kinds of results. I was involved in some of the studies; in others I was not. My involvement doesn't seem to matter.

3. The middle, or average, person—
   a. conducts seven distinct learning projects in one year;
   b. spends an average of 100 hours per learning effort;
   c. spends a total of 700 hours per year.

There was a national survey in the United States funded by the U.S. Office of Education and carried out by Patrick Penland at the University of Pittsburgh. He is in the Graduate School of Library Information Services there. Libraries try to serve all learners, not just those who come and learn in groups or classrooms, so I think it was appropriate that a library school be the one to carry out the national survey of adult learning. The basic findings reported that the middle person (that is, half the people were higher, half the people were lower) conducts one of these major learning efforts in seven quite distinct areas of knowledge and skill in one year. That is a startlingly different finding from any other picture of adult learning that was in existence before we came along with a sort of simpleminded request: "Tell us everything you have been trying to learn and how you do it."

We find people are learning seven quite different things. Some things are connected with their home and family, some with hobbies or musical instruments, and some with their jobs and other areas of life as well, such as community or volunteer work.

Another finding was that each of these learning efforts takes about 100 hours, making the total about 700 hours a year, which is quite startling. And we were very fussy. We didn't accept just vague claims that they learned something. We wanted to know precisely what they did. We would ask people for particular information. We asked what they read or what particular film they used. People had to tell us the actual efforts in which their *major intention* was to learn about this particular knowledge or skill.

4. In whose hands is the day-to-day *planning* of what and how to learn? Twenty percent of all learning projects are planned by a *professional* (someone trained, paid, or institutionally designated to facilitate the learning). The professional operates in a group (10 percent), in a one-to-one situation (7 percent), or indirectly through completely preprogrammed nonhuman resources (3 percent). Eighty percent of all learning projects are planned by an "amateur." That is usually the learner himself or herself (73 percent), but occasionally it is a friend (3 percent) or a democratic group of peers (4 percent).

Maybe the simplest way to understand the picture of adult learning that we have come up with is to compare it to an iceberg. The iceberg represents the total mass of adult learning, the total bulk of all the adult's learning efforts. With a real iceberg, the highly visible portion above the surface of the water is only a small fraction of the total bulk of the iceberg. The same is true of adult learning. The highly visible part that we have all paid attention to for years is the people learning in classes, correspondence courses, conferences, workshops, and so on.

That is a very important part, but as we ask people to tell us about the full range of their learning, what we find is that the bulk of it is below the surface. The bulk of it is not visible until we have gone below the surface and can really probe, can really try to get people to tell us about the other things they have been learning and how they have gone about it. As it turns out, the visible part is about 20 percent, and the invisible part is about 80 percent.

Twenty percent of adult learning is planned by a professional—by somebody who is paid to lead a class or a group or by someone who is paid to teach in a one-to-one situation, such as a driving instructor. Or it can be someone who is designated by an institution to lead a group, such as a church group, in which the person is not paid but it is his or her volunteer responsibility to lead that group. We considered any learning in which somebody was designated to be the official, responsible teacher as professionally led.

The remaining 80 percent of adult learning (which is a highly conservative number) is not particularly visible. That is because most of it is planned by the learner himself or herself. Most of it is self-planned, self-guided, as the person goes along from day to day.

There are a couple of other things included in the 80 percent. There are self-help groups, which are becoming increasingly common. They are a fascinating phenomenon. Alcoholics Anonymous is the old standard, but there are quite a few others now for all kinds of needs. These self-help groups are groups of peers with the same problems. There is no expert; there is no designated leader or teacher.

The other phenomenon I included in the 80 percent is learning from a friend. For instance, a friend teaches you how to drive a car, or you ask your father to teach you how to drive a car. If you have a driving school instructor, however, that is included in the 20 percent of visible adult learning.

5. The most common motivation is some anticipated *use* or application of the knowledge and skill. Less common is satisfying curiosity or wanting to possess the knowledge for its own sake. Rare (1 percent of adults' learning efforts) is undertaking a major learning effort to earn credit.

6. Details, integration, and implications are provided in my *Adult's Learning Projects: A Fresh Approach to Theory and Practice in Adult Learning.* It is available from Publications Sales, Ontario Institute for Studies in Education, 252 Bloor Street West, Toronto, Ontario, Canada, M5S 1V6.

It may seem that I am talking about a survey in Tennessee, a survey in Nebraska, what we found in Canada, in Ghana, and so on. I think it would be a lot more relevant for you if you took a few minutes to look at your own learning efforts in the last year. What have you been trying to learn? What kind of knowledge? What kind of information? What kinds of skills? Take three or four minutes to jot down some of the things you have been trying to learn that are connected with your job, your family, your home, your sports, or whatever. It can be any kind of knowledge or skill. It can be the kind of things that you learn in schools or classes. Or it can be other quite mundane things—raising kids, how to get a kid to sleep, coping with a particular disease, learning a foreign language, learning about a particular country if you are going to be traveling there. Anything at all.

If you start to run dry in your own list, here is a list we used in our interviews to help people recall things they have been trying to learn. It might help you think of something that you have been trying to learn.

a sport or game; swimming; dancing; bridge
current events; public affairs; politics; peace; biography
sewing; cooking; homemaking; entertaining
driving a car
home repairs; woodworking; home-improvement project; decorating
   and furniture
a hobby or craft; collecting something; photography
raising a child; discipline; infant care; child's education
nature; agriculture; birds
mathematics; statistics; arithmetic
speed reading; effective writing; public speaking; vocabulary; literature
science; astronomy; man in space
health; physical fitness; posture; clothes; appearance

history; geography; travel; some region or city or neighborhood
personal finances; savings; insurance; investing; purchasing something
psychology; effective relationships with other people; groups; leadership; social skills
typing; data processing; mechanical skill
some personal problem; mental health; an emotional problem; an
  illness or medical condition
various careers; choosing an occupation; finding a job
gardening; landscaping
something related to a job or responsibility or decision
musical instrument; singing; music appreciation
professional or technical competence; sales skills; how to teach or
  supervise
some aspect of religion; ethics; philosophy; moral behavior
current changes in society; the future; problems in cities; pollution;
  sociology

"Passages" of Adulthood and Triggers to Learning   The best-seller
Passages by Gail Sheehy awakened millions of Americans to the fact
that adult life is not a flat plateau of "maturity" after the turmoil of
adolescence. Rather it is marked by stages, crises, challenges, disasters,
and triumphs. The landmark study "Americans in Transition," under-
taken through the Exxon-funded project Future Directions for a Learning Society (which subsequently developed into the College Board's
Office of Adult Learning Services in New York City), probed the implications of this fact for adult education.

Insightful analysts of adult life had always known that occasions of
growth can be plentiful throughout life. "No doubt the greatest opportunities for self-renewal and new growth," John Gardner had noted
some years earlier, "occur at those periods of life when one's role
changes." But this pioneering inquiry into what causes adults to learn,
using interviews with a national sample of almost 2,000 Americans, put
hard statistics behind these intuitive perceptions.

The findings of Aslanian and Brickell enable adult educators to better predict which adults among their potential clientele will study
what topics in what numbers; to better anticipate what kinds of institutions they will choose and what credentials they will want; to better
foresee the times, places, and teaching methods they will prefer and
the prices they will pay.

Over and above these pragmatic benefits, better answers to the
question, What causes adults to learn? yield a fresh perspective—and a
most hopeful one—on the quality of life for Americans. As Willard
Wirtz said in commenting on the Aslanian-Brickell study: "A society
worried about reported limits to its growth will recognize that while
Americans in transition are typically individuals encountering uncertainty and often difficulty, the enlargement of their opportunities represents a new frontier for the democracy's expansion."

This selection first appeared in *Americans in Transition*, published by the College
Board in 1980.

"Passages" of Adulthood and Triggers to Learning

Carol Aslanian and Henry Brickell

The findings [of "Americans in Transition"] are a rich source of information: some raise questions that remain unanswered; some answer questions that were not even asked; and some confirm the hypotheses with which we opened the study. Further research, of course, may confirm or disprove the findings. But the answers arising from this particular set of findings seem quite clear. They are summarized and supplemented by our interpretations here.

1. *We have indeed become a learning society.* The fact that half of the adult learners interviewed had studied at least two different topics in the past year is evidence of the intensity of adult interest in learning. The fact that adults had studied every imaginable topic—surgery and sales, sewing and sailing, Swahili and swine-breeding—is evidence of the breadth of adult interest in learning.

Any nation in which half of all the adults, as well as virtually all of the childen, learn something significant every year is without question a nation of learners.

2. *We have become a society in which adults learn everywhere.* It is not simply that some adult learning takes place outside formal education institutions; it is that most of it does.

This means that learning has become a characteristic of adult behavior, a pervasive and perhaps even a necessary aspect of adulthood in our society. It has become an activity without a fixed, predictable location—an activity that can and does take place anywhere. This means, in turn, that social institutions other than schools are gradually being redesigned to accommodate adult learning activities and, in many cases, to provide them.

3. *Many adults learn in formal educational institutions.* Approximately half of these learners attend four-year colleges; the other half divide themselves about equally between two-year colleges and local school districts. The remainder enroll in technical institutes, proprietary

159

schools, correspondence schools, and every other kind of school available. Almost all these educational institutions were originally designed for children and youth. Adults have slipped into the seats alongside their children and have become almost as numerous, greying the green campuses, making junior colleges familiar places to senior citizens, and preserving the jobs of thousands of professors while confronting them with a new breed of students. It seems inevitable that the new adult students will change the schools and colleges. Already, campuses have become quieter; could the influx of adult students be one of the reasons?

Sooner or later, eagerly or reluctantly, forced by circumstance or excited by opportunity, schools and colleges will have to accommodate this new clientele. Indeed, the process is already well under way.

4. *Many adults learn in institutions for which education is not the primary function.* Such institutions include the workplace, churches, prisons, libraries, museums, the armed forces, and others for which education has become a significant function.

All institutions that deal with adults are becoming, to some degree, teaching institutions. Their reasons undoubtedly are quite diverse. A company may teach to make its work force more productive; a library may teach to build adult traffic and boost circulation; and a church may teach to help its congregation deal with its teenagers. But in all cases, the teaching function improves the institutions' other functions and makes them more successful.

Noneducational institutions may be better places for adults to learn than educational institutions because their teaching is accessible, convenient, realistic, immediate, and applicable. If so, educational institutions can learn from them, and the first thing they might learn is to pattern their own offerings accordingly if they want to attract adults.

5. *There are virtually no kinds of voluntary organizations—associations of boat owners, minority advocacy groups, societies of senior citizens—which do not arrange some kind of instruction for their adult members.*

If de Tocqueville were to return to the United States today, he might well observe that Americans create organizations partly so that they can learn together. He probably would go on to note that as their members become more skillful, the organizations function better.

6. *Some adults take private lessons.* Private lessons include instruction in the fine arts, home arts, sports, and foreign languages.

Private lessons subtract the social factor from the learning formula and leave two adults: one who knows and another who wants to find out. The content may be trivial, but the learner is serious. It may be expensive but, in the eyes of the 12 percent who learn this way, it is worth it.

7. *Many adults learn completely on their own.* These adults proceed without regular teachers or formal instruction, buying or borrowing whatever books, tools, magazines, and supplies they need. They watch television, ask friends, observe relatives, help fellow workers, or use trial and error until they finally get it to grow or run or look right or make sense. These adults demonstrate not only the independence but also the resourcefulness of adult learners. If schools and colleges want to understand their competition in the adult learning market, they have to realize that their greatest, toughest competitors are adults who learn on their own. What does the competition have to offer that the schools and colleges do not? Several factors give the individual adult learner a distinct advantage: Twenty-four-hour-a-day availability of instruction; variable-length lessons ranging from five minutes to five hours; a wide choice of locations, furniture, and lighting; food and drink on demand; and an instant end to boredom by closing a book or flipping a switch. What school or college can match—or should match it? Perhaps none. But that is one way to a larger share of the adult learning market.

8. *Adult learners differ in several respects from nonlearners.* Learners are younger, better-educated, wealthier, disproportionately white, employed (working at jobs in higher occupational categories), unmarried or married with a few young children, and more likely to live in urban areas or in the Pacific Coast states.

It is unfortunate that such clear cut differences exist between the adults who do and do not learn. Cannot adults of all types benefit from lifelong education? Why, for example, do the lesser-educated and the minorities not seek to learn as often as others? If we could answer this question, we would be better able to influence public policy to encourage them to do so.

9. *Most adults do not learn for the sheer pleasure of learning.* For most learning is not its own reward. Many enjoy the process of learning; some do not. Many enjoy knowing something new; some do not. But neither the process nor the possession is the reason most adults learn and neither, in itself, is enough to make most of them learn. Most learn because they want to use the knowledge.

While this finding is certain to disappoint most educators—who like to think that learning, both acquiring it and possessing it, are inherently rewarding apart from any use to which it might be put—they should understand that most adults use learning as the means to some other ends. The value of the learning lies in its utility. Educators will have to deal with that fact if they want to deal with adults.

10. *Adults learn in order to cope with some change in their lives.* Regardless of their demographic characteristics, almost all the adult learners interviewed pointed to their own changing circumstances as their reasons for learning. Further, adults who learn because of one kind of transition differ from those who learn because of another.

As we had hypothesized, it is being in transition from one status in life to another that causes most adults to learn. Adults learn what they need to know in order to be successful in their new status. Adults enter a learning experience in one status and expect to leave it in another. They will be disappointed if they go out exactly as they came in. The test of the learning is the success of the transition.

We believe that combining demographic characteristics and status change explains the correlation of demographic characteristics with adult learning. That is, younger, better-educated, wealthier whites working at responsible, demanding jobs and living in urban areas, particularly in the Pacific Coast states, are experiencing an extraordinary rate of change in their lives, and therefore are learning at an extraordinary pace.

Adults never outgrow their need to learn. Change touches the life of every adult, although it touches life at some points more often than at others and it touches some lives more often than others. Whenever change comes, early or late, and to whomever it comes, rich or poor, learning is one way of dealing with it. There are no types of adults, black or white, educated or not, blue collar or white collar, who do not use learning to accommodate the changes in their lives.

The learning a person undertakes is related to the transition he or she is undergoing. The transitions a person undergoes are related to his or her circumstances in life. Because those circumstances are measured by demographic indicators, the indicators correlate with the transitions, as shown in the following diagram.

These relationships explain, for example, why workers and students learn primarily to make career transitions, while homemakers, widows, and retired persons learn primarily to make family and leisure transitions. As demographic indicators change to keep up with changes in life circumstances, they will continue to correlate with learning and the life transitions that cause them.

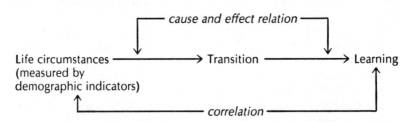

11. *Learning can precede, accompany, or follow life transitions.* Some of the adults interviewed were learning to cope with a change that had already taken place; others with a change still under way; and others with a change that lay ahead.

Learning can help an adult prepare for a future transition, deal with a current transition, or cope with life in a new status that he or she has already entered but cannot handle successfully.

Learning before a transition presumably is the best way. But adults cannot always plan their lives well enough to prepare for all changes ahead of time. Further, some institutional arrangements make it impossible. Military training, for example, is not available to most adults until they enter the armed forces. Company training is not available until an adult takes a job at the company. It is true, of course, that both military training and occupational training are scheduled immediately after an adult enlists or is hired. This suggests that the date of induction or hiring can be best understood as a triggering event, with the training preceding the adult's transition to actual job responsibilities.

12. *Transitions—and the learning needed to accomplish them—occur unevenly in the several areas of adult life.* More than half are career transitions; a smaller but substantial fraction are family or leisure transitions; a few are art, health, or religious transitions; almost none are citizenship transitions.

The major purpose for adult learning is to acquire occupational skills: The occupational motive outweighs all other motives combined.

There are several possible explanations for the predominance of career transitions. The first is that careers are more turbulent than other aspects of adult life; second, that career changes are more likely to require learning; third, that learning opportunities are more plentiful for career shifts; and fourth, that many adults think they can handle other kinds of life changes without learning anything new. But there is yet another explanation, simpler than any of these, which is probably the best. We present it next.

13. *The number of transitions in each life area corresponds exactly to the amount of time adults spend in each life area.* The adults interviewed spend about 80 percent of their time with their careers and families, for example, and trace about 80 percent of their learning to changes in their career and family lives.

We conclude from this that the best way to explain what adults learn is to point to how they spend their time. Occupational topics dominate adult learning because occupational matters dominate adult living. Changes occur in every aspect of adult life and adults have to learn to cope with all of them. An adult selects the learning needed for living. Thus, the adult learning pattern follows the adult living pattern. A high school student or a college student may wonder what some courses have to do with life, but an adult does not speculate. An adult knows exactly what the relationship is; otherwise, the adult will not attempt to learn.

We are talking here about the pattern of voluntary learning, which accounts for most adult learning. There is some involuntary adult learning, but it is difficult to force adults to study irrelevant topics. To do so ordinarily requires some type of compulsion, as in the military, in prison, as a condition of employment in a company, or as a course requirement for a degree in a college. Even with young people, mandating that they study irrelevant subjects works best if combined with compulsory school attendance. Relevancy, of course, is always in the eye of the beholder.

14. *Adults who learn because their lives are changing more often learn several things at once, more often learn career skills, and more often learn in formal educational institutions.* Conversely, those who learn for other reasons frequently learn informally about a single topic unrelated to careers.

We have several interpretations of this. One is that adults in transition have to juggle several problems at once and, thus, must learn more. Another interpretation is that learning is more urgent and more utilitarian for these adults. Another reason is that what they need to learn—usually about their careers—is so important that they seek out qualified teachers in schools and colleges. Finally, the new situations they are entering are rewarding enough, economically and otherwise, to merit the investment of time and money that formal schooling requires.

15. *Every adult who learned because of a transition pointed to a specific event in his or her life that signaled, precipitated, or triggered the transition and thus the learning.* Getting hired or getting fired, getting married or getting divorced, getting sick, getting elected, or moving to a new city were the kinds of events that told the adults it was time to learn.

For adults in transition, specific life events set the time on the learning clock: to know their life schedules is to know their learning schedules.

The need, the opportunity, and even the desire are not sufficient to cause most adults to learn at a particular point in time. There are millions of potential adult learners who need, want, and have the chance to learn. But it will take specific life events to convert most of them from latent learners into active learners. Decisions to learn may be pending for a long time, but the timing of their entry into the learning arena will be determined by particular events that permit—or force—them to enter it.

16. *Triggering events occur unevenly in the several areas of adult life.* More than half are career triggers and almost all of the remainder are family triggers. Only a tiny fraction occur in other life areas, chiefly health.

The pattern is much like that for transitions. However, leisure disappears here as a category which leads us to conclude that while there are leisure transitions, there are no leisure events powerful enough to trigger life transitions and thus require learning to deal with them.

17. *The number of triggering events in each life area corresponds closely to the amount of time adults spend in each life area.* Adults spend about 80 percent of their time with their careers and families, and about 90 percent of the events triggering learning occur in their career and family lives.

The pattern again is much like that for transitions. The configuration of events triggering learning follows the configuration of all other life events. Career and family living account for most adult time and, thus, for most learning triggers.

18. *While the topic an adult chooses to learn is always related to the life transition requiring that learning, the topic is not always related to the event triggering the learning.*

We conclude that the kind of life change an adult is making—career, family, leisure—dictates the kind of learning the adult must accomplish—typing, cooking, tennis, etc. This is understandable enough. But the event triggering the decision to go to work as a typist may be a divorce; the event triggering the decision to learn to cook may be a heart attack; and the event triggering the decision to play tennis may be a job change.

The value of knowing what kinds of transitions cause adult learning lies in being able to predict *what* they will learn. The value of knowing what kinds of events trigger adult learning lies in being able to predict *when* they will learn.

Learning, "Flow," and Happiness The widespread *use* of learning to cope with the challenges of life was amply documented in Aslanian and Brickell's study. But what about learning for its own sake—the so-called joy of learning that has been cited so often but rarely studied precisely? To what degree is learning an integral part of the good life, a key to happiness?

University of Chicago researcher Mihaly Csikszentmihalyi has looked closely at those intense experiences of "flow" in the lives of both elite professionals and blue-collar workers. He finds that learning that is intrinsically motivated and self-rewarding (rather than pursued for some extrinsic goal) generates such feelings as Abraham Maslow studied in his "peak experiences." His essay presents a model of how to "go with the flow" by constantly adjusting one's self-chosen challenges to one's self-developed skills. Thus, one can promote constant personal growth without falling into the trap of either boredom or frustration. The model is useful both as an instrument of personal life management and as a way of structuring the learning experiences of adults.

The author concludes by calling upon adult educators to create the social conditions, as well as empower their clients, to make possible more such learning-for-its-own-sake experiences throughout our lives. "Learning is essential not only because of what one can do with the knowledge, but also because of how one feels while one is learning and the kind of person one becomes as a result of the experience."

This selection is the full text of a hitherto unpublished paper entitled, "Motivation for Lifelong Learning," written for the National Institute of Education in 1979 under a grant administered by the Syracuse Research Corporation.

166

Learning, "Flow," and Happiness

Mihaly Csikszentmihalyi

Why do people learn? If we could only answer that modest question, we would be well along the way toward understanding and implementing lifelong learning. If one knew what motivates people to learn, one could facilitate its occurrence and channel it in directions that are socially or ethically desirable. But of course that question is not as simple as it sounds; in fact, no generally useful answer can be given to it at this time. In this paper, I will attempt to deal in depth with some dimensions of the motivation for learning and to relate these to other approaches. Before doing that, however, I will have to set down some of the ground rules for what kind of learning we shall be talking about and what kinds we shall exclude from the analysis.

Learning is an increase in complexity in the information-processing capacity of an organism. It can be consciously pursued, or it can involve changes that happen accidentally as a result of the organism's interacting with his or her environment or reflecting on previous experience in an unintended way. In the first case we have deliberate, voluntary, intentional learning; in the second, spontaneous, incidental, unplanned learning. Although many learning theorists would claim that much of the change an organism goes through is due to incidental learning, we shall consider here only the deliberate kind.

Deliberate learning can be either intrinsically or extrinsically motivated. When a person chooses to learn and feels responsible for his or her choice, the motivation is intrinsic. This stance corresponds, it seems to me, to what Warren Ziegler calls the "praxiological proposition." On the other hand, learning can in fact be extrinsically motivated. For most people, the thirteen-plus years spent in formal educational institutions involve learning that is experienced as forced rather than chosen, and over which one does not feel responsibility or ownership. Among adults the proportions might well be reversed, but even in the second half of life much learning is forced on us by changing conditions. The dangers of extrinsic motivation in learning have been amply documented.[1] To educate people under compulsion is costly in terms of social resources because it requires an expensive system of rewards and deterrents to be viable; and it is destructive of the individual's agentic powers, thereby increasing anomie and alienation. For these reasons, we shall here be concerned primarily with intrinsically motivated learning.

Learning that is intrinsically motivated can be either autotelic or exotelic. Autotelic learning is pursued for its own sake. In it the experience of active change involved in learning becomes its own reward. The goal is contained within the learning process. Exotelic learning is directed to an outside goal: the outcome is prized rather than the process itself. In practice, the distinction between these two modes of acting is not always clear. A person might first decide to learn to play the piano for exotelic reasons—for instance, because he or she would like to be a good pianist. Playing itself is a chore, a painful discipline. With time, however, the goal of becoming a good pianist may recede as the primary motivational factor because the experience of playing is so rewarding that it can sustain the process by itself, at which point the motivation becomes essentially autotelic.

I will try to develop a model of learning that is *intentional, intrinsically motivated,* and *autotelic.* I will argue that these three criteria define a psychological state that contains a powerful force, for good or for ill. In such a state persons will expend great energies without the need of external rewards. When this force is directed to ethical ends, the social system is strengthened; if it is wasted or harnessed to destructive purposes, it becomes a great danger.

I will further argue that any intentional, intrinsically motivated, and autotelic activity must lead to learning, that is, to changes in the complexity of the organism. Moreover, I shall propose that this kind of learning is the avenue for personal growth that approximates most closely the state of happiness.

Happiness as Personal Development

From earliest times, a majority of people have identified happiness as the ultimate goal of life. There has been no problem in agreeing that happiness is a subjective feeling, but beyond this point sharp differences arise in terms of the origins of this state and in terms of strategies for reaching it.

The great variety of attempts to pursue happiness can be reduced to one of two complementary approaches: to maximize pleasure or to minimize pain. The first is the hedonist approach, manifested in our days by that component of the American Dream that stresses material success, comfort, pleasure, and ever increasing consumption. The second solution is typified by the Epicurean stance of *ataraxia,* or serene acceptance of the inevitable, and the stoic notion of right living in harmony with the natural forces in the environment. While less popular at this time, the course of reaching happiness through minimizing pain is still an option chosen more or less self-consciously by a number of people in our culture. It seems clear, for instance, that current concepts of mental health, coping, and adaptation are continuous with stoic prescriptions of how to reach happiness.

What is common to both these approaches is that they are essentially homeostatic. The seeking for constantly new sources of pleasure in the hedonistic stance can barely disguise the fact that the experience of pleasure is limited by the inherited capacities of the organism. Thus, the pursuit of pleasure, no matter what novel forms it takes, always seems to lead back to the same cycles of arousal and release. The pleasures of food, sex, rest, and intoxication may produce positive subjective states, but they do not lead the organism to change. Avoidance of pain as a basic stance is also inherently a homeostatic goal, though less so than the pursuit of pleasure. The various disciplines required to curb one's drives and to cope with external changes—from yoga to psychotherapy, from *ataraxia* to Calvinist asceticism, from Tantric rituals to monastic practices—tend to change the organism, to refine conative skills, and thus lead to personality growth. Yet the ultimate goal of such procedures is still homeostatic in that they aim at maintaining the person at a level of quiescence or integrity, protected from the buffeting of fate.

The American Dream, that vague if powerful collective expression of hope that has been the most attractive asset of this society in the eyes of the rest of the world, includes goals that go beyond the homeostatic processes of pleasure seeking and pain avoidance. More clearly and consistently than in perhaps any other society, people in ours have claimed that it is possible for men and women to fulfill their potential by growing in skills, in knowledge, in wisdom. Not for any specific adaptive reason, not as a response to environmental pressure, but simply for the sake of actualizing latent possibilities.

Historically, policies created to implement personal growth have been channeled into educational institutions. It made sense to expect that the unfolding of personal potential would be best achieved within schools. Thus, it is through schooling that we have attempted to escape from homeostatic circularity into an ever spiraling growth pattern. Unfortunately, the school systems inherited from previous ages were not designed for such a purpose. The structure of schools, their curricula, their connections to the rest of societal institutions are encrusted with a variety of status-maintaining functions. Thus, all too often schools limit themselves to sorting young people into the social roles they are expected to assume; only rarely are they able to stimulate patterns of lifelong growth. It is not surprising that formal education has now lost some of its credibility as the main vehicle for personal growth and fulfillment.

Despite this setback, it is worth considering how education is related to happiness. Perhaps if we succeed in clarifying the connections between learning, growth, and happiness, it will become easier to understand what went wrong with education and what could be done to set it right.

The thesis of the present argument will be that the state of happiness is best described by the developmental rather than the homeostatic models. Pleasure and absence of pain are rewarding conditions, indispensable to maintain psychic processes on an even keel. But happiness also depends on something else: the feeling that one is growing, improving, changing to approximate a barely intuited ideal state. That process is by definition a process of learning broadly defined. One might conclude that learning is necessary for happiness, that learning *is* the pursuit of happiness.

The rest of this essay will elaborate on this theme. In order to develop the argument with some conceptual rigor, it will be necessary first to outline a model of the self and its dynamics. It is on this model that the later analyses of growth and learning will be based.

A Systemic Model of the Person

Happiness is a state experienced by persons. Experiences are changes in the state of the self. The self is an information-processing system. Through the allocation of *attention,* which represents psychic energy and is in limited supply, the self can produce and then process information about its outer environment and its inner states.[2] For example, if I say, "I feel feverish," I am relating the fact that I am aware of certain changes in my physical state that suggest the presence of illness. The "fever" as an experience is not diffused in the body but describes a certain state of my consciousness, or self. If I think, "I am bored," this again refers to a state of my information-processing system. In this case consciousness reflects on its own state and produces the information "I am bored."

All of this sifting and relating of information is accomplished through allocation of attention. Since attention cannot be split indefinitely, the amount of information that can have an effect on the self is limited by the availability of attention. Hence, the amount of attention available determines the kind of experiences one can have and therefore the content of one's life over time. It is impossible to "experience" a symphony and a poem at the same time, or to balance a checkbook and process a philosophical argument concurrently. It is difficult to feel happy and sad at once, and the intensity of one experience will be at the expense of the other. How one allocates one's attention will determine the content and quality of one's life.

For practical purposes it is convenient to differentiate two ideally contrasting states of the self. The first might be called psychic entropy. This obtains when the information-processing system, or self, is in a state of disorder. In this state attention is withdrawn from the outside world to reconcile conflicting information in consciousness. Conflict is the result of a mismatch between information being processed and goals or intentions developed by the self. The ensuing subjective experiences are anxiety, self-pity, jealousy, boredom, and so forth. They are all characterized by self-consciousness, that is, the *involuntary* turning inward of attention to restore order in the self. Thus, psychic entropy is a state of disorder in the self system that results in decreased efficiency of that system, inasmuch as less attention is left over to relate to new information.

The opposite state might be called psychic negentropy. This is a condition in which the information processed in consciousness does not conflict with other information available to the self. The self system is in harmony, and no attention needs to be allocated to its internal functioning. If attention is turned inward, it is done so voluntarily to reflect or to plan, not to negotiate inner conflict. The subjective experiences of psychic negentropy are what we call fun, involvement, enjoyment, serenity; and they are characterized by lack of involuntary self-consciousness.

Psychic disorder is not necessarily "bad," nor its opposite "good." There is no way to avoid information that conflicts with expectations held by the self, and the self develops by integrating new material into itself, part of which is bound to produce conflict. Entropic self-consciousness is often the necessary precondition for artistic accomplishment and creativity in general. At the same time, a person who devoted most of his or her psychic energy to introspection would not have enough attention left to relate adaptively to the environment. Moreover, while psychic entropy is subjectively experienced as a negative state, negentropy is exhilarating. The former might be justified as a means to achieving the latter, but psychic order is in itself the goal.

Entropy and negentropy do not apply only to states of the self. They can be seen as attributes of the information exchanged *between* people as well; thus, they characterize states of social systems. For instance, a classroom as a social system is in a state of entropy when the information provided by the teacher does not match the students' expectations, or vice versa. In such a case the teacher's actions will produce information that creates conflict in the students. Instead of paying attention to the lecture or the assignment, the students are conscious of boredom, worry, or anger, or else they withdraw into fantasy. Negentropy of a classroom system would consist of all of the students and the teacher processing the same information without being distracted by extraneous thoughts and feelings. Order and disorder are useful concepts to describe the states of individual selves as well as the states of social systems, ranging from two-person dyads to entire nations.

The Conditions of Psychic Negentropy

How does it feel to be in the state of psychic negentropy? And what are the conditions that help produce it? Psychologists, whose province it would be to answer such questions, have seldom attempted to do so. In general they have instead devoted their efforts to exploring the various manifestations of psychic disorder. Among modern scholars, some exceptions are Maslow's description of "peak experiences," Laski's collection of reports of ecstasy, and Bradburn's survey studies of happiness.[3]

In a series of studies started ten years ago, we conducted interviews with several hundred people who were intensely involved in enjoyable activities: artists, athletes, chess players, dancers, rock climbers, and so forth. We expected that such an elite group would constitute the extreme tail of the normally distributed population in terms of familiarity with psychic negentropy. From their accounts we hoped to be able to reconstruct the essence of the experience. These studies were later replicated with more "normal" samples: professionals, high school students, engineers, secretaries, assembly-line workers, and groups of elderly people.[4]

The descriptions obtained from these studies agree to a remarkable extent about what the experience of enjoyment is like and about the conditions that facilitate its occurrence. For the sake of brevity we shall refer to the negentropic experience as "flow," which was a term often used by our early respondents to describe their feelings while involved in an enjoyable activity.

The flow experience is one of deep concentration on a limited set of stimuli that are accepted by the person as being relevant. These stimuli might be the opponent's serve for a tennis player, a set of musical notes for a composer, or the patient's anatomy for a surgeon. Concentration precludes the person from thinking about, or even noticing, those stimuli that are temporarily "irrelevant" to the task. Thus, a chess player in a tournament is typically unaware for hours that he or she might have a splitting headache or a full bladder; only when the game is over does awareness of one's physical condition return. Such an intense concentration is sustained in part by the activity's having clear goals and providing clear feedback to the person's actions. The climber suspended on a rock wall knows what he has to do and is constantly aware of whether his moves do or do not help him achieve that goal. Composers have a set of sounds "in their minds" that they wish to reproduce on paper, and each note they write down approximates more or less closely the effect they wish to achieve.

Concentration on a manageable and clearly structured stimulus field leads to a total immersion in the activity, with no attention left over to think about one's self as separate from the interaction. Thus, people report a loss of awareness of time passing, a loss of self-consciousness, of self-doubt, of any of the ego-related concerns that one experiences in everyday situations where goals, feedback, and concentration are more loosely or contradictorily structured. And finally, the flow experience is unanimously described as being exciting, fulfilling, enjoyable—an experience that is rewarding, a goal in itself rather than a means to some external reward.

These findings suggest that in the flow experience we might have a model for that optimal state of being on which a theory of happiness could be built. Flow differs from the homeostatic approaches to happiness because it consists neither in seeking to satisfy a limited and closed set of needs for pleasurable stimulation nor in attempting to avoid unpleasant sensations. Studies of the flow experience show that people obtain positive negentropic states by seeking out new stimuli that might be threatening, like dangerous mountains or the depths of the sea. Enjoyment does not derive from the satisfaction of instinctual needs but from the achievement of *emergent* goals, that is, from one's ability to respond to opportunities in the environment that one learns about, or actually *discovers,* in the course of one's life.[5]

But what are the conditions that make the experience of flow possible? As one might expect, psychic negentropy typically occurs in activities that are ordinarily classified as play or leisure. Yet the important finding from our studies is that any activity can produce flow. It is not the objective, culturally sanctioned nature of the activity that determines whether the experience will be entropic or negentropic; what counts are more subtle parameters in the structure of the activity. A game of tennis does not necessarily induce flow in the player, nor is working at the assembly line necessarily a sign that the worker's consciousness is in a state of psychic entropy.

What, then, are the structural parameters in a situation that mark the presence of flow? In the first place, it is necessary that there be *something to do,* that the person be faced with opportunities for action, or challenges. Next, it is necessary for the person to have appropriate skills, or the capacity to respond to the challenges at hand. When the skills and challenges balance each other, the situation usually produces flow. If the challenges are too high relative to the skills, entropy ensues in the guise of worry or anxiety. If the skills overwhelm challenges, self-consciousness appears in the form of boredom (see figure 1).

Figure 1. A model of the flow experience

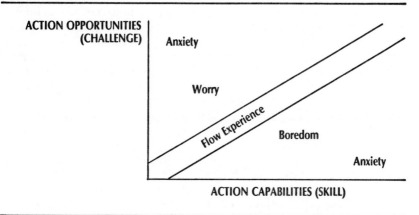

In addition to the balance between skills and challenges, a flow activity (that is, an activity that tends to elicit the flow experience in people who practice it) usually has clear rules and clear goals and provides clear feedback. The stimuli relevant to the activity are clearly identified to facilitate concentration. As a result, a flow activity is able to provide a self-contained little world in which a person can act with total involvement and without self-doubts. The most obvious example of a flow activity is an athletic context, such as a football game. Here the relevant space is limited by the gridiron, the relevant time is indicated by the game clock, the uniforms separate the actors from the audience and the team from its opponents. Rules, goals, and challenges are clear. After each play the results of one's actions are measured in terms of yards gained or lost. In this well-structured little world, one can act with total involvement for a little while and experience flow.

But what is important to realize is that one doesn't have to play to experience flow. Every activity can be enjoyable because every activity has the potential of being structured like a game. There is no inherent reason for work to be painful, nor for learning to be dull.

To understand the experience of psychic negentropy, it is essential to keep in mind that the conditions that produce it are both objective and subjective. For instance, the amount of challenge present in a situation will depend on what is actually there and on what the person perceives to be there. To most people, a vertical slab of rock does not present opportunities for action; it is something to be glanced at and immediately forgotten. To a rock climber, it might constitute an exquisite sequence of challenges to be savored for hours or days. The same is true of skills. While some people consistently overestimate their own abilities, others think they can do less than they are "objectively" able to do. Thus, the ratio of challenges to skills cannot be accurately predicted by knowing only the external parameters of a situation.

That point has some very important practical consequences. It implies that to make a person happy in a given situation, it is not enough to change the external conditions; the person's perception of the situation must be changed as well. People need to be able to restructure their interaction with the environment to bring their skills in line with the challenges. It is possible, for instance, to enjoy even the most objectively "boring" situation by developing enough cognitive challenges and skills. That is what the discipline of yoga and other meditational techniques teaches. Similarly, musicians, poets, and mathematicians are able to transform even concentration camps into tolerable experiences because they can interact with a symbolic world of challenges and skills they have internalized. The best policy for increasing negentropy in everyday life, however, would consist in a two-pronged approach that aims to restructure both the objective and the subjective structure of activities. It is necessary to transform the typical tasks of life into flow activities and, at the same time, to teach people how to reach flow even when what they have to do is not inherently conducive to the experience.

Perhaps by now the relationship between happiness—or the state of psychic negentropy we have called "flow"—and what Warren Ziegler is calling the "learning stance" has started to emerge. The connection will become clearer in the following sections, but at this point it might be convenient to state its development thus far. For a person to experience flow, he or she must be able to recognize opportunities for action in the environment and must have the skills to deal with them. It is clear that some people are born with or acquire skills in a specific area and thus have a privileged entry into one type of flow activity; for example, physical build, a good singing voice, a special talent or early training may set a person up for competence in a certain activity. But in addition to such specialized skills, there is a more important, more general skill available to everyone. That is the ability to transform any situation into a flow activity, the capacity to restructure one's environment to achieve a balance between challenges and skills. A person with this meta-skill sees opportunities where others don't or learns new ways to cope with challenges if they threaten to be overwhelming.

This basic meta-skill seems to be a good description of the "learning stance." It is also very similar to what I understand Kenneth Benne to mean by his "methodological character," or one's tendency to seek out new learning through conflict and doubt. How it relates to psychic negentropy, and how it can be affected by training and policy decisions, will be explored later. At this point it should be emphasized that the flow model suggests that such a learning stance is not just a means to an adaptive end. The importance of this basic kind of learning does not lie only in the fact that it can provide skills necessary to cope with this or that problem of existence. The learning stance is a necessary skill by itself, regardless of its outcomes, because it offers the closest approximation of happiness that human existence can provide.

The Dynamics of Personal Growth

I do not intend to imply that people are happy only when they are learning to cope with new challenges or when they are deeply involved in a demanding flow activity. As the model in figure 1 suggests, flow experiences occur also at the lowest levels of challenges and skills, provided these are in balance. In fact, the results of our ongoing research suggest that day in, day out, the most enjoyable times in people's lives consist of rather trivial, low-key experiences. About one-third of the reports concern pleasant occasions of sociability: talking around the dinner table, admiring a friend's new car, sharing gossip around the office water cooler. Another third of the time, people explain why they feel exceptionally good in terms of being rested, well fed, relaxed, or in tune with the weather. Finally, a third of the time the good feelings come from something the person is doing, from the activity itself. On the whole, we are now estimating that about 15 percent of the best everyday experiences occur in the context of learning, which includes such things as trying out a new recipe or a new hairdo, as well as more conventional tasks such as learning a new language or improving one's tennis game. On the other hand, people report that of the worst daily experiences, fewer than

3 percent involve new learning. More than a third of the worst experiences are due to boredom experienced in routine, repetitive activities.

If it is true that people in general are happiest when they are relaxed in an undemanding situation, what is the justification for suggesting that the flow model is crucial for understanding happiness? The reason is that the prevalence of happy experiences that are extremely low in challenges and skills should not obscure the fact that restful occasions are enjoyed because they contrast with the more challenging encounters of daily life. Without the latter, the times of relaxation begin to pall. The charged experience of deep involvement is enjoyable in its own right, and it gives value to the low-key occasions in which neither challenges nor skills are high.

But the most important feature of the flow model in the present context is its implication for understanding the growth of the self. An example might serve to illustrate the dynamics involved. Let us imagine a beginning chess player, who plays against other beginners. In terms of the flow model, one would predict that he enjoys playing the game because challenges and skills are matched. His situation is represented by position A in figure 2. As time passes, and our imaginary player keeps playing, one of three possible outcomes is likely to occur. One is that both the player and his opponents learn new skills as a result of practicing the game. If this is what happens, then the player will move to position C in figure 2: he will still be in flow when he plays. A second possibility is that the player improves, but his opponents do not. In this case, our player will find himself at B_1 and will tend to get bored when playing. If he gets bored, he will either stop playing chess or find himself some more skillful opponents, thus moving back up into flow at position C. A third alternative is that our player's opponents improve much faster than he does; in this case he will soon find himself in position B_2. At this point the player does not enjoy the game because he knows he will keep losing, and the experience becomes frustrating. He has the option of quitting the game or of returning into flow, either by finding opponents with fewer skills (i.e., back to position A) or by improving his own skills until they match the opponents' (up to position C).

In other words, positions at the lower end of the flow diagonal are inherently unstable. People must progress upward along the diagonal if they wish to keep enjoying whatever they are doing. If they do not move, boredom or worry is likely to ensue. Incidentally, the same argument explains why some activities are more conducive to flow in the long run than others. A game of tick-tack-toe, for instance, soon becomes boring because it cannot offer new opportunities for action. Chess, on the other hand, provides an almost unlimited range of increasing challenges.

But what does a move up the flow diagonal imply? What is the difference between positions A and C in figure 2? It is not necessarily true that the quality of the experience changes as one matches higher challenges with greater skills. Playing with a puppy can be as involving a negentropic state as playing a Beethoven violin solo is. The difference between A

Figure 2. Dynamics of flow: A hypothetical transition from a low skill, low challenge state (A) to three possible alternative states

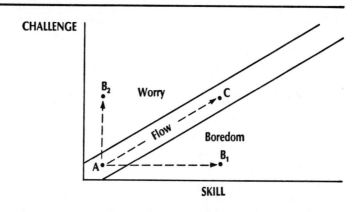

and C on the diagonal is that C is a more *complex* experience. It means that the opportunities for action are more difficult to meet and that the abilities being used are more refined. Higher up the diagonal, behavior is more complex because more differentiated responses are required to meet the demands of the situation. Therefore, the experience might be described as being more "deep," since presumably more cognitive and affective skills are involved and the attention is more concentrated. It follows that a person who stays in flow in several different activities will necessarily become a more complex person because the dynamics of the flow process must become more complex as a condition for continued enjoyment. This increased complexity of the self is what one means by personal growth. Thus, to be happy one must grow.

It is now possible to see more clearly the role connection between learning and happiness. Happiness requires that one be able to find increasingly complex opportunities for action and that one be able to improve one's appropriate skills. That ability, which seems to come naturally to children, apparently often atrophies by early adulthood. Some people, exposed to a constricting environment, never realize their inner resources or the presence of surrounding opportunities. Others are overwhelmed by demands in their milieu early on, and they find that the only way they can cope with the entropic forces is to restrict their perception of opportunities. For them, the French definition of human development applies: first an age of illusion, followed by an age of disillusion, ended by an age of indifference. The only way to break this vicious cycle is to maintain one's ability to grow, to find ways of getting deeply involved with the world around. That is the ability that we are calling the learning stance.

Our research with representative blue- and white-collar workers in the

Chicago area suggests that people differ greatly as to how often they report experiencing deep flow. About 10 percent claimed never to have felt anything like it; the rest were rather evenly distributed along a continuum ranging from once a year to several times a day. Of course, it is difficult to know whether such interview reports are accurate reflections of the experience. Convergent validation, however, suggests that what people say in this respect might be true. The more often people report flowlike experiences, for instance, the more satisfied they are with every aspect of their lives and the more involved they are with their work.[6] In our sample, adult workers report that about 40 percent of their deep flow experiences take place while they are working on their jobs, and the rest occur about evenly in situations of sociability, in hobbies and sports, in passive leisure activities like reading or listening to music. These preliminary findings confirm three important predictions derived from the model: (a) flow can be experienced in a variety of situations, including work; (b) people differ greatly in terms of where and how often they experience flow; and (c) those who experience flow more often, regardless of context, are more involved and more satisfied with their lives.

Some Principles for Development of the Learning Stance

These considerations lead us back to policy issues. While it is clear that research in this field is still in its infancy, and much more data need to be collected before we can be sure of our facts, one might hazard some suggestions about what can or cannot be done to increase happiness by affecting the learning stance.

In the first place, the argument thus far provides a different philosophical justification from the ones that usually underlie policies in adult education. The point is that opportunities for learning in later life should be made available not only in response to specific needs such as occupational retraining, certification, the improvement of health, and cultural enrichment. These are important reasons, but an even more central one is that learning opportunities are necessary for negentropic personal growth. Learning is essential not only because of what one can do with the knowledge, but also because of how one feels while one is learning and the kind of person one becomes as a result of the experience.

It follows that the content of learning must be seen as much broader than the usual utilitarian subject matter of adult education. The question should be, What kind of opportunities are most conducive to the development of personal potentialities? We need to know more about the sort of activities that adults find intrinsically rewarding and growth producing. The most obvious policy direction would then be to make such activities available to larger segments of the population.

To a certain extent, we already know that people spontaneously take on a variety of learning opportunities in their lives. Allen Tough has shown that average adults spend almost ten hours each week engaged in learning efforts. That is an impressive investment of psychic energy, but before one knows how to interpret what it means, one would want to know a bit more about the quality of these learning experiences. How complex are they? How much growth do they provide? How integrated is the change produced with the rest of people's lives? My impression is that answers to these questions would spell out a less optimistic picture than the numbers alone suggest. Our data—which were not collected specifically to find out about learning and are therefore far from conclusive on this score—suggest that although most adult learning efforts are intrinsically motivated, they are usually exogenous. In other words, they are means to specific, and usually short-term, ends. While this type of learning is invaluable for coping with the day-to-day problems of existence, it is essentially a homeostatic response that may not lead to growth and complexity.

An enlightened policy would not restrict itself to enabling people to learn skills that are easiest to acquire. The flow model suggests that a person will engage spontaneously in activities that are enjoyable and that initially these will be activities of low complexity, unless the person's capacities are already developed. The temptation is to satisfy immediate needs for involvement by providing activities that not only require few skills to begin with, but that also never make substantial demands on the person's abilities; therefore, they are structurally incapable of nurturing growth. We should remember that in Latin *education* meant "to lead out" and that educational policy should aim to assist people to move upward along the diagonal of complexity. Fashionable but trivial learning opportunities are in the long run literally self-defeating; they keep people busy for a little while, but they fail to start them on a pattern of growth.

Perhaps the main priority for lifelong learning at this point is the development of symbolic skills. Strictly speaking, of course, all learning involves symbols, even learning how to bake bread or how to fix the plumbing. But here I mean learning to operate within a symbolic subworld like mathematics, music, chess, poetry, or art, which provides greater opportunities for growth. How does mastery in such a subworld contribute to happiness? The advantage of symbolic action systems (like poetry, for instance) is that they offer an almost unlimited range of opportunities in which negentropic states can be experienced. Symbolic systems have two main limitations. First, they require a certain level of skill to enjoy in the first place and thus need a large initial investment of psychic energy. Second, compared with achievements based on power of money, symbolic skills are generally seen as useless and hence not worth bothering with. This problem can be resolved, at least in principle, since whether people perceive an activity to be useful depends to a great extent on the amount of attention others devote to the activity. Hence, a policy directed to enhance happiness through learning might be able to support symbolic accomplishment by devoting increasing attention to it and so generating enough attention to make the activity self-sustaining. An excellent example in this direction is the work of the poet Kenneth Koch. He has trained ghetto children and a group of semi-illiterate older persons to express their most intimate feelings in poetry.[7] Having learned the tools of poetic expression, these essentially alienated people were able to make order in their experiences through symbolic means—psychic order. The temporary flow became a way to a more permanent one. Such methods are a national resource to be studied and applied by anyone concerned with lifelong learning.

The importance of symbolic systems goes beyond the fact that they can provide a way of ordering people's experiences and thereby create states of psychic negentropy and growth. They also have implications for the future of our society. As long as our values are exclusively material and utilitarian, people's energies will be devoted to secure increasingly expensive material goals: bigger homes, more energy-intensive appliances, more powerful means of transportation. It is clear by now that this course can lead to only two alternatives: either we destroy our planet by seeking happiness in material objects, or we shall have to scale down our appetite, in which case intense frustration and demoralization can be expected.[8] Education in symbolic skills might be one way out of this ruinous course. To the extent that a person becomes able to act in subworlds that operate on different principles from the everyday environment, subworlds that run on information rather than oil, to that extent he or she might become less dependent on the material world and more able to find satisfaction in symbolic rather than material rewards. One should add, of course, that "material" rewards are also symbolic; the problem is that focusing people's energies exclusively on this one set of opportunities has upset the ecology almost beyond repair. Attempts to improve the learning stance should therefore not disregard ephemeral symbolic skills in favor of simpler, more concrete training. In fact, creative efforts to reconstitute legitimate alternative realities in the present barren materialistic landscape might be the most important contribution a policy in this field can make.

Having pointed out some general principles pertaining to the *content* of what should be included in the learning stance, the question arises: How should this content be transmitted? Clearly "formal education" can be only a small part of the answer. Classroom instruction works only for students who are already motivated to learn in a classroom setting. To affect the learning stance, one must recalibrate people's motivation to become involved with learning in the first place. The ability to restructure situations to make the interaction with them enjoyable, and hence growth producing, is presumably a meta-skill one develops fairly early on. We need to know more about when and how it is acquired because it is likely that the most efficient way to enhance lifelong education is by maintaining more and more children on the growth path. At present we know a great deal about how children learn to read and to count. But we know next to nothing about how children learn to enjoy learning and about how to foster this skill. Yet that is what we need to know if we wish to enhance what Brewster Smith[9] called the "benign spiral" of self-development, or what we are calling the learning stance.

At present, the structure of a young person's environment is not the most conducive for the development of a learning stance. Community resources for intrinsically motivated learning are sorely inadequate and overshadowed by the effects of television, that ubiquitous pacifier. In our research with adolescents, we found that while youngsters enjoyed watching TV less than anything else in their daily lives, and enjoyed sports and games most, they still spent almost four times as much time in the former activity than in the latter.[10] Television mimics activity and purports to convey information, but those who watch it do not act and therefore cannot get feedback and learn about themselves. Sports and games require a greater output of psychic energy to get started in; but once that initial expenditure is made, they become autotelic, and one grows by practicing the necessary skills.

What about schools then? Surely they are the institutions expressly designed to instill the learning stance, and young people spend a large proportion of their time in them. The problem with classroom instruction is that the material presented by the teacher (which constitutes the "challenge" for the students) is by necessity aimed at an average level of complexity in relation to the individual skills of the students in the class. For many students the material is too easy, and they will be bored; for others it is too difficult, and these students will be anxious. Although it is true that some classes are seen by some students as enjoyable as flow activities, and even though enjoyment of a class is a better predictor of a student's semester grade than scholastic achievement scores or grade point average,[11] in general school is experienced as boring or threatening most of the time, and making it more enjoyable is not one of the priorities of educators. It is typical, for instance, for an inner-city school in budgetary difficulties to curtail its art, music, or physical education program. Yet these are the activities that children in general enjoy most, and for many children with low academic skills they provide opportunities for growth otherwise unavailable. If we also consider that art, music, and sports are some of those symbolic systems our culture needs to develop in order to survive, the shortsightedness of such policies becomes even more obvious.

What young people need in order to acquire a lifelong learning stance are opportunities for action and respected adult models from whom they can learn. Socialization into the learning stance requires that young people be exposed to adults who are doing complex things and *who enjoy themselves*. A teenager will not be wholeheartedly motivated to be an engineer as long as he sees engineering as something unreachable or boring. Our interviews with adolescents reveal that the greatest positive impacts in their lives were made by adults who cared for them, who did difficult things at the level the youngster could understand, and who seemed to enjoy the interaction. In addition to parents, these were athletic coaches, summer camp counselors, work supervisors, and teachers.

It is unfortunate, however, that the most widely available cultural role models for young people are figures from the entertainment world. Posters of rock stars, fashion models, and movie actors decorate the walls of their bedrooms, shrines where youths invest their psychic energy. These cultural heroes are merchandised by the media as examples of psychic negentropy: people who have no problems, who have fun, who can satisfy every one of their whims.

These few observations have indicated some of the principles for establishing a viable learning stance in young people. But what can be done to maintain it in adults? The principles remain the same throughout life: opportunity and example are still the major factors. Given the social roles of adults, however, some specific points should be raised.

Most adults spend about half of their waking hours at work and spend additional time working in their homes. For the vast majority of people, the jobs they do were not designed to foster the learning stance or to provide enjoyment. Since the Industrial Revolution, almost every occupation has been affected by Taylorean criteria of efficiency, which boil down to the question: How should a person act to produce more in a shorter time? From a purely materialistic rationality, this question is a sensible, even elegant one. Like an athletic event, it sets down simple rules for a race in which new records can be attained again and again. But as the only principle for organizing human effort, the productivity criterion not only stifles growth by channeling it into too narrow a course; it becomes actually self-defeating in its own terms because people eventually refuse to let their actions be dictated entirely by requirements set up by production engineers.

Of the worst experiences that our sample of workers reported in an average week, the largest single category—28 percent—was due to aggravation with a routine, boring job. That was twice the frequency with which they complained about physical inconveniences like being tired or feeling ill. These workers each wore an electronic pager for a week, and they were randomly "beeped" during the day; whenever the pager beeped they filled out a brief report on where they were, what they were doing, and what they were thinking about. In addition, they rated their experience at the time along two dozen dimensions. We learned, for instance, that when these workers are on the job they actually work only about 60 percent of the time; the rest they talk, daydream, or do other things unrelated to their task. As one would expect, the less they enjoy their job, and the *fewer flow experiences they report outside their job,* the less time they spend working at their task.[12] It seems that even in terms of productivity one should consider enjoyment as one of the main factors in designing jobs.

Satisfaction with one's job is best predicted by the amount of *variety* and *challenges* one finds in the task. These variables correlated with overall work satisfaction many times higher than the amount of salary the worker is paid.[13] These trends clearly suggest that the opportunities to learn and to grow are as essential to the person who is working as they are in life generally. Yet very rarely are these requirements built into the way jobs are structured.

If one were to ask, "Why is productivity so important?" the answer would be some variation of "Because material products will make our lives more happy." It then makes little sense to give up our present happiness in exchange for a hypothetical future one. "Deferral of gratification" is a valuable skill to have, but when it becomes a way of life built into the social structure, it ceases to make sense.

Some researchers have claimed that it doesn't matter whether workers enjoy their jobs or not, provided they can dispose of their free time at will. But when at least half of one's waking time is spent doing routine things on the job, and then another quarter or more has to be employed in routine maintenance tasks like dressing, driving, shopping, and cooking, it is difficult to use the remaining energies for starting a complex activity. It is much easier to watch TV or go bowling or drinking. Here the challenges are few, but one is comfortable with the skills one has. These activities rarely get more complex, but there is enough day-to-day variation in the stimuli experienced to give the illusion of change, if not of growth.

Given this situation, it is difficult to see how the learning stance of adults can be significantly improved without seriously restructuring working experience. Under present conditions only those people who are fortunate enough to have developed an already strong learning stance succeed in making routine jobs an opportunity for further growth. In a welding shop we studied, where more than a hundred workers were assembling railroad cars amidst an infernal din and extremes of temperature, there was a sixty-year-old immigrant with a fourth-grade education who illustrates the rare exception. Joe, who was a line worker on the lowest end of the status and pay scale, was respected by management and co-workers alike for his uncanny ability to spot and repair malfunctions in any of the machinery used in the plant. "Without Joe," many of the others said, "this place would have to close. He keeps this plant running." Joe described his uncanny ability to repair mechanical defects very simply. Early on in his life, he said, whenever a machine malfunctioned, he would ask himself, "If I were this thing and I couldn't do my work, what would be wrong with me?" Having identified with the machine, he would then patiently find out what interfered with its functioning.

The ability to experience flow at work generalized to the rest of Joe's life. At home he had bought three empty lots adjacent to his house, where over the years he built an elaborate rock garden in which he planted hundreds of cacti and succulents. He also installed an underground sprinkling system he designed so that rainbows would form over the garden when the water was turned on. Finally, he placed a system of spotlights next to the sprinklers so that he could make rainbows even at night. Joe had a library of about four hundred books on gardening. Every week, he claimed, he tried to read at least one book on plants, preferably cacti.

In a modest, self-effacing way this poor, uneducated laborer had succeeded in transforming his life, at work and outside it, into a complex growth experience. I can think of no better example to illustrate the learning stance. As William Westley noted, flow in one's job can liberate a tremendous amount of psychic energy. Workers whose jobs are redesigned to allow greater variety and challenge will volunteer their free time for civic activities and will become politically involved. Changing from psychic entropy to negentropy at work makes a great deal of attention available, from grousing to constructive use.

Joe's case is an exception, showing that even under the most inauspicious conditions a person who has developed a learning stance will be able to achieve psychic negentropy and growth. Such exceptions, however, do not relieve us from the responsibility of trying to restructure work and community life to make them more conducive to complex learning. If we reduce the number of what Westley calls "role traps" in occupational settings, a great amount of energy for learning and growth could be generated. Westley's own method of "sociotechnical design" is a good example of how this could be done in practice, so I need not go into that issue here.

If one looks at the causes of the most enjoyable and least enjoyable experiences in everyday life, one finds that in addition to work *other people* are the primary source of both negentropic and entropic states. One-third of the best experiences are explained in terms of enjoying the company of whomever one is with, and about the same percentage of the worst events are due to arguments or other interpersonal tensions.

That suggests that the way one relates to others is a central factor in determining happiness. But can sociability contribute anything to personal growth? In our research with adolescents, we found that teenagers ranked "being with friends" throughout the range of complexity of the flow diagonal, from the very lowest to the very highest level of challenges and skills (this tended not to be true of other activities, which were ranked either only at the low end of complexity, like watching TV, or only at the high end, like playing the piano or participating in athletics). This seems to reflect the fact that interaction with others is remarkably flexible: it can be a relaxing homeostatic activity similar to watching television, or it can be a challenging, growth-producing experience. It is probable that friendships and love relationships, like games, lose their power of attraction when they cease being enjoyable—that is, when they cease to maintain the optimal ratio of challenges and skills.[14]

Would it be very unorthodox to propose that concern with the learning stance be extended to include interpersonal skills? In addition to being crucial to personal happiness, these are also necessary to maintain social negentropy, by facilitating exchange and integration of information among persons. Here again, the issue is *not* to teach social skills directly. The strategy would be to provide more opportunities for structured interaction, responsibility, and leadership. Of course, people spontaneously make such opportunities available to themselves already: they form religious sects and chess clubs, Elvis Presley fan clubs and professional associations, and so forth. But if the principles derived from the analysis of the learning stance were to be applied to provide opportunities for more and more complex social activities, the overall growth due to interactions could surely be improved.

Elise Boulding describes with great eloquence the complex interpersonal skills that women possess and use in our society. She points out the enormous contribution that women's nurturance makes to collective well-being and the fact that this contribution goes almost entirely unnoticed. Part of the problem is that this contribution cannot even be *measured.*

While we can quantify the material effects of a change in the GNP, we cannot express the difference that energy invested in reducing interpersonal entropy makes. Clearly it is a priority for any healthy society to recognize nurturant skills and to encourage their development. Another set of interpersonal problems is that addressed by Jerome Ziegler and Kenneth Benne. They talk about the learning community, the societal organization of problem finding and problem solving. This involves the institutionalization of flow into political action and urban planning and lifts the issue of entropy and growth from the level of the individual to that of the social system. I will not attempt to deal with these issues, except to say that the energy for community action must ultimately come from individual motivation, and thus the conditions for getting people to grow and learn that I have tried to explore in this paper should be relevant to making the learning community possible.

Suggestions for Research

Any of the above ideas for enabling the development of the learning stance must remain tentative and vague until we have firmer knowledge concerning the relevant facts. Thus, it is proper to conclude these considerations with some indications about what questions might be most important to investigate to establish a firmer factual basis for implementing policies.

In the first place, we need to confirm the following relationships: (a) that, other things being equal, one enjoys more an activity from which one learns; (b) that the more opportunities for enjoyment one has, the more happy the rest of one's life is; (c) that the more opportunities for enjoyment one has, the more productive one becomes; (d) that growth in symbolic and nurturant skills is inversely related to material needs and consumption; (e) that enjoyment liberates energy for productive and community action. Each one of these propositions opens up a broad field of research with potentially vital contributions for the theory underlying the learning stance.

Next, it is necessary to find out how the learning stance develops. The following questions need to be addressed at this level: At what point do children show stable differences in the ability to concentrate? to derive enjoyment from the use of skills? How can such differences be affected? How can the range of stimuli to which children respond spontaneously be increased?

Some recent research by Holcomb[15] bears on these issues. She found that college students who reported a wide range of enjoyable activities were able to reverse perceptually ambiguous figures much easier, and showed lower cortical activation levels when paying attention to sensory stimuli, than students who rarely reported enjoying themselves. These findings might mean that the learning stance has a physiological basis— either inherited or acquired. It seems that those who can enjoy themselves in any situation are able to restructure sensory input at lower energy costs. Related to this issue are studies on stimulus overinclusion and anhedonia, which show that inability to control access of stimuli into consciousness, and absence of enjoyment, are crucial symptoms of schizophrenia and related diseases.[16]

Finally, there is a whole host of research that needs to be done concerning the evaluation of policies attempting to affect the learning stance in adults, if and when such are implemented. Of particular interest would be interventions aimed at restructuring jobs and those that try to increase symbolic and interpersonal skills. In the meantime, while waiting for research directly dealing with these issues to be started, it would be important to reinterpret already existing studies in related areas to see what light they shed on the learning stance. The topics of most direct relevance would be those dealing with the development of competence and attentional processes in children, and work satisfaction, intrinsic motivation, and psychological well-being in adults.

The pursuit of happiness has been too "soft" an ideal to generate much interest among either academics or politicians. Perhaps a recognition that happiness consists in complete involvement with a challenging task, from which learning and growth result, will make it possible for us to take this ideal seriously. If this happens, the learning stance might become a high priority research and policy goal, as it deserves to be.

Notes

1. P. Goodman, *Compulsory Mis-education* (New York: Horizon, 1964); U. Bronfenbrenner, *Two Worlds of Childhood* (New York: Pocket Books, 1973); R. DeCharms, *Enhancing Motivation: Change in the Classroom* (New York: Irvington, 1976); E. L. Deci, *Intrinsic Motivation* (New York: Plenum, 1975); M. Csikszentmihalyi, "Intrinsic Rewards and Emergent Motivation," in M. R. Lepper and D. Greene (eds.), *The Hidden Costs of Reward* (New York: Erlbaum, 1978): 205–216; M. Csikszentmihalyi and R. Larson, "Intrinsic Rewards in School Crime," *Crime and Delinquency*, 1978, 24(3): 322–335; and M. Csikszentmihalyi and P. L. Mayers, "Intrinsic Motivation and Learning in High School," manuscript submitted for publication, 1979.

2. M. Csikszentmihalyi, "Attention and the Holistic Approach to Behavior," in K. S. Pope and J. L. Singer (eds.), *The Stream of Consciousness* (New York: Plenum, 1978): 335–358.

3. A. Maslow, *Towards a Psychology of Being* (Princeton: Van Nostrand, 1962); A. Maslow, *The Farther Reaches of Human Behavior* (New York: Viking, 1971); M. Laski, *Ecstasy: A Study of Some Secular and Religious Experiences* (Bloomington: Indiana University Press, 1962); and N. M. Bradburn, *The Structure of Psychological Well-being* (Chicago: Aldine, 1969).

4. M. Csikszentmihalyi, *Beyond Boredom and Anxiety* (San Francisco: Jossey-Bass, 1975); P. Mayers, "Flow in Adolescence and Its Relation to School Experience," unpublished doctoral dissertation, University of Chicago,

1978; P. Mayers, M. Csikszentmihalyi, and R. Larson, "The Daily Experience of High School Students," paper presented at the meetings of the American Educational Research Association, Toronto, 1978; and H. R. Gray, "Enjoyment Dimensions of Favorite Leisure Activities of Middle- and Old-aged Adults Based on the Flow Theory of Enjoyment," unpublished doctoral thesis, Pennsylvania State University, 1977.

5. M. Csikszentmihalyi, "Intrinsic Rewards and Emergent Motivation," in M. R. Lepper and D. Greene (eds.), *The Hidden Costs of Reward* (New York: Erlbaum, 1978): 205–216; and M. Csikszentmihalyi, "Love and the Dynamics of Personal Growth," in K. S. Pope (ed.), *On Love and Loving* (San Francisco: Jossey-Bass, 1980).

6. M. Csikszentmihalyi and R. Graef, "Flow and the Quality of Daily Experience," manuscript submitted for publication, 1979.

7. K. Koch, *Wishes, Lies and Dreams: Teaching Children to Write Poetry* (New York: Chelsea House, 1970); and K. Koch, *I Never Told Anybody: Teaching Poetry Writing in a Nursing Home* (New York: Random House, 1977).

8. M. Csikszentmihalyi, "The Release of Symbolic Energy," paper presented at the American Art Therapy Association meetings, Baltimore, 1976; M. Csikszentmihalyi, "Attention and the Holistic Approach to Behavior," in K. S. Pope and J. L. Singer (eds.), *The Stream of Consciousness* (New York: Plenum, 1978): 335–358; and M. Csikszentmihalyi and E. Rochberg-Halton, "People and Things: Reflections on Materialism," *The University of Chicago Magazine*, 1978, 70(3): 6–15.

9. B. Smith, "Competence and Socialization," in J. A. Clausen (ed.), *Socialization and Society* (Boston: Little, Brown, 1968).

10. M. Csikszentmihalyi, R. Larson, and S. Prescott, "The Ecology of Adolescent Activity and Experience," *Journal of Youth and Adolescence*, 1977, 6(3): 281–294; and P. Mayers, M. Csikszentmihalyi, and R. Larson, "The Daily Experience of High School Students," paper presented at the meetings of the American Educational Research Association, Toronto, 1978.

11. P. Mayers, "Flow in Adolescence and Its Relation to School Experience," unpublished doctoral dissertation, University of Chicago, 1978.

12. M. Csikszentmihalyi and R. Graef, "Flow and the Quality of Daily Experience," manuscript submitted for publication, 1979.

13. R. Graef, M. Csikszentmihalyi, and P. Griffin, "Flow and Work Satisfaction," unpublished manuscript, University of Chicago, 1978.

14. M. Csikszentmihalyi, "Love and the Dynamics of Personal Growth," in K. S. Pope (ed.), *On Love and Loving* (San Francisco: Jossey-Bass, 1980).

15. J. H. Holcomb, "Attention and Intrinsic Rewards in the Control of Psychophysiologic States," *Psychotherapy and Psychosomatics*, 1977, 27: 54–61.

16. A. McGhie and J. Chapman, "Disorders of Attention and Perception in Early Schizophrenia," *British Journal of Medical Psychology*, 1961, 34: 103–116; and R. Grinker, "Anhedonia and Depression in Schizophrenia," in T. Benedek and E. Anthony (eds.), *Depression* (Boston: Little, Brown, 1975).

Part IV

THE PRACTICE OF
ADULT EDUCATION

Success Stories of Adult Learning   The bottom line in adult education is Better People. These distinct and vivid, but also representative, success stories portray such results. Naming names and documenting circumstances, these profiles reveal both the ways in which individual lives are enriched through lifelong learning and the ways in which our society benefits.

Courage, perseverance, patience, and plain hard work are some of the ingredients of these success stories. Students and teachers alike display these qualities.

Compiled by the National Advisory Council on Adult Education, these portraits pull flesh-and-blood people out of the cold statistics. Dedicated, resourceful people are at work every day in the field of adult education, learning and creating together. In these pages their dreams, their dedication, and their rewards are dramatically evident.

Such stories can be useful in advocating adult education in two ways. For the already advantaged, they can increase awareness of the learning needs of other adults and the social value of public investment in the field. For the less advantaged adults, such stories can entice them to turn to learning as a way to improve their lives.

These eight profiles were published by the National Advisory Council on Adult Education in 1978 as *Success Stories of Adult Learning.*

Success Stories of Adult Learning

Samuel C. Brightman

Too "Dumb" to Finish High School

At 5:30 in the morning Charles Rumble and his wife sit down in the comfortable kitchen of the solid house he built with his own hands in a pleasant section of Springfield, Ill., and she reads to him for an hour from the textbooks he uses as an adult education student at Lincoln Land Community College.

Rumble is getting his college education the hard way, which is the way everything in life has come to him. Once a skilled construction worker who was disabled in accidents, Rumble is going to college and leading a full and rewarding life because of the interest and ingenuity of an adult education administrator and adult education teacher and because of his own determination to control his life.

Rumble does not learn by listening because he is blind, but because he has dyslexia, a learning disability that jumbles words and letters. To get an idea of what books are like for Rumble, imagine that the words you are looking at now were swirling around into different patterns of words and letters much as the patterns change in a kaleidoscope. Try to imagine learning what you learned in the classroom without the written word to return to when your memory is shaky. Keep this in the back of your head as you read about Charles Rumble.

Rumble is a pleasant, chunky, muscled man, articulate, zealous in an amiable way, and utterly free of self-pity. His zeal is in the cause of other adults with learning disabilities. Having received from adult education the learning opportunity that was not provided him in his childhood, Rumble is dedicated to helping other adults with learning disabilities to receive the same opportunity. That is the purpose of his continuing education and of an organization he has formed which publishes "Not For Children Only," a newsletter devoted to obtaining educational assistance for adults with learning disabilities.

Rumble's father had a learning disability and all but one of his broth-

191

ers had the same problem. His one son is also afflicted, but, with today's resources in the public schools for the handicapped, is doing well in the sixth grade.

During the depression of the thirties, Charles Rumble's father lost his farm and his business of renting farm equipment and doing the threshing for other farmers. He became an operating engineer and a skilled mechanic.

Charles Rumble had a hard time of it in the public schools. His learning disability was not diagnosed. He was a "retard" to other children and their parents, who told their children not to play with him. The unhappy boy spent hours in the woods alone, miserable.

He was nearly 17 when he quit school and worked in a greenhouse as a laborer. Then he was apprenticed into the operating engineers union to which his father belonged. Along with his learning disability, he had also inherited from his father unusual manual skills and the ability to understand how things work by looking at them. (He can make complicated auto repairs by looking at the pictures in a shop manual.)

So in the fifties, Rumble learned to work various construction equipment and eventually became a heavy crane operator. He noted that he worked steadily except when his equipment broke down and that the master mechanic, who was better paid, worked only when something needed repair. Since the master mechanic had less work and more pay, Rumble decided to learn to become a master mechanic. He wound up not only with the ability to make complicated repairs himself, but with the ability to teach mechanical skills to others.

He moved around the country and was making as much as $1,000 a week with overtime on the Feather River tunnel project in California when he hurt his knees badly in a fall on the job. The money was good, and he wrapped his knees in elastic bandages, endured the pain, and kept on working. But finally he had to have an operation. He devised a special set of homemade bandages to support his knees and went back to lighter work. The big money days were over and he supported his family for 3 years by repairing various appliances, mostly wheelchairs. Then he decided to return to Springfield and use his operating engineer's card to get work there, work where he would not have to walk.

About that family he was supporting. In school Rumble admired a pretty girl who didn't pay much attention to the class "dullard." When he began to make good money as an operating engineer he decided to attract the attention of the young lady. He did. Some of his fellow workers were buying jacked-up hot rods with fancy paint jobs and fat tires to impress the girls. Not Charles Rumble. He showed up at high school in a shiny new MGA sports car, pretty much of a novelty on the prairies in those days, and offered the young lady a ride.

Once Charles Rumble gets your attention, he is persuasive. They were married. If you're a car freak, you will be interested to know that there is a rare MGA, just like the courtship car which was totaled when a truck pushed it off the road, sitting in Rumble's garage. He and his son are restoring it carefully and slowly. The engine and transmission are as good as new, but the body work and upholstery take time to get done right. Rumble has a schedule on this job. He plans to have the restoration completed in time for his boy to take his driver's license test in it 3 years from now.

Back in Springfield, Rumble began to make good money, running a concrete spreading and finishing machine. Then he fractured his coccyx in a tractor accident. After an operation he suffered so much pain that he could not sit on any equipment. His knees would not hold up for construction work. Rumble was totally disabled, getting social security disability and also drawing a comfortable sum from insurance he had taken out in the big money days.

But the pain was intense and eventually led to overuse of drugs. Rumble wound up at the pain management center at the Mayo Clinic in Rochester, Minn. Two big things happened there. He learned to "manage" his pain. And his "stupidity" or "retardation" was diagnosed as dyslexia.

Back in Springfield, he went to the Department of Vocational Rehabilitation. They looked at his papers from Mayo and turned him down as "untrainable," sentenced to a life of doing nothing.

Rumble then went to the adult education people in the Springfield public schools. The administrator was Jack Pfeiffer who put Rumble into a satellite adult basic education program conducted in the basement of the St. John's African Methodist Episcopalian Church.

The new student was a big challenge to a young teacher named Evelyn Deimel. She hit upon the notion of using the tapes provided to teach blind students to pass their GED tests. She was ingenious enough to look for a printed text to match the tapes and lucky enough to find one. In 1976, using tapes and dictating his answers to the questions, Charles Rumble passed his GED test. It was as big an occasion for Jack Pfeiffer and Evelyn Deimel as it was for Charles Rumble.

Now Charles Rumble is continuing his studies, seeking the skills and academic credentials to aid other adults with learning disabilities. In addition to his adult education classwork, he travels around the country working to organize adults with learning disabilities to obtain public assistance in learning. The bureaucracy is not always responsive.

Recently a bureaucrat in the Illinois State Board of Education asked him to turn in a State-supplied cassette recorder, "Property Control No. 17848, no later than June 1978," because dyslexia "does not fall within the category of visual impairments."

But Rumble has worked out that problem. He uses a cassette as many of us use scissors and paste. Where we store clippings and articles in file cabinets, Rumble files and stores bits of tape with material he wants to recall and use.

Rumble has disability income and his wife works at a data processing company. This gives them enough funds to travel with their children to places of historic interest, in keeping with the fact that Rumble and his son learn best by seeing and doing.

The house Rumble built is snug and shipshape, unusual in its living plan and in the imaginative two-level greenhouse he has added on one side. There is a well-equipped workroom. Rumble built the house from a do-it-yourself kit. He used the pictures. The blueprints were needed to obtain the building permit and to guide the electrical and plumbing contractors he was required to use.

Rumble likes wheels. He has a van which he bought for $300. He rebuilt the motor and transmission, finished it inside and put in a CB radio and a tape player sound system. The final paint job on the outside is not completed but Rumble keeps turning down $5,000 offers for the vehicle. And there is a Japanese truck with a small trailer to haul the sleek fiberglass soapbox derby racer Rumble's son has built. There is a Cadillac, once faltering, which Rumble got in trade for a VW wagon. That car is near the 200,000-mile mark and running like a top. All Rumble has bought for the car is tires and tuneup kits. And finally there is that MG in the garage.

It is a full and rewarding life, made possible by Rumble's indomitable spirit and a big assist from the adult education people in the Springfield public schools. It is also a busy life and Rumble's day doesn't really begin at 5:30 in the morning when his wife starts reading to him from his textbooks. Before that he helps his son roll the newspapers for his paper route.

A "Connecticut Yankee" in Adult Education

If you think of higher education in Connecticut as rich kids from all over throwing frisbees at Yale and sturdy white yankee descendants of revolutionary soldiers studying at Storrs, think some more. Think about Allan Thomas, a 26-year-old black alcoholic court-martialed veteran who is a freshman at the Housatonic Community College in Bridgeport.

A few years ago Thomas appeared certain to remain in the ranks of life's losers. Now he's a little ahead of the game and working hard to stay there. Adult education played a key role in the turnaround.

Allan was born in Derby, an industrial town, in 1952. He lives in Ansonia, a similar town nearby. His father was a masonry laborer. His mother died when he was 10 and his father stopped work to attempt to care for his 12 children. Welfare funds and odd jobs provided his income. By Allan's account a good portion of that income went for alcohol, which has been a nemesis for both father and son.

Allan says he was "passed along" in grade school and "put down" by the teachers in high school, which was about 12-percent black. He says there was an unspoken message to go to vocational school or go into the Army—that the black son of a black drunk was not going to become a doctor or lawyer or businessman.

Even before high school Allan started drinking. After he quit school when he finished the ninth grade he was "on the street" doing odd jobs— and drinking. Within 2 months he was arrested for breaking and entering a grocery store next to a bar and taking $30.

The judge game him the choice of joining the Army or going to jail. At age 18, Allan Thomas joined the Army at New Haven. After boot training at Fort Dix he went to Texas for training as a missile crewman and finally wound up in a mountainous post near the border between East Germany and West Germany. There were about 40 blacks in a garrison of 250 and Thomas says there was some racial friction. He got into booze, pot, hash, and acid, all, he said, easily obtained from other soldiers who got them from German civilians. Thomas was working as a cook and in the motor pool.

Why didn't he get into the Army's education program? He says the commanding officer decided who could take available GED courses on the Army's time and troublemakers like himself were not about to get this privilege.

Near the end of his hitch, Thomas got into a poker game fight with a white noncom. Thomas pulled a razor. He was court-martialed and spent 14 days in the Mannheim Military Prison.

Despite the court-martial conviction, Thomas got out in 1972 with an honorable discharge, with papers which erroneously said he was a high school graduate, and about $2,000. He capsulated what happened next as "I got married and settled down."

He is ironic. What happened is that he drank away the money in 2 months and didn't get a job for 6 months. He lived with his father, who was also drinking heavily. They didn't drink together but had a kind of tacit understanding not to say anything to each other about their aberrations when they were into the booze.

Finally he got a job as a furnace operator in a brass foundry. And he got married.

Joeanne Ballaster quit school in the ninth grade. Her parents were divorced. She said her mother had an alcohol problem and she lived with a sister. She didn't have a job and there wasn't much to do. She married Thomas when she was 16 and he was 22. They have a 5-year-old son. Joeanne is white. Mixed marriages are not unusual in Ansonia, but among the poor of both races who live on menial jobs and welfare there is no particular social opprobrium for such marriages.

Thomas was not fired from the brass company job for drinking but he says that drinking caused the bad performance at work that caused him to lose the job. And he says he abused his wife and son when he was drinking and was near a divorce when he reenlisted in 1975. He was given the rank of E4, which entitled him to government housing. First he went to Fort Lee for training in the Quartermaster Corps as a petroleum storage specialist. His wife and baby lived with him in Hopewell and he commuted to duty. When his training was completed he went to Fort Hood in Texas, a station not regarded by its alumni as a Shangri La. The family lived in military housing there, but Thomas was still unsettled and unhappy. He was drinking hard and when he would try to quit drinking he would rely on pot for his needed "high." He was court-martialed on a charge of dealing in pot but won acquittal. When his second hitch ended in 1977 the Army had no burning desire to retain him and he had no burning desire to remain in the service.

The troubled family went to Brooklyn. They stayed with his wife's sister. Thomas, who is tall, well-built, and articulate, found a job as a clerk in a liquor store. It was a fox and chicken coop arrangement that was doomed to failure. Thomas said he was drinking more and more and he began to sip the merchandise. He was fired from this job and the family returned to Ansonia. He moved in with his father and sent his wife to get on welfare by saying he had left her. She found a place to live in what residents of comfortable suburbs would probably describe as a run-down working class neighborhood.

Somehow, Thomas says, he managed to quit drinking after the return to Ansonia. He had injured a leg badly in a drunken fall in Brooklyn. He had begun to face the fact that bad things took place when he was drinking heavily—lost jobs, the fight in Germany, the fall in New York, and the arrest for burglary.

Articulate as he is, Thomas does not do very well in describing how he quit drinking. He is involved with the work of Alcoholics Anonymous, but says that movement did not get him on the wagon. "I just bumped into myself one day," he says. This may mean little to most people and may be an adequate explanation to many of those who once drank heavily and are engaged in the day-to-day exercise of staying dry. Staying dry one day at a time for—they hope—the rest of their lives.

Why the drinking in the first place by someone who has the ability to organize his thoughts, has a good appearance (the ravages of drink may cause him to look older than his years later on but they don't show now and didn't show when he was younger) and good manual skills and muscular coordination?

Now that Thomas has started studying sociology he has done some introspective thinking about that. He has reached no hard conclusion but he thinks that his troubles began when his mother died and that he was the victim of some discrimination in school, partly racial and partly economic, probably unconscious. He thinks that grade and high school teachers tend to be more sympathetic to students from their own backgrounds and from families which share their lifestyles and values. But he puts the primary blame on himself. Not that he wallows in guilt. He is more interested in his future than in his past and his primary concern is with the present. He is living one day at a time.

At the unemployment office he met a Veterans Administration representative who urged him to use the veteran's stipend available for those studying to pass the GED. He went to the adult learning center in an old bank building on Main Street in Ansonia and met Walter Zielinsky.

Zielinsky has been a friend and counselor ever since. He is a former high school economics teacher who got into adult education as a moonlighter. He likes working with adults and believes that adult education is a vital force in keeping society functioning in economic problem areas like the Derby-Ansonia region where he is in charge of adult education. Zielinsky works day and night and runs adult learning programs day and night. There is a lot of paperwork involved in helping adults to get help from a variety of programs so that they can learn the skills needed to function in a society with a glut of unskilled labor. There is also a lot of people work involved. Zielinsky does not shirk at either task.

Zielinsky tested Thomas and started him in adult basic education and a GED prep program to pass his GED test. Thomas got into the bottle again. He dropped out of his GED program. But he came back. To get the VA stipend, 25 hours of study a week are required. Zielinsky tries to make sure that there are 25 hours of real concentrated learning. Thomas started his studies in March 1977. He passed the GED test in January 1978. Zielinsky had worried that Thomas was not ready and would fail and quit. But Thomas made it. Zielinsky then steered him to the Housatonic Community College. He received a VA stipend, worked at odd jobs, and his wife worked in a nursing home. Thomas started out to carry 16-credit hours his first semester, but found the going rough and dropped 2 hours. Now he has 14 hours of credit and is looking for work before he returns to college for another semester. His wife is not working.

The family lives in a somewhat dilapidated apartment in a drab neighborhood. The apartment is being spruced up. The landlord is supplying the materials and Thomas and his father are putting up the sweat equity.

Thomas is proud that he is able to help his son with the boy's school work. It is something that he missed in his childhood.

Thomas is working with Alcoholics Anonymous to help other veterans with drinking problems. His training at the community college will enable him to be an urban professional assistant, probably he will become a social worker helping the poor in Ansonia, he believes. Whether a 4-year degree is ahead is uncertain. Thomas would like to get the 4-year degree, but 3½ years of college work for a man with a wife and child will not be easy and Thomas is cautious about setting distant goals. He is still living one day at a time. Thomas has become something of a social activist. There is an antidiscrimination suit against a landlord who had a vacancy when Joeanne Thomas applied for an apartment but who said that there was not a vacancy when her black husband showed up to sign the lease. He feels that race played a part in his troubles in school and in the army. The adult education he is achieving is giving him the confidence to fight back at what he considers racial prejudice and discrimination.

As long as Thomas keeps his head on straight he will have a friend and helper in Walter Zielinsky. Zielinsky sees each adult student as a separate problem. He tries to find teachers who are good at personal relations. Together they try to get people like Allan Thomas back into the mainstream of society.

The young son of Joeanne and Allan Thomas wasn't quite sure what the stranger was doing in the house talking with his father and mother and he went outside to play after a while. Watching the father watch his son, the reporter had to think that Thomas was going to stay in the mainstream. Living one day at a time.

He Survived

If you listened to a tape of the teacher guiding the small class through an animated discussion of the obligations of employers and employees to each other you would probably assume that you were overhearing a conventional teacher in a conventional class of a conventional postsecondary institution.

You would be wrong. The class was at the Technical-Vocational Institute (T-VI) in Albuquerque, N. Mex. The students were adults of all ages and colors. The teacher and many of his adult students were dropouts who became eligible for training at T-VI by passing a GED exam.

This story is about the teacher, a Ph.D. teaching adults at the "trade school" institution which prepared him to get his high school equivalency certificate at the age of 49—34 years after he quit school and ran away from home. The teacher's name is Orlando Stevens, and during the 34-year gap in his schooling he was: A circus roustabout, a sailor, a soldier, a prisoner of the Japanese Army, a loafer, a deputy sheriff, president of a printing union local, owner of a printing company, a civil leader in Albuquerque, and a skilled amateur painter in oils.

Orlando Stevens was born in New Mexico in 1916. His father was an electrician with the street railway who came there from Ohio. The father was half-English and half-French and his wife was half-Spanish and half-Cherokee. In an era when ethnicity is fashionable, this ancestry is a sort of credential for Orlando Stevens' activities in the field of cultural awareness. In public school in the tough mission district of San Francisco where he lived when his father took a job with the street railway company there, Orlando's ancestry led to a lot of playground fights and scorn from teachers who did not think much of children with names like Orlando.

Orlando was 15 when he left the ninth grade and ran away with a circus. He spent 3 years as a roustabout and clown and then enlisted in the Navy. He was in training to become a pharmacist's mate when he was given a hardship discharge. His father had died years before and his mother was suffering from asthma in the damp climate of the bay area. Orlando and his mother returned to New Mexico. Orlando's Navy medical skills helped him to get a job in a hospital. One of the doctors there headed a National Guard medical unit and suggested that Orlando join the unit. He did.

The unit was called to active duty in 1941 and sent to the Philippines. Stevens was captured at Bataan. He made the long march. He spent 3½ years in Japanese prison camps. As a master sergeant in the Medical Corps he was sometimes the senior American medic in his compound and was assigned to the Japanese to treat the prisoners. He learned enough Japanese to prompt Senator S. I. Hayakawa, the noted semanticist whom he met recently, to ask, "Where in the hell did you learn to speak Japanese like this?" Enough of his Spanish ancestry shows in his face so that no one is surprised at his fluent Spanish.

Stevens was on a Japanese prison ship that was torpedoed by Americans off Formosa. The 300 survivors of the 1,500 Americans on the ship were recaptured by the Japanese and taken to Formosa, which is where he was when he was liberated. It was a couple of years before the Army cured him of diseases he contracted while a prisoner and gave him a 100-percent disability discharge. He bought a car with his back pay and bummed around the country for a year with an Army pal and then returned to Albuquerque where another Army buddy had been elected sheriff. He made Orlando a deputy and assigned him to escorting extradited prisoners. Finally this gave Stevens his fill of traveling. He married and took a GI course in photography and lithography.

He joined the union, became president of his local, and then bought his own printing company, which he headed for 16 years. His skill at lithography had caused T-VI to employ him as an instructor. While he was teaching there he sold his printing business. The president of T-VI, Louis Saavedra, suggested he might want to take some courses in education and make teaching his new career.

When Stevens revealed that he had never finished high school, Saavedra told him about the GED test and helped him to engage in a crash adult education program which enabled him to pass that test in 2 months. Still teaching lithography, Stevens studied drafting and technical illustration at T-VI and began teaching those subjects.

Saavedra suggested Stevens might want to go to the University of New Mexico for some further study. Stevens didn't know that his GED certificate made him eligible. Still teaching at T-VI, he got his bachelor of university studies degree from the University of New Mexico in 2½ years. He was 53 and had become interested in the field of cultural awareness, partly as a result of serving in South America in an Agency for International Development education project conducted by the University of New Mexico.

He was teaching classes for that institution when he decided to obtain a master of arts degree in education, but a youthful department chairman did not want to accept a man in his fifties with a GED-university studies background instead of the conventional high school diploma and youthful undergraduate college experience. Some friendly faculty members suggested he sue, charging age and race discrimination. His threat to sue brought his admission, and, despite some bruised feelings in the department, he got his master's in 1 year and then went on to get his Ph.D. This meant another year and a half of taking courses plus additional months to complete his dissertation. During all this time Dr. Stevens (he is proud of his doctorate but loathes being called doctor so this is the last Dr. Stevens in the article) was still teaching. He didn't stop working at 5 o'clock and spend the evening with his family. His marriage grew strained and finally ended with divorce.

Stevens taught for a while at El Rito, N. Mex., and then returned to Albuquerque to teach at T-VI and the university.

Sometimes adult education solves all kinds of problems. After many years of marriage Stevens was sort of rattling around as a single when an adult female student in one of his classes asked him to her apartment for some homecooked food. He is happily remarried—to this student—and lives in a comfortable home decorated with some of his oil paintings. One is a self-portrait, striking with its raw, bright colors. It depicts Stevens as a clown. To keep busy he is active in an Elks lodge project which entertains youngsters from broken homes and disadvantaged families. Stevens used his circus experience to play the clown for the children. Another portrait is somber. It shows a Spanish-Indian woman, her face strong but lined. Her stooped shoulders and her gnarled hands in the foreground reflect the hardship and poverty of life in the desert, a life Stevens understands.

Despite the fact that his intense drive to complete his self-chosen goals in formal education broke up his first marriage (or maybe because of it), Orlando Stevens is keenly sensitive to the needs of self-development. He is outgoing, laughs easily, teaches skillfully, and leads a full life. Saavedra and Dr. John Aragon at the university were among those already diplomaed who helped him to obtain his education and now he, in turn, spends a good deal of time helping adults to meet their educational goals.

Was life easy for Orlando Stevens in the post GED years? "No." Was it worthwhile? "Yes."

It took a good deal of time to get Orlando Stevens to look back and provide the information you have just read. At 62, Orlando Stevens is looking ahead to new adventures of the mind and spirit in adult education.

Pennsylvanians Change Their Lives for the Better

The poised woman saying a few gracious words of thanks to the comfortable, middle-class group that filled the handsome conference center at Hershey, Pa., could have been a suburban matron receiving an award for highway beautification from a State convention of conservationists. That was the scene. But it was deceiving.

The meeting was a State convention of adult educators. The woman they were honoring was a ninth-grade dropout who ran away from home to marriage with a construction worker and a life of drudgery on a small farm. Her work began at dawn and ended long after dusk. Adult education had enabled her to change herself and to change her life. She was being honored as the winner of a statewide "adult education success story contest" conducted by the Pennsylvania Department of Education's Adult and Community Education Division. The award was made at a State conference of adult educators after a committee had studied accounts of adult education accomplishments from many school districts within the Commonwealth.

Pennsylvania has a strong program of adult learning and the contest winner, Katrina Ferraro, was only one of many persons a reporter talked with in a 2-day visit to the State who have found purpose and fulfillment through adult education. It is a State where adult learners can find community support as well as help from those who are paid to teach. Many of the adults who have benefitted from this program have found ways to support adult education after they have received their GED certificates. More about that later.

Katrina Ferraro was the second to the youngest of nine children. Her father had immigrated to Erie at age 15. He worked there as warden at a girl's home and then moved to nearby Waterford, where he ran a restaurant. Katrina had a hard time in school. She repeated the second grade and she quit school while repeating the ninth grade. She left home and got a job working in an auction barn run by the grandparents of her husband-to-be. She married him when she was 16 and he was 23. He had been raised by his grandparents on a small farm. He had little education and earned a living by farming and doing construction work. He loved animals. Even when working on construction jobs he got up in the dark to tend to his livestock and he was back caring for them long after dark. His wife shared the burdens, living in homes that sometimes offered less protection from the cold of western Pennsylvania than the barn.

The marriage was in 1963. Katrina had her first of six children when she was 17. Fourteen years after she left school she went to an adult basic education class conducted by the Penncrest School District. With the help of her instructors, working at her own pace, she resumed her education. Her attendance was sporadic because of the burdens of raising children on an isolated farm, but she studied for her GED test. The first time she failed. She studied some more and in 1976 she passed it and received a Penncrest School District High School Diploma.

The adult education people in Penncrest helped her to get a job at the Penncrest Day Care Center. She likes working with children and the income made it easier for her to study. She earned enough that her children could be taken off the day care rolls. Katrina also achieved self-confidence and a new idea of what life is about from her return to learning.

The Ferraro marriage has been rocky at times. Education changed some of Katrina's values. It also gave her confidence in her ability to communicate with other people, including her husband. There has been a family conference and some changed priorities. The children have time to study. Making the house livable for the family has become a higher priority than making the barn comfortable for the livestock.

A reporter visiting Katrina at the day care center finds her comfortable with the children and enjoying her work. She says that the course she took at Edinboro State College to enable her to be certified as a day care supervisor has enabled her to be a better mother to her own children as well as to help the children of others. She goes to Edinboro to study early childhood education. She wants that to be her career. Life is still hard, but education has brought a change. Before Katrina became involved in adult education, she says, "I didn't even know there was a world out there." A reporter who spent some time with her found out that the biggest reward she has found from her return to learning is not the improved economic conditions she now enjoys but the ability to do more for herself and for others. She is proud of her ability to teach children and of increased skills in relating to other people. "Things have improved at home now," she says.

It may be just a coincidence that the fellow who is in charge of adult education for the Penncrest School District, Art Pergamasco, was a dropout who got into college by passing the GED examination, and went on to make teaching his life career.

The nominees in the Pennsylvania success story contest follow no fixed pattern. In Lancaster there is Sally Kusuplos, born Soultana Goropoulos in Athens, Greece, daughter of a shoemaker.

Sally was 17 when she met Spiros Kusuplos, then 36. He was running a restaurant in Lancaster, where he was born. He was in Athens on a special mission—"to marry a blond Greek girl." There was a chaperoned Old World courtship. They were married 10 days after they met. He returned to Lancaster and she followed him later, arriving in 1957. She studied English in phrase books and do-it-yourself manuals and helped her husband with his business, which grew to include an interest in a local resort. In 1976 she enrolled in the adult education center in Lancaster. In 9 months she progressed from the fifth grade level to passing her GED examination.

The family is in comfortable circumstances, are leaders in the Greek community, and Mrs. Kusuplos is president of the Women's Auxiliary of the Blind Association of Lancaster.

Sally Kusuplos was proud to take part in the formal graduation ceremony that is conducted for GED graduates in Lancaster. She welcomes publicity which encourages adult learning. She is now taking courses at the same State college where her son is a full-time student.

Sally's pride in her GED graduation is not unusual in Lancaster. Each successful GED class—the graduates get a regular diploma—is graduated with as much pomp and ceremony as in a regular high school. Learning to read and write is a matter of pride, not of shame, in Lancaster. It is there that the first GED alumni association was organized by Mrs. Laura Whitted, who was 1970 valedictorian at the GED ceremonies, and who recently was named by the Governor to the State Advisory Council on Vocational Education. In addition to this, Mrs. Whitted works as a remedial reading aide, is raising a family (the oldest is at Pennsylvania State), taking courses at Millerburg State College, and singing in the choir at the Ebenezer Baptist Church. She keeps pretty busy, but as she said at her graduation in 1970, "This is a beginning from which we can step outward and upward—a lot of doors have been opened to us—doors of higher education, doors of better employment. We should try in some little way to help our community."

Mrs. Whitted had a cannery job when she came to the area. After completing her GED she opened the door to equal education opportunity by encouraging the school district to give the regular diploma to adults passing the GED examination.

Another nominee in the success story contest is Barbara Drew, in Erie. She looks like a teacher, talks like a teacher, and she is a teacher. But her route to this career was not exactly typical. She dropped out of school in the 10th grade, was married, had 2 boys and 1 girl, was divorced in 1970 and remarried 3 years later. After she obtained her GED certificate she went on to college while working as a teacher's aide. The Federal model cities program and the career opportunities program gave her the opportunity.

There's a man who was broke and badly into drugs. He enrolled in a GED course and an adult vocational education training program in welding. Now he teaches welding. In his spare time he works as a volunteer in the training of the retarded.

There is the widow who went from illiteracy to the GED certificate and from the mental confusion of five valiums a day to none and a job in nursing. There is the prisoner who is still in prison, but he learned to read there and became the foreman of a work crew. He will have job skills to enable him to stay out of trouble when his sentence is finished. There is the Indian woman who went from an alcoholic rehabilitation program to a GED certificate and is now taking vocational training. There is the Vietnam refugee who entered this country in 1975 and is about to receive a 2-year certificate in electronics.

These people came into richer lives through a variety of programs—adult learning centers, conventional night school classes, English as a second language course, one-on-one tutorial programs. They must be doing something—make that several things—right in the adult learning programs in Pennsylvania.

Learning to Live with Change in Kentucky

Pamela Crouch Donaldson is smiling and seemingly at ease as she moves about the pleasant room where students not much younger are studying at their desks. The atmosphere is friendly and comfortable.

The adult learning center where Pamela is serving as a paraprofessional instructor is located in Mount Sterling, which is the county seat of Montgomery County, which is in the part of Kentucky where the rich and fashionable "Blue Grass" section ends. To the east the land slopes up to the poverty of Appalachia.

This was once a farming county with tobacco one of its main crops. It was not unusual for boys and girls to begin to work full time on the farm when they finished the eighth grade. Farming was labor intensive in those days and the dropout who didn't work on his family farm could find a job as a hired hand for some other farmer.

There are only some 16,000 persons in the county and Mt. Sterling has a population of 5,000. The economy of the county is now based upon agriculture, service and manufacturing. Many who live on small farms must also work at the typewriter factory or the electric motor factory to make ends meet. Not too many years ago, this was a county where the husband was the breadwinner and the wife stayed home and cared for the children. Now the pattern of both spouses working is becoming as prevalent in this rural country as it is becoming in the cities and their suburbs.

Young people who drop out of high school can no longer find a job on a farm. The light industries the city is successfully seeking mostly won't hire anyone without a high school education. Those already working in the factories who have not completed high school are encouraged to obtain a GED certificate. Factories make study rooms available for those workers and the school district sends instructors there.

Some years back the Montgomery County Board of Education became the first school system in Kentucky to adopt the concept of community education. The school system has about 4,000 pupils in K–12 and serves 6,000 to 7,000 persons of all ages in adult education, recreation, cultural and social service needs.

All of these facts, and some others that will follow, are relevant to the story of Pamela Crouch Donaldson, the teacher who does not appear to be much older than her students. And these students, these adult basic education students, look young, particularly since the reporter saw a grandmother working on her ABC's at the Montgomery County Learning Center he visited. Learning and recreation are all together in the Montgomery County system. Next to this grandmother were a half dozen other elderly women working on a quilt. When they were brides, it was a custom to get together to make quilts for use in their homes. This one, a beautiful example of a disappearing art, will be sold at a handicraft fair to help support the community education program of Montgomery County. But most of the ABE students are younger than the quilting group.

The setting where Pamela Donaldson is teaching is relaxed but the students are intense at their work. They need their GED certificate and they want to prove that, even though things went wrong in high school, they are able to learn. And Pamela is not as relaxed as she seems.

Not yet 30, raised in poverty and hard work, Pamela is going through a painful personal crisis. She is coping with it because of her own strength, because of the confidence she obtained from completing an adult basic education program and training to become a paraprofessional teacher herself, and from the support of the friends she has made through the Montgomery County community education program.

Pamela was born in 1951 in Frenchburg, east of Mount Sterling. She lived with her parents on a small farm. Her father owned some land and worked as a tenant farmer on the land of others to eke out a marginal existence—life in a frame house without running water and indoor plumbing. She made good grades at the Salt Lick Elementary School in Bath County but she dropped out of the Bath County High School after 6 weeks. Her older brothers and sisters had moved on. She was needed to work on the farm. And she was not happy in high school. She was shy and poor and her clothes were not as stylish as the garb of the other students.

Pamela was 14 when she left school. She worked on the farm and finally got a work permit and a job in a company that made T-shirts. She shared a room in town with another girl and had her first date, with Gary Donaldson. He was the first boy friend she took to meet her parents. Five months after they met she was married to him.

Her husband had her quit her job. He worked in a typewriter factory and had a 2-year degree from a business college. He believed that a wife's place was in the home. Like it was when he was young. Their first child died in birth. The second child, a boy, is now 7 years old. While this boy was in kindergarten and the family was living in Camargo, outside of Mount Sterling, Pamela became acquainted with a neighbor, Marjory Pelfrey. She was a paraprofessional in an adult learning center at Jeffersonville and she told Pamela about the GED program and suggested she try it. Pamela took a test and enrolled in the adult learning center to acquire the knowledge to pass her GED. She studied while her boy was at school and she worked at home. She started in October and by the next March she was able to pass the GED test.

She learned of an opening in the paraprofessional program and went to see Don Patrick, the community education director for the Montgomery County schools. Patrick, an energetic chap who seems to know everyone in the community and to have a finger in almost everything that is going on, supervises, among a myriad of duties, the adult basic education program in the county. He arranged for the shy, young GED graduate to take a special training course at nearby Morehead State College and she went to work teaching candidates for the GED certificate in one of the adult learning centers. She also continued her own training. Patrick believes that the people who have gone the dropout GED route are effective in teaching and motivating adults with similar learning problems. It seems to work.

Gary Donaldson had been supportive of his wife's effort to get her GED certificate. But her new career was a different matter. Things had not been going well for him on his job. He believed that his wife should have the food on the table whenever he got home and this was not always the case when his wife began teaching and studying.

Not long before a reporter went to Mount Sterling to look at the adult basic education program, the domestic problems of Pamela Donaldson came to a head. There was a violent family argument. Pamela called the police. Her husband had a gun and he resisted the police. They filed charges against Gary Donaldson.

The court gave him a 2-year sentence. Pamela went to see the judge.

She said that her husband had mental problems as well as a drinking problem and she urged that he be given a chance to respond to treatment. He is now undergoing therapy provided by the company where he works and he is on probation which requires him to undergo this therapy. The couple is divorced. Gary Donaldson is living with his parents (although they supported Pamela when the family troubles came to a head) and Pamela lives with the child in their house. Her paraprofessional wages barely enable her to keep going and Don Patrick is attempting to find a stipend program that will enable her to obtain the additional education she wants and support her child.

In a matter-of-fact way Pamela tells this story and remarks, "I am sure that I would have submitted to wife beating and child beating and tried to hide it if I had not enrolled in the adult learning center. I found confidence in myself after I passed my GED test and was able to hold a job teaching others."

When you read that statement it may come through as a stilted "testimonial," not so when you are talking with Pamela. She knows there's rough going ahead but she's convinced she can manage, thanks to that casual suggestion by Marjory Pelfrey.

From the Hiring Hall to the State Legislature

When educators with their Ed.D's and Ph.D's come before the House Education Committee of the Washington State Legislature to testify on pending bills, the hearing is presided over by someone with a different "D"—a GED certificate. The chairman of the committee is a GED graduate named Arthur L. Clemente, a man whose full-time occupation these days is public service, a man who is a successful [intermediary between] the blue-collar world and the white-collar world.

Art (nobody calls him Arthur) Clemente does not have a college degree nor is he planning to seek one, but his success in life is connected with his off-again, on-again participation in adult education. For those who measure education by a collection of certificates, Art Clemente might not be regarded as an educated man. For those who measure learning by doing, Art Clemente would probably be regarded as a man who has been well educated by a combination of real life and classroom learning.

Clemente's legislative service is a part-time job. His full-time occupation is labor staff representative for the Washington State Council on Alcoholism's Labor-Management Task Force. In this job he deals with the white-collar management of corporations and with their blue-collar workers, using the experience he has had in both worlds. He is also using the skills he has obtained in college classrooms since he obtained his GED certificate back in the forties, and information from extensive planned reading.

Clemente was born in 1925 in Hoquiam, in Grays Harbor County. His family had an egg farm and the men worked in the woods. His father became a moulder in a foundry and the family lived in Seattle during the depression years of the thirties.

In 1942 Clemente dropped out of the West Seattle High School in his second year. Clemente didn't have a particularly good time in high school. Part of the district was the "Ocean View" section where homes faced Puget Sound. The other side of the hill was called "The Gulch." That is where you would find the children of Italian immigrant laborers. West Seattle High School was a more pleasant place if you came from the "Ocean View" side, where the parents had educations and white-collar jobs. After he quit high school, Clemente had laboring jobs in a foundry and on wartime construction projects. In 1943 he joined the Marines and served in the Pacific. When he left the Marines in 1946 he worked in Portland, Oregon, as a construction laborer. He had been briefed in the Marine Corps on the GED program and took preparatory training and his GED test at Reed College in Portland. He obtained his GED certificate the same year he left the Marines.

Clemente's counselor at Reed recommended that he go to college under the GI bill, but Clemente broke his legs in an auto accident and ran up substantial medical bills. He decided to skip college and go to work to pay the bills.

He worked in the construction trades along the west coast and in Alaska. In 1954 he became a journeyman in the Cement Finishers Union. On his return from Alaska in 1966, he decided to run for union office. He was elected treasurer of his local. He was part of a movement by younger members who wanted to open up the union to a bigger apprenticeship program and to take control from what these younger members regarded as conservative leadership with narrow interests. Under the new regime blacks were admitted as apprentices.

Clemente turned to adult education courses for the skills he needed to become an effective union official, taking courses in communications, bookkeeping, public speaking. He was not seeking a piece of paper to show that he had skills, only the skills he needed to do his job.

Eventually he was elected president of his local and became a delegate to the Building Trades Council and to the Labor Council.

He became interested in politics and government as a result of this experience and in 1970 he ran for the State legislature from a district near Everett in Snohomish County north of Seattle. He lost and ran again in 1972. This time he won. The job took up a good deal of time and he did not run for reelection to his union office. The legislative job pays only $3,200 a year plus a $40 per diem when the legislature or a member's committee is in session. So Clemente returned to working out of the hiring hall on construction jobs. Then he obtained a Snohomish County job as a construction inspector.

Meantime the Central Trades Council was building up its community services department and it obtained a grant for a program to combat alcoholism. Clemente was picked to head the program. He dealt with management and with workers and had a staff of counselors. And he studied to learn more about the problem, attending seminars and reading the literature of alcohol problems and treatment. His success in this position led to his present one where his responsibilities are heavy and the reading he does to keep up with developments in the field occupies much of his spare time. So Clemente is not planning to run for reelection to the legislature.

In the legislature he feels that his chief accomplishment was legislation which puts on the State the burden for funding public education in the basics and leaves it to the local school districts to fund enrichment activities.

Today Art Clemente is contributing to society in his full-time job and in his part-time job. The public learning opportunity that has been available to him in his adult years has not resulted in any one spectacular achievement nor in any single dramatic event. But it has helped to shape his life. Without adult education, Art Clemente might be pouring cement or sweating in a foundry instead of shaping legislation and combating a serious social problem. Public learning opportunity was available for Art Clemente when he wanted it. He used it. It worked.

From the Bayous to Baton Rouge

The odds that Marie Audrey Breaux would ever complete high school were prohibitive when she was a little girl walking barefoot from a marginal farm in the soggy bog land of the Louisiana bayou country. When she married at the age of 14 and began to bear children those odds became astronomical. This story is written about Marie Audrey Breaux because she beat the odds. Today she is a college graduate and a supervisor in the Adult Education Division of the Louisiana Department of Education.

Marie was one of three daughters of a black "crop equity" farmer who lived on land outside Jennings in Jefferson Davis Parish. Life there was so hard during the depression of the thirties that a day's food for the family sometimes consisted of rice handpicked from corners of the field where the harvesting machine had missed a few plants. As white and black families alike found the going too tough to stay on the land, the one-room school for blacks was closed. Marie went long distances and sometimes boarded with relatives to get some more grade school education, but she was "out of school for good" when she married Joseph W. Meno in 1946. She was 14. He was 23, an Army veteran who had dropped out of school. He learned some carpentry and radio repair under the GI bill and worked at just about anything he could find.

But despite their poverty, the Menos took over the raising of three children in addition to their own six. The way that happened was that Mr. Meno's brother's wife died and he left the children in their care while he went west looking for work.

In those days the State's allocation of funds for adult education was around $500 a parish but the Jefferson Davis Parish did have a modest adult education program. It accomplished a good deal more than might have been expected because of a white man named Gordy Shirley who was assistant school superintendent of the Jefferson Davis Parish. He tried to get both blacks and whites to come back to school.

It wasn't easy because it was the custom in many families for the children to go no further than the eighth grade even though the family might be well enough off to have put their children through college.

Maybe Gordy Shirley believed in education because he had a hard time getting his own. He was one of a large family of boys whose family had a farm north of Jennings in Beauregard Parish. Everybody in the Shirley family worked to get the oldest boy through college and when a boy graduated he was expected to send help for a younger brother. Gordy was near the bottom of the list and times were hard, but he made it and went into teaching.

One of the reasons Marie went back to school was because she couldn't read enough to shop, or understand simple instructions when her children required medicine. The ability her husband had to perform simple computations seemed far beyond her reach.

Today Marie Meno is confident and self-assured. It is the confidence that comes from years of overcoming obstacles that looked insurmountable when she first faced them.

She didn't believe she could learn when she went back to school through adult education. The first time she took her GED she failed. But she continued to study and she passed. And she was able to get her husband back to school.

But there were rewards. The GED diploma got Marie into McNeese. The GED diploma got Joe a steady job with Gulf Utilities. He learned on the job and was promoted. He now has a good job with Gulf in Baton Rouge. The combined earnings of husband and wife have enabled them to get most of their children through college and to buy a comfortable home in Baton Rouge. At Jennings, Marie drove her visitor in a new air-conditioned car to see the gravel road on which she used to walk to school.

But this is getting ahead of our story. After Marie completed her struggle and graduated from McNeese, Gordy Shirley helped Marie to get a job teaching adults in Jennings. She was pregnant when she graduated from McNeese in 1962. She still put in hours raising her children when she worked at her full-time teaching job. When the Federal Government started putting funds into adult education the program expanded in Jennings. Eventually Marie became supervisor of the integrated adult education program for the parish. The Federal funds for adult basic education meant a lot in all of Louisiana.

A word is in order here about Joseph Meno. The bayou country of the fifties is an unlikely spot to find a husband who would work at two jobs and borrow money to provide his wife with more education than he had. Joseph Meno is something special. He passed his GED and the two of them received their adult high school diplomas at the same time. It was a cap-and-gown ceremony. They are proud of the picture of them at graduation that is in their scrap book, along with photos of the frame house they lived in and improved during the years they lived in Jennings and nearby Welsh.

It took Marie 3½ years to get her GED. Then she went to a special program at McNeese State College in Lake Charles. When she finished that she decided to take the 4-year course. Gordy Shirley encouraged her. Her husband worked day and night to help her make it. She would get up and fix breakfast for the children and drive to Lake Charles in a rickety car, take her classes, come home, work in the house, do homework, fall asleep over her books, doze a while, and get up and repeat the process. Her husband was borrowing money at 25 cents interest on the dollar during part of this period.

Then the family ran out of money to keep Marie in college. Gordy Shirley helped her get a Federal NDEA loan of $250. That $250 was the margin of success for Marie.

This account has not given the flavor of the drudgery and weariness that husband and wife went through during these years. A visitor who goes around the parish with Mrs. Meno can see why she loves it and why now, even though the family home is in Baton Rouge, the Menos retain their house at Jennings and return to it on vacation. A visitor can sense the charm of the country, but even though he grew up in a different small town with different crops grown on the land around it, he can also sense how harsh life was for the Menos during those years.

When Marie took a visitor to their comfortable home in Baton Rouge, Joe had a pot of gumbo on the stove. He likes to cook, and it's a good thing, because he did a lot of cooking while Marie was battling her way in education. He's a good cook, by the way. The two of them recounted their days in Jennings in a matter-of-fact way that made it all sound easy. When the visitor questioned the borrowing of money at 25 cents on the dollar, Joe said, "When you need to buy money for something worthwhile, it's better to borrow the money and do what you need to do than to fail to get what you need."

In 1969 when the Louisiana director of adult education asked Marie to come to Baton Rouge and become a supervisor, Joe got a transfer from Gulf Utilities and the family made the move.

The Menos are comfortable and secure now. She is taking graduate work. Their youngest child is in junior high school. Their oldest daughter is teaching.

The three adopted children are back with their father in California. All the Meno children are doing well in school or in their jobs.

The Menos don't really see why anybody wants to make a big deal of what they did by writing about it. They talk about the long struggle without a touch of self-pity. They don't want to claim they have done anything special. But they make sure that Gordy Shirley is in the story. They want everyone to know that he is a very fine man.

Body Wrecked—Life Saved

The paralyzed black man with the afro and big plastic glasses tells a reporter he's going to finish college and become a sportscaster. His name is William Haskins.

Fran Cohen believes he can do it because she is a therapist who believes that handicapped persons can become what they have the will to become.

The two of them share this belief because Del Doss, who runs the adult education operation of the St. Louis public schools, believes that adult education should come to the pupil when the pupil cannot come to the classroom.

Bill Haskins is a high school dropout who was paralyzed in an automobile accident. He lives at the Harry S. Truman Restorative Center in South St. Louis. It's a place that Harry Truman, a spunky man who overcame a few handicaps himself, would be proud to have his name on. It's an institutional building containing everything possible to depress a visitor. But a reporter leaves it refreshed, convinced that people are better than he thought them to be when he entered.

It is the place where the reporter met the Rev. P. D. Parker, a one-legged black man who has a sunny smile and a voice that makes ordinary conversation sound like a hymn.

It is a place where the reporter saw Robert Bechtold driving a Rube Goldberg battery-powered wheelchair stuck together by volunteers after 6 years of work under the prodding of Fran Cohen. Bechtold is 47 years old. He never drove until a couple of months ago when the wheelchair was completed. Bechtold operates the wheelchair with the lone finger that is strong enough to push a lever. He is happy when he drives the wheelchair (the course is a little erratic) and this makes everybody happy—patients, staff, and a visiting reporter.

Bill Haskins edits the patients' newspaper. It's lively. The headlines on a story about Bechtold reads, "Look Who Is Driving," and ends, "gangway everybody. Bob's driving!!!"

Bob Bechtold is an adult education student learning to read. Bill Haskins got his GED after studying with teachers sent to the center by Del Doss. Del sent them there because Fran Cohen, a professional therapist who came to the center several years ago as an unpaid volunteer after her children became old enough to fend for themselves, went to the city school system and suggested the need for adult education services at the center.

"P. D.," as the reverend is known to one and all, studied to pass his GED while he was learning to use a wooden leg. He is a steelworker by trade and his theological credentials seem to run more to experience in storefront church preaching than courses in a cloistered seminary. The public rehabilitation center has no funds for a chaplain, so the Lutheran Church provides this service. After P. D. passed his GED test and took a two year course in communications at Forest Park Community College, the Lutheran Synod hired him as a chaplain at the center. It was a good move. P. D. is a mellow man, both in the street definition and in the dictionary definition, and his ability to read the Scriptures and sing hymns is coupled with a strong empathy with the halt and blind.

Del Doss and Fran Cohen are proud of the patients they serve at the Truman Center and they are particularly proud of Bill Haskins. He was a tough case. His good mind had withdrawn from life almost to the point of no return when he came to the center.

Haskins was born in 1952. His mother was a school teacher. She and Haskins' father, who owned a liquor store, were divorced when he was a baby and he was raised by his mother and grandmother. They owned a four-family flat in a working-class neighborhood mostly occupied by blacks. He went to public elementary school and then transferred to a Lutheran church school. Next he went to a public high school and dropped out after 1 year. He hung around a YMCA and school playgrounds, playing ball and "being cool." He was a tall, strong youth who liked athletics and was bored in the classroom. He was sent to a probationary high school for problem youths and things didn't work out there. He was back on the streets.

On May 12, 1970, he played some schoolyard basketball. Then he got into a Mercury with some friends and they were going down the street when a Road Runner laid down some rubber alongside them and the drag race started. The Mercury didn't make it around a station wagon that pulled out suddenly in its path. Haskins had a broken neck. He was paralyzed.

Pain and self-pity followed for 7 years until, as Haskins tells it, he looked up at the ceiling on his 25th birthday and said, "Billy, get off your butt."

After the accident Haskins was in traction for a long time. He could move his arms and neck but he could not use his fingers. Neither his body nor his mind responded to therapy in various hospitals and rehabilitation centers. He went home. His mother died when he was 20 years old. Eight months later his grandmother died. He was unable to manage the four-family flat his mother owned. He lived in various nursing homes. His father tried to help, but the two did not get along well. His father and stepmother see him but there is still some friction. Two of his brothers and sisters are in college. But Haskins had become something of a loner. He says he had "just given up and just lay there."

When he went to the Truman Center he came into the life of Fran Cohen and vice versa. She is energetic and effective. It is probable that some in the bureaucracies involved in the rehabilitation of the handicapped that do not share her zeal may find her pushy and abrasive. No one doubts that she believes in the power of positive thinking.

She got the shop at the center to make a contraption that fastened sticks with rubber ends to Haskins' wrists so that he could turn the pages of books. She got Haskins to start studying in adult basic education and work toward his GED with the help of the teachers Del Doss was providing.

It was slow going. It was hard work. There was a young medical student from Washington University there, working as a volunteer. He tutored Haskins in mathematics. Haskins got sympathy and help from all of these people and a little pushing when he became discouraged or mired down in self-pity. Haskins started out flat on his back. He was—or felt he was—unable to sit up. But as he studied, his body changed. He took his GED sitting up in bed. Then he waited.

One day his stepmother came to visit. She brought along an envelope and asked Haskins if he had any idea what was in it. After some speculation they opened it and to the surprise of Haskins (but not of his stepmother and some of those who helped him with his studies and just happened to be around) the envelope contained his GED certificate.

Knowledge is power—certified knowledge, that is. Upon getting that GED certificate, Haskins asked for a wheelchair for the first time. He was pretty proud when he showed Fran Cohen that GED certificate. Fran Cohen is not the kind to let anyone, even someone who is paralyzed, rest on his academic laurels. In short order, she had an assistant dean from the Forest Park Community College talking with Haskins.

The college sent John Sabin, an instructor in broadcasting, to give Haskins instruction. The course lasted for 15 weeks and at the end Sabin wrote to the area vocational rehabilitation director recommending help for further instruction. As a result Haskins is scheduled to attend classes on campus at the Forest Park Community College.

Adult education has been a pretty good partner with the rehabilitation folks at the Truman Center. It has given Bob Bechtold the ability to move his mind to new places along with the ability to move his body with his custom-made wheelchair. It has given P. D. Parker the skills to give cheer and hope to the disabled and provided him with a rewarding new career. Adult education has given Bill Haskins a strong start toward assuming control of his destiny.

Education in the Shoe Shop The success stories presented in the foregoing selection stressed the achievements of individuals who had benefited from the offerings of adult education institutions and programs. But to give a complete picture, there is another mode of life-long learning that should be portrayed: the informal and collective learning that occurs in any healthy community. It needs to be stressed because it is usually invisible, rarely recognized, and almost never documented and celebrated.

Moreover, this approach underlies some of the most exciting experiments in adult education, such as the Highlander Research and Education Center in Tennessee. The best short portrayal of this kind of learning as part of community life is the following essay by Frank Adams.

Adams was awakened to this phenomenon at Highlander. He subsequently wrote the history of the center in *Unearthing Seeds of Fire.* The importance of such learning was well put by the editors of the *Harvard Educational Review* when they printed excerpts from Adams's book: "If our judgments about educational change were based on conventional histories, our vision of alternative futures would be constrained. We would probably come to the conclusion that a small number of school professionals and prominent social reformers have alone been responsible for initiating and maintaining worthwhile reforms. . . . Yet there are other histories. There is a history of 'common-folk' struggling to become, and becoming, their own leaders."

This account of education in the shoe shop gives us a glimpse of that process.

This selection, reprinted from the magazine *The Radical Teacher*, was written in 1977 under the title "Learning and Change in the Shoe Shop."

Education in the
Shoe Shop

Frank Adams

If you agree that the community is but one of many teachers, as the ancient Greeks believed, then the idea of teaching in a cobbler's shop may not sound preposterous. The job I do is fix shoes and make leather sandals while, at the same time, attempting deliberately to use the community I live in as an educative force for social change.

The shoe repair shop, called the Awl-Soles Shoe Repair & Leatherworks on the few bits of paper necessary to keep a very small business going, is in the county seat of a rural, quite poor, political subdivision of northeastern North Carolina. So-called progress has been fended off in Gates County and Gatesville, its county seat. There are no fast-food hamburger drive-ins, no air-conditioned malls, no superhighways. Traffic gets heavy—compared to what we are used to—for a few minutes around nine a.m. and five p.m. Local wits call it the rush minute.

The shop is across the street from the post office, and next door to the weekly newspaper office. People come and go all day, stopping usually to exchange greetings or gossip. Just around the corner on Main Street is the county's largest grocery store. There you can buy excellent sharp cheddar cheese, chain saws, New York or California wines, hog jowls, wire screening, seeds and fertilizers, nuts or bolts. The school administration offices, headquarters for the county's largest employer, the county library and courthouse, and welfare offices are in sight of the shoe shop half a block away.

Here, as in most rural places in the South, the tradition of sitting around talking in a store endures. In the past, these gatherings were the places we could learn without appearing ignorant. Valuable information could be learned about farming or logging, or road conditions if the weather was bad, who was doing what in politics, and what happened in the last session of court. We could find out what was happening in the world beyond from the drummers who stopped in, too, peddling this or that. To insure that nobody got the idea we were there for less than serious trading, someone usually provided a checker board. Having grown up in a similarly rural community thirty miles away, I knew the importance of country stores in our culture as learning centers.

But I also knew that much of the talk in these places was racist, or sexist, baseless tittle-tattle, often mean-spirited and usually politically reactionary. Only when I saw how Jake and Edith Easterling of Poorbottom Hollow, Kentucky, and Joe Begley of Blackey, Kentucky, nearby, used the community stores they ran did I realize the potential of such places for social change.

For years, the Easterlings and Begley have been in the thick of efforts to end poverty, to stop strip-mining, to insure that their neighbors were not trampled on by government and the rich. They and their Appalachian neighbors have not always won the fights they got into, but they seldom got pushed around because they didn't know who was pushing, or because they misjudged their opposition, or because they acted as individuals, not collectively.

I was on the staff of Highlander Research and Education Center in New Market, Tennessee, when I came to know the Easterlings and Joe Begley, and how they used their stores. What they were doing naturally in their native communities, I felt could be duplicated as an experiment in education at the grass-roots level. So, when my work at Highlander was finished, I learned the cobbler's trade, collected the necessary equipment second-hand, and opened the shoe shop/education center trying to answer these questions:

Can greater social use be made of what might be described as accidental learning? Could talk in a country store become one means of focussing knowledge about civic affairs so that racist, sexist and exploitative power relationships were altered? Would it be possible to provide low-cost, independently financed informal or community education in the South without depending on grants or fund-raising? Could small, community-based education centers become enclaves for a social movement?

Before attempting to answer these questions, some sense of what happens in the shoe shop during the day, and of the shop itself, should be briefly shared. Besides all the necessary equipment to repair shoes and for making sandals, there is a small table (with a checker board, of course), three chairs, a rocker, and a couple of stools. While the shop is small, it has a sense of space because of two huge windows which run from the ceiling almost to the floor and look out on Court Street's daily activity. Bright yellow and orange paint on the machinery and furniture liven the atmosphere. A few plants soften the shop's interior lines. A bulletin board holds a spate of meeting notices and news items, plus a bumper sticker or two proclaiming, "Legalize Freedom."

The curriculum does not grow from a fixed notion of what should be taught, nor from a textbook or ideology, but rather from the life of our county, its households, its schools, its religious ceremonies, its festivals, and its public affairs. While I'd like to fancy myself an unbiased teacher operating in the traditions of a university professor orating on all sides of an issue, I am not. Civic affairs, in general, and poverty, powerlessness, sexism and racism, in particular, are issues which affront me, and which most directly impair life in Gates County and in the world. So these issues are discussed frequently in the shop, and I hasten to add, often with greater care for gathering the facts, for examining the human factors involved, and for exploring the alternative courses of action than has been my experience in a college classroom. To do otherwise, could be hazardous to your health.

After all, the explicit aim of discussions in the shop is to put what we learn together about our common problems into collective use; to act on what we know to be unjust or unlawful in Gates County.

There is no daily agenda. Who comes in, and what is on their minds, and what they will talk about, is what is talked about. In this sense, the learning is accidental. Sometimes, I continue fixing shoes while talking with the one or several persons present. At other times, I stop and join them around the checker table. Frequently, I provoke conversation. "Have you heard . . ." or, "What do you think about . . ." As often, I contribute nothing when several people are discussing an issue they have begun talking over. In this sense, too, learning is accidental. But we are all peers; learning takes place horizontally rather than vertically as is the circumstance in a traditional classroom.

There are, of course, patterns of continuity. Very few civic problems have easy solutions. The process by which individuals arrive at the point where they feel confident enough of themselves to act publicly on a civic problem differs from individual to individual and is painfully slow, although usually evident. People, however, do get issues on their minds and come back repeatedly to talk again about still another aspect of what's troubling them. Some community issues loom so large that many people want to talk, and these on and off conversations may last over a period of several weeks, or even a month or two. There is no formula for when or how to ask the essential question, "What can we do about it?" Sometimes it is obviously too soon to ask; other times the opportunity is lost in a fleeting second. Nevertheless, the question must be raised. Action must result. Collectively.

Some "customers" come by regularly; others only when they have some shoes to be fixed. Still others come when they feel the pinch of a social problem they have heard discussed in the shop. They are young and old, black and white, men and women. We have talked about the particulars of taxes, politics and candidates, prisons, Alex Haley's *Roots,* peanut acreage allotments, revenue sharing, the school system's short-comings and strengths, the preservation of a beautiful millpond as a state park, the shortage of doctors. We have mourned the death of a good neighbor, and celebrated some good times. We have told a few jokes, usually on ourselves. But as we talk, as a teacher, I always keep in mind to ask how we can empower ourselves to meet our self-defined problems collectively.

What has happened in Gates County as a result?

An unqualified response would be unjustified; the shoe shop has been open only two years. Insufficient time has elapsed to warrant any final judgments. I learned at Highlander that ten to fifteen years are required to "unearth the seeds of fire." Too, it would be impossible as well as improvident to suggest that some events would not have taken place were it not for the shoe shop. However, for those in the country who work hard to maintain the status quo, and who hold power, the shoe shop is given credit for virtually anything which results in social change. The shop is a thorn in their sides. But their talk about it brings in new "customers." And while their charges about its effectiveness are exaggerated, the shoe shop affirms what the ancient Greeks believed, and what Paul Goodman used to say frequently about learning, "The job we do, the environment we live in, and the social culture of our communities educates us."

For example, on the most rudimentary level, blacks and whites, men and women, young and old have found the shoe shop a place where they can talk as equals. About 56 percent of the county's population is black. Old segregationist traditions continue. In this part of North Carolina, blacks are to be seen and not heard, are to work, not think. So to see a black man or woman introduced to a white person, then to watch them shake hands, then talk as equals, is to see Jim Crow wither. For a woman to be taken seriously in the discussion of civic issues is to dismantle another rural South taboo. For the young to have a place where they can talk to adults about drugs and sex without fear provides an example of what could be rather than the continued constraint of what is. These "little" events happen regularly in the shoe shop.

The alteration of individual consciousness is not the only result. Organizations have sprung to life from talk in the shoe shop. As so often happens when people talk together who have been kept apart by design, tradition or fear, they find each has pretty much the same problem, and, frequently, that problem derives from the same source. Once this commonality can be discovered by each person, and experienced if not savored, then it is not difficult to encourage them to release their own individual potential and energy, and not merely seek relief from their problem. Getting organized with others seems a natural way to solve civic problems. The teacher's task at this point is to search through repeated questions, or the piling on of uncontested fact, until one spark will evoke the first action. This takes time and patience.

For example, within days after the shoe shop opened in September, 1975, one of the county's two overworked doctors shut down his practice to join the Coast Guard. He moved away. The community was shocked. He was a life-long resident. For more than two months after his departure, medical care became the chief topic of conversation. Slowly, by persistently asking the question "What can we do to start a community-controlled medical clinic?" at what seemed appropriate moments in the conversation, an informal group started meeting in the shoe shop once or twice a week without call or formal resolve. A young lawyer assumed a leadership role in the discussions. Blacks were assumed to be included both in the discussions and in the resulting organization. They needed medical care, and had taken part in the talks from the outset. The aid of the county's part-time public health director was enlisted. A countywide fish fry was held to raise money to buy five acres of land for a clinic site. The search was begun for two doctors, a dentist, a physicians' assistant, and others who would work in the clinic. Plans were drawn for a $350,000 primary care facility for two doctors, and a dentist. Emergency room care would be provided at a nearby hospital. State-level support was secured, and a grant of $52,800 was given by a private foundation. The clinic is expected to open within a year. Rich and poor, black and white, professional and blue collar, men and women sit on the controlling board.

A second organization also grew out of the shoe shop talks. One mother after another would come into the shop hauling an armload of shoes with a child or two in tow. Taking advantage of what I saw—mothers burdened with shoes and children—I started asking what each mother thought about day care centers, and why they thought there were no centers in the county. By accident one day, two young women, one black and one white, arrived in the shop simultaneously. After getting to know each other's names, I raised the questions with them. They started telling each other how a center would help, and how when they were children there always seemed to be a grandmother or aunt around to help tend children. It was a good talk between strangers. And I knew it could continue—they would come back for their shoes.

When the young black mother returned, she had obviously been thinking about our talk, and asked, "Do you suppose a day care center could be started here?" From that question grew a countywide organization calling itself Alternatives for Children in Gates County, Inc. Its members include men and women in equal proportion, not by design or mandate but by interest. They have devised their own goals, written their own by-laws, filed their own forms for state and federal tax exemption, held enough fund-raising events to buy a small building, and wrote their own Title XX contract for the local department of social services. Despite many setbacks—the most common being the refusal of owners to rent vacant houses to them because the center would be integrated—the first center for ten children will open in June, 1977. Three teachers, a director, and volunteers—all from Gates County—will be employed. A second center for 14 children is being planned. A grant of $56,000 was secured to train staff, bring the buildings up to federal certification standards, and to buy equipment. State officials in charge of day care services say the drive in Gates County to establish day care is the only one of its kind in the state. It is being done completely by the citizens.

Both organizations used the shoe shop as a meeting place, as a place where messages could be left and delivered. The day care organization used it for bake sales. Larger meetings were held in various public buildings. In each, I took an active part in the development process but held no office and was only an informal part of the decision-making and discussion process.

Even a quasi-governmental organization emerged from the shoe shop. A few months back a local Baptist minister and a young black who works in a shipyard across the state line in Virginia got to talking one Saturday about the gulf between the races in Gates County. A few weeks later, again in the shop for a shoe-shine, they picked up their conversation, with the minister adding this time his idea that the county needed a human relations commission. They asked if I knew anyone with the North Carolina Human Relations Commission in Raleigh who could help them get one started. I agreed to find out, and, if possible, to arrange a meeting. In the months following, quiet meetings were held in homes around the county, each meeting attended by more persons than the previous one. Plans were laid for an organization. By-laws were drawn up. A public meeting was planned with the state director to attend. This was followed by the selection of a delegation to attend the county commissioners' meeting to formally request that they establish such a group.

There were a few tense moments. A young woman who worked with the agricultural extension service was threatened with being fired by her white boss. The Ku Klux Klan temporarily revived in the county. Both developments only underscored the minister's points when he and the other citizen-elected delegates appeared before the commissioners. The idea was approved. A fifteen-member commission was formed and started work bridging the color line.

These events have not shaken the world. No dramatic headlines have been written about them. And, unless I were to describe in greater detail the nature of the political fabric in Gates County, one could say that no significant alteration in power relationships resulted.

Five years ago, when my wife and two children moved to the county, there were no means by which blacks and whites could come to know one another save in the traditional dominant-subordinate roles, the old boss-servant shuffle. Today, as a direct result of educational experiences in the shoe shop, there are three such organizations. Indirectly, two others have come into being. One is an arts council; the other is an investment club formed among the local school administrators. Through all of these, the long suppressed wisdom and talent of people of both races and sexes are merging. New leaders have emerged.

People slowly have come to believe they can participate in public meetings. Again, five years ago no citizen attended meetings of the board of education. Today, upwards of twenty are frequently there. The schools are no longer run as a private club.

Blacks have gained a new self-image and esteem. Five years ago there was no black elected or appointed official in county government. Today, two blacks sit on the school board, one each sits on the county planning board, on the Alcoholic Beverage Control Board, and on the department of social services board. Of thirty-six members on the county board of elections, eighteen are black. Blacks are equally represented on the local Democratic Party committee with whites. There has been some shift in the balance of power.

Still another factor has to be considered. Each of the organizations which grew from the shoe shop talks has created jobs, often for people with little or no formal education. In a county with an unemployment rate standing regularly at seven percent, where 43 percent of the homes have no running water or electricity, and where each year is recorded the highest infant mortality rate in North Carolina, jobs are important. Moreover, these jobs have community esteem.

All is not roses, however. The shoe shop does not produce enough income to support my family. The economics of the cobbler's trade and the size of our community work against such hopes. It pays its own way and supplements my wife's income as a school teacher. On the other hand, I waste no time writing grant proposals to foundations, guarding what I judge needs to be said educationally for fear of losing tax-exempt status, or mailing pleas for donations.

Further, as an advocate of adult residential education, the shop has limitations. People can carry on extended conversations in it, but the format prevents implementing the powerfully educative opportunities which result when people live together for short periods of time, break bread over the table, or make music together. To counter this shortcoming, when discussions on issues seemed to warrant, I have arranged to use a regional meeting place for larger, overnight or weekend workshops.

But essentially, the shoe shop as an education center must be seen as the point of a spear, a place where previously half congealed thoughts can be said out loud, and where a response can be gotten, so that action results. The shop functions on three essential levels within the context of adult education: first, it permits a multi-level response to a whole range of issues; second, it provides linkages or a means of referral between groups and issues in our community and groups and issues in other communities nearby and in the region; and, third, through conversation with such a diverse group as the customers during the course of a day connections can be and are made between seemingly disparate issues and problems.

Yet to be seen is whether the idea can be duplicated. No experiment in education is worth its salt if it can't be done by others elsewhere. The Danish Folk Schools succeeded not because Kristen Kold managed to implement the ideas of Bishop Grundtvig, but because the school he started could become a reality elsewhere until, after numbers of them had opened, a powerfully revitalizing social movement formed. Then social change resulted.

Notes

1. For a history of Highlander Research and Education Center, New Market, Tennessee, see Frank Adams, *Unearthing Seeds of Fire: The Idea of Highlander.* Winston-Salem, N.C.: John F. Blair, Publisher, 1975. And Aimee Horton, "The Highlander Folk School: A History of the Development of Major Programs Related to Social Movements in the South, 1952–1961." Unpublished dissertation, University of Chicago, 1971.

2. For a well-done bibliography on the folk school movement, see Rolland G. Paulston, *Folk Schools in Social Movements: A Partisan Guide to the International Literature.* Pittsburgh: University Center for International Studies, University of Pittsburgh, 1974.

Now I Am Only Interested in Learning   The founding father of humanistic psychology came to the conviction, some years ago, that he was no longer interested in trying to *teach* other people. For himself, as well as for his students, *learning* rather than *teaching* must now be at the center of the process of education.

Many practicing teachers have had the same intuition, but few have had the courage to stand up and say so publicly—either because they were afraid to assert such a heretical notion or because it would seem like a betrayal of their profession.

For adult educators the message in Rogers's credo is in the courage as much as the concept. What Rogers says is true. But equally important is his faith in his own perception, his willingness to "own" his feelings. The challenge for us is not merely to hear and understand his message but also to ask ourselves, What do *we* perceive and feel about adult learning that we should be brave enough to express and act on with comparable courage?

This selection is excerpted from the chapter "Personal Thoughts on Teaching and Learning" from the book *Freedom to Learn*. It was originally part of a paper entitled, "Classroom Approaches to Influencing Behavior," presented at a Harvard Conference in 1957.

Now I Am Only Interested in Learning

Carl Rogers

I will try to digest some of the meanings which have come to me from my classroom experience and the experience I have had in individual therapy and group experience. They are in no way intended as conclusions for someone else, or a guide to what others should do or be. They are the very tentative meanings, as of April 1952, which my experience has had for me, and some of the bothersome questions which their absurdity raises. I will put each idea or meaning in a separate lettered paragraph, not because they are in any particular logical order, but because each meaning is separately important to me.

a. . . . *My experience has been that I cannot teach another person how to teach.* To attempt it is for me, in the long run, futile.

b. *It seems to me that anything that can be taught to another is relatively inconsequential and has little or no significant influence on behavior.* That sounds so ridiculous I can't help but question it at the same time that I present it.

c. *I realize increasingly that I am only interested in learnings which significantly influence behavior.* Quite possibly this is simply a personal idiosyncrasy.

d. *I have come to feel that the only learning which significantly influences behavior is self-discovered, self-appropriated learning.*

e. *Such self-discovered learning, truth that has been personally appropriated and assimilated in experience, cannot be directly communicated to another.* As soon as an individual tries to communicate such experience directly, often with a quite natural enthusiasm, it becomes teaching, and its results are inconsequential. It was some relief recently to discover that Søren Kierkegaard, the Danish philosopher, had found this too, in his own experience, and stated it very clearly a century ago. It made it seem less absurd.

f. *As a consequence of the above, I realize that I have lost interest in being a teacher.*

223

g. When I try to teach, as I do sometimes, I am appalled by the results, which seem a little more than inconsequential, because sometimes the teaching appears to succeed. When this happens I find that the results are damaging. It seems to cause the individual to distrust his own experience, and to stifle significant learning. *Hence I have come to feel that the outcomes of teaching are either unimportant or hurtful.*

h. When I look back at the results of my past teaching, the real results seem the same—either damage was done—or nothing significant occurred. This is frankly troubling.

i. As a consequence, *I realize that I am only interested in being a learner, preferably learning things that matter, that have some significant influence on my own behavior.*

j. *I find it very rewarding to learn,* in groups, in relationships with one person as in therapy, or by myself.

k. *I find that one of the best, but most difficult, ways for me to learn is to drop my own defensiveness, at least temporarily, and to try to understand the way in which his experience seems and feels to the other person.*

l. *I find that another way of learning for me is to state my own uncertainties, to try to clarify my puzzlements, and thus get closer to the meaning that my experience actually seems to have.*

m. This whole train of experiencing, and the meanings that I have thus far discovered in it, seem to have launched me on a process which is both fascinating and at times a little frightening. *It seems to mean letting my experiences carry me on, in a direction which appears to be forward, toward goals that I can but dimly define, as I try to understand at least the current meaning of that experience.* The sensation is that of floating with a complex stream of experience, with the fascinating possibility of trying to comprehend its ever-changing complexity.

I am almost afraid I may seem to have gotten away from any discussion of learning, as well as teaching. Let me again introduce a practical note by saying that by themselves these interpretations of my experience may sound queer and aberrant, but not particularly shocking. It is when I realize the *implications* that I shudder a bit at the distance I have come from the commonsense world that everyone knows is right. I can best illustrate this by saying that if the experiences of others had been the same as mine, and if they had discovered similar meanings in it, many consequences would be implied:

a. Such experience would imply that we would do away with teaching. People would get together if they wished to learn.

b. We would do away with examinations. They measure only the inconsequential type of learning.

c. We would do away with grades and credits for the same reason.

d. We would do away with degrees as a measure of competence partly for the same reason. Another reason is that a degree marks an end or a conclusion of something, and a learner is only interested in the continuing process of learning.

e. We would do away with the exposition of conclusions, for we would realize that no one learns significantly from conclusions.

I think I had better stop there. I do not want to become too fantastic. I want to know primarily whether anything in my inward thinking, as I have tried to describe it, speaks to anything in your experience of the classroom as you have lived it, and if so, what the meanings are that exist for you in *your* experience.

The Shape of Adult Education in the Eighties   The adult educator must constantly monitor, analyze, and understand the fast-changing society in which he or she operates. In fact, the successful practitioner and planner must be *ahead* of the culture's changes to anticipate what adults will want and need to know. What kind of signs should we look for? How should we analyze them?

Here, one sharp observer identifies six such influences that will continue to shape the field in the 1980s. Jerold Apps, professor of adult education at the University of Wisconsin in Madison, shows how population structure, inflation, consumerism, the status of women, politics, and the mood of society toward education will have profound effects on adult education. His speculations range from the kinds of new students who may be showing up on college campuses to the seeds of a new "planetary consciousness."

Most of Professor Apps's prognostications are still valid despite the fact that his analysis was published in mid-1980, prior to the election of a new national administration that signaled a national shift in a new political direction. This continuing relevance suggests that the forces discerned here are indeed fundamental.

But even more important than the specific predictions is the author's penetrating way of thinking about our professional future. Each of us in the field of adult education is challenged to engage constantly in such serious reflection on our role in a changing society.

This selection was first published in *Lifelong Learning: The Adult Years* in June 1980.

The Shape of Adult Education in the Eighties

Jerold W. Apps

Many people in our society mark time by decades. They record events, even societal moods, by ten year blocks of time. These people write and talk about what happened in the ten years just passed. Many speculate about what is likely to happen, given certain sets of circumstances, in the coming decade and beyond. Not to be outdone by these future speculators, I would like to examine adult education from the perspective of six influences that are important now, and will likely continue to have an effect on adult education as we move farther into the 1980s. Many influences could be mentioned, but I have selected the following: (1) changing population structure, (2) inflation, (3) consumer movements, (4) status of women, (5) politics, and (6) mood of society toward education.

Changing Population Structure

The median age of the U.S. population is slowly creeping higher. In 1975 it was 28.8. For 1980 the predicted median age is 30.2, and for 1990, 32.8.

The number of people in the 24 and younger group is in decline, those in the 25–64 age group are increasing in numbers. For instance, in 1975, 93.9 million people were 24 and younger. By 1990 predictions indicate a drop to 89.9 million for this age group. In 1975, 97.3 million people were 25–64. Predictions for 1990 suggest 123.8 million in this age group. During this same 15 year period of time predictions suggest those 65 and over will increase from 22.4 million to 29.8 million.

Implications for Adult Education. The number of potential participants for adult education programs is obviously increasing. But with decline in the youth population many elementary, secondary, and even some colleges face the possibility of closing.

The effects of school closings relate to adult education in some interesting ways. The late 1940s and early '50s resulted in some heated debates about closing one room country schools and consolidating rural school districts. Though often angry, citizens were interested in discussing and making decisions about education during those years. They debated the purposes of schools, the future of education, the contributions of education to society, the financing of education, and much more.

Today, with discussion about closing community schools because of declining enrollment, a similar situation is developing. Citizens are becoming vitally interested in education and are asking questions similar to those asked by Midwestern farmers 30 years ago.

With millions of citizens once more talking about education, it would seem an excellent time to bring adult education into these discussions: what it is and how it can fit into the lives of people. A closed public school may be a community facility for adult education. Former elementary and secondary teachers, with additional training in adult education, may be potential teachers of adults. And maybe for the first time with large numbers of people we can begin discussing lifelong learning that truly spans birth to death. Perhaps we can begin to examine what the relationship of elementary and secondary education should be to adult education in its various forms.

Colleges and universities are likely to change rather dramatically in the 80s, particularly in terms of who attends them. Most will have fewer students, some may have to close. David W. Breneman, a Senior Fellow at the Brookings Institution, was recently quoted in the *Chronicle of Higher Education* as saying, it is "entirely possible that 200 to 300 small colleges may close their doors during the 1980's."

Projections by the Federal Government's National Center for Education Statistics indicate a total college and university enrollment of 11,048,000 in 1988 compared to the fall of 1979 enrollment of 11,500,000. Projections indicate that private institutions may decline by 7.4 percent from 1979–1988, and public institutions may decline by 3.1 percent during the same time.

The number of part-time students attending colleges and universities is increasing rapidly but not enough to offset predicted declines in numbers of traditional students. According to the National Center for Education Statistics, 32 percent of all two and four year college students enrolled in 1970 were part-time. By 1978 the percentage of part-time students had increased to 41 percent. If the trend continues, predictions indicate that by 1985 close to 50 percent of the enrollment in two and four year colleges will be part-time (approximately 65 percent for two-year campuses and 35 percent for four-year).

Nevertheless, the complexion of colleges and universities, whether four year or two year, is likely to change considerably during the 80s. We may well see the graying of the campuses. For example, at the University of Wisconsin–Madison, of 40,233 students enrolled for the 1979 fall semester, 11,982 were 25 and older (about 30 percent).

Is the field of adult education as we now know it ready for a rather dramatic increase in potential participants? Will these potential participants look more to traditional providers of adult education such as colleges, universities, and vocational schools, or will they look more to newer, nontraditional forms of adult education such as learning exchanges, community organizations and the like? What problems will colleges and universities face in attempting to adjust administrative arrangements, teaching-learning approaches, and an overall attitude given increasing numbers of students 25 and older?

Inflation

Our recent annual inflation rate is approaching 18 to 20 percent nationally. Much of that figure is due to increases in the costs of gasoline, heating fuels, and other petroleum products. Remember 1969 when gasoline was 35 cents a gallon, and the U.S. bought a barrel of oil from OPEC for $1.80? And we only imported about 22 percent of our crude oil. Compare those figures with 1979 when gasoline soared toward $1.50, and OPEC oil sold for about $30 a barrel with nearly 50 percent of our crude oil imported. In addition, food, clothing, utility, and housing costs are up.

Shortages of energy and increasing costs for nearly everything will force Americans to examine their lifestyles, their leisure time patterns, their travel to and from work. Many values we have come to accept during the past 25 years will be examined: planned obsolescence; convenience foods; throw away bottles and cans; if something breaks, toss it and buy a new one; live for today; "do my own thing"; and money will buy anything.

The country will need to examine how agriculture should be done, how business and industry will operate, how human life will be lived.

Implications for Adult Education. Many people with low incomes who might benefit from additional education leading to a higher paying job may not be able to afford the extra education. On the other hand, many persons will look to additional education so they can make a career shift, with a higher salary in mind.

The College Board's 1978 report, *40 Million Americans in Career Transition,* indicates 36 percent of the population 16–65 (40 million) were in some type of career transition in 1978. Of the 40 million, 60 percent or 24 million were planning additional education as part of their career change.

In many families it may become necessary for both spouses to work to meet family expenses. Wives may see education as an entry to better paying jobs. Many persons may look to education so they can learn basic skills such as plumbing, carpentry, and furniture repair.

Because of the increasing costs of education, self-directed learning could come into its own in the 80s. Much education could be done in local communities with people sharing their knowledge and skills rather than going to an adult education provider for this kind of help.

For many years, colleges, universities, and vocational/technical schools have been traditional providers of adult education. The National Center

230 Jerold W. Apps

for Education Statistics, in a 1975 study of participation in adult education, reported that two and four year colleges and universities and vocational/technical schools provided 40 percent of all adult education courses available in this country. But 60 percent of the courses were offered by employers, grade or high schools, community organizations, government agencies, labor organizations, churches, and others.

Increasingly, business and industry are offering adult education opportunities to their employees. In 1975, 12 percent of all adult education courses were offered by employers.

As we move into the 80s, many private firms are making adult education opportunities available to the general public, often in direct competition with courses offered by college and university outreach efforts.

Much adult education is based on the assumption that people will travel some distance to meet—in a workshop, in a conference, in some type of face-to-face gathering. Can we continue to accept [that] assumption of how to do adult education given the anticipated energy situation? Are we prepared to offer alternatives while not being seduced by the mechanistic element in our society that suggests that nearly everything, including education, can be done electronically?

Is adult education prepared to make changes in how it is carried out, not only because of increased costs, but because it is immoral to use as much energy as we have in the past?

Consumer Movements

People are increasingly more aware of their rights as consumers. They complain about shoddy goods and poor quality service. People are more careful about what they buy in the first place, whether it be goods or services.

During the 70s, automobiles by the millions were recalled by manufacturers for one reason or another. Present day legislation insists that advertising be truthful, whether the product is a can of baked beans or a graduate degree. The consumer in this country has spoken and has been recognized.

Implications for Adult Education. All adult education offerings, no matter what the topic, must be of high quality. In this decade, it is not at all remote to expect some malpractice suits being filed against adult educators because what they said they had to offer was not what the learner received.

Although there is little or no evidence to support the contention, some claim the consumer movement has influenced mandatory continuing education. In a large number of professions—law, medicine, dentistry, engineering, psychology, architecture, veterinary medicine, optometry and others—professionals are required to participate in continuing education to maintain their right to practice. There is no clear evidence that forcing a professional to gain new knowledge will insure a more competent and caring practitioner. Because a professional has new knowledge does not assure that the professional will be more competent. At the present time, every state mandates some forms of continuing education for its professionals.

Of course, with mandated continuing education, providers of educational opportunities meeting the mandated requirements stand to benefit greatly from increased enrollments. There is much debate, both pro and con, concerning mandatory continuing education and the role of adult education providers. The 80s will likely see the issue even more sharply focused and debated. Will adult educators, particularly those from institutions offering continuing professional education, be willing to face the issue of whether or not continuing education should or should not be mandated?

From a content perspective, consumers will likely continue to pressure adult education providers to offer classes, courses, independent study materials and the like on consumer topics ranging from how to purchase a house to consumer rights when dealing with insurance salespersons.

Will adult education providers continue to offer such classes and workshops, or will they, on occasion, help citizen groups organize to obtain this information without attending a class?

Status of Women

Though sex bias is still rampant, women made some gains in the 70s. Today, one can find women who are carpenters, bricklayers, doctors, lawyers, gardeners, janitors, police officers, and judges. Some people argue that women have really made little progress, that what we see is token and cosmetic, and that much work remains to be done if women are to achieve equality in society. Nevertheless, there is some evidence in the direction of equality for women.

Implications for Adult Education.   For one reason or another, women are returning to education by the millions. One of the fastest growing student groups on college and university campuses are women 35 and older. In 1972, 418,000 women in this age group were in college. By 1976, the figure had grown to 700,000, an increase of 67.5 percent. During these same years, the enrollment of men students 35 and older grew from 365,000 to 489,000, an increase of only 34 percent.

After several years away from college, many women are returning to finish interrupted undergraduate degree programs. Women who have been employed are returning to school—community colleges, universities, technical colleges—to change careers. Some women who never attended college are enrolling after their childen are grown or after a recent divorce. Some women, many who already have college degrees, are returning to school to find more meaning in their lives. An increasing number of women are enrolling in adult education courses to become more self-sufficient. They are learning how to care for their autos, how to fill out income tax forms, and how to budget family incomes. Many are interested in improving their health and appearance and enroll in weight loss and exercise programs.

Many of these reasons are the same for men who are returning to education. But it has always been accepted for men to do this—with some exceptions. It has only recently become acceptable for women.

Will women continue to return to school in the 80s as they have in the past decade? What are the implications for adult education providers, particularly colleges and universities, if they do? Will "business as usual" be accepted by these women?

Politics

At the beginning of the 80s, the world is once more tilting toward a cold war attitude. Already, increasing numbers of politicians are advocating higher defense budgets and more attention to protecting the United States' interests in world affairs.

In this country, beginning in the 60s and continuing throughout the 70s, large numbers of people have become disenchanted with costly, federally funded programs designed to solve major social problems—poverty, illiteracy, urban blight, unemployment, and many more. The current national mood is a more conservative one with much discussion about ways and means of cutting federal budgets rather than adding new programs.

At the state and local level, a similar mood grew and developed in the 70s with California's Proposition 13 taking honors for receiving the most publicity. Major cities also experienced great difficulty in simply remaining solvent—New York and Cleveland, for example. At the end of 1979 Chicago's School Board said it was broke and presented its teachers with empty pay envelopes as Christmas presents.

Special interest groups came into their own in the 70s, and many of them were quite successful in the political arena. These special interest groups represented a wide variety of concerns and interests—environmental, anti-nuclear, beef boycott, opposition to more four lane highways, legalization of marijuana, and banning of the draft forever—to name only a few.

Implications for Adult Education.   Tax supported traditional adult education programs such as the Cooperative Extension Service are being carefully examined by federal and state budget makers. More than ever before, traditional providers of adult education are asked to justify their very existence. Every indication suggests this will continue into the 80s.

Even with the possibility of fewer tax dollars needed for elementary and secondary education because of declining enrollments, the competition for education tax dollars will likely continue to be keen in this decade.

The once promoted idea that adult education should develop and present a united front to budget decision-makers, particularly at the national level, seems to be an impossibility based on experience during the 70s. The failure of the Congress to fund the Lifelong Learning Act is a case in point. It appears that we are entering a decade of intense competition among adult education providers as well as with other agencies depending on tax dollars for programs.

During the past 20 years, those adult education programs that appeared to be innovative and nontraditional had the best chances at the federal money trough. If this trend continues, old, established agencies such as Cooperative Extension will likely need to relook who they are, how they should be organized, and what they can do given the situation of the 80s. People are no longer convinced of the value of an agency that insists on telling people how good it has been rather than emphasizing its worth for the present and the future.

As we look to the 80s, will more nontraditional adult education programs in nontraditional settings become successful in gaining tax dollars? Will those long standing tax supported adult education programs that have not kept up with the times be phased out? Will tax supported adult education providers who are keeping up-to-date also die because they are not able to obtain sufficient funds?

Mood of Society Toward Education

Many people in this country are unhappy with elementary and secondary education. Employers point out example after example of high school graduates who can neither read, write, or handle numbers. This negative attitude is carrying over into adult education. William C. Rodgers, writing in National University Extension Association's *Continuum* (September, 1979), said,

> Adult education is too important to be left to the adult educators. One look at the dismal quality of the public schools should convince anyone of the danger of turning any kind of education over to specialists in education. Their low level of competence and their disrespect for subject matter (since their own is so watery) makes them particularly dangerous in dealing with educated adults.

John Holt, Ivan Illich, and others have offered alternatives to compulsory schooling for children. Thousands of taxpayers are insisting on a "back to basics" movement for education, eliminating the "frills" and concentrating on reading, writing, arithmetic, citizenship and little else.

In adult education, we have seen increased emphasis on adult practical literacy education, "demonstrated mastery of basic and life skills necessary for the individual to function proficiently in society." Adult basic education programs emphasizing literacy training have continued to receive taxpayer support and interest. Education for job preparation has been positively received and supported by many people as evidenced in the rapid increase in vocational education program participation. Continuing professional education, whether mandated or not, is on the rise throughout the country. All of these, in my judgment, are reflections in adult education of citizens' interest in "basic education," that which is practical and which can be quickly applied.

On the other hand, there are the beginnings of a new consciousness in the country. Theodore Roszak in his new book, *Person/Planet,* talks about the rights of people to self-discovery, to finding what it means to be a human being. Increasingly, people are questioning the heavy emphasis of education on narrow vocationalism, because at best such education only prepares one for the next job, certainly not for a life of living.

Much education today is education for survival in a complex society. While everyone is obviously interested in surviving, many persons are interested in discovering and developing their inner powers of growth, creativity, and renewal. They want more than survival education.

In a time of social, economic, political, and technological change, people are once more recognizing aspects of human life that are unchanging and universal. Thus, the great literature, art, and music of the past continue to speak to the human condition of the present, and of the future.

It is easy for adult education agencies and institutions to develop programs that seem to respond to what people want. It is much more of a challenge to go beyond the wants of people and deal with inner needs—needs that some people have not even recognized in themselves.

Perhaps in the 80s we will remember that adult education is much more than agencies and institutions, certificates and continuing education units, teachers and students. Perhaps we should re-read Eduard Lindeman's classic book, *The Meaning of Adult Education,* where, in 1926, he wrote, the purpose of adult education ". . . is to put meaning into the whole of life."

We have become so caught up in how to finance adult education, how to market it, how to add gimmickry to our teaching, and how to evaluate and communicate our successes that we sometimes forget what adult education is and what it can accomplish. We forget, sometimes, that outstanding adult educators are often ordinary people without degrees or vitae. We forget that adult education can occur, and does, in taverns, garages, cow barns, and tenement houses. We forget that adult education is as natural as life itself.

Missing Links in the Learning Society "A learning renaissance for adults" is how our time is characterized by K. Patricia Cross, distinguished research scientist at the Educational Testing Service and lecturer in higher education at the University of California at Berkeley. She hails this rebirth of concern for the life of the mind as being just as significant to the twenty-first century as the original Renaissance was to the fifteenth.

But she also perceives that there are ominous gaps in who is getting what knowledge. There is a pressing need to strengthen the links between learners and opportunities; that strengthening may provide many of the most exciting career opportunities for adult educators. Already, whole new kinds of agencies and professional roles, such as that of the educational brokers, have emerged to meet some of the needs Cross sees.

This selection first appeared in *The College Board Review,* Winter 1979-80.

Missing Links in the Learning Society

K. Patricia Cross

Centuries ago, Aristotle, Jesus, Socrates, and the other great teachers of ancient times taught adults, not children. Today their methods would be considered formal education, as they consisted largely of lectures or sermons, teacher-student dialogues, and adult discussion-groups. Their curriculum, too, was one that we would associate with formal education, for it emphasized not so much how to do things as how to think about things. The lessons of the ancient teachers were heavy with the abstractions of ideas and values and the life of the mind. Now, in industrialized nations throughout the world, there is a renaissance of lifelong learning and a rebirth of the notion that learning is a lifetime activity, as important for adults as it is for children.

For a relatively short span of history—actually only several hundred years—civilization advanced through concentrating on formal schooling for the young, and adults were largely forgotten by educators. I call our times a renaissance of education for adults because a rebirth of attention to the life of the mind is occurring that is as significant to the twenty-first century as the original Renaissance was to the fifteenth century.

Yet I'm afraid that those who read about education today are likely to conclude that we are experiencing something more akin to the Dark Ages than to the Renaissance. Almost daily, we are treated to a one-sided picture of education in which test scores are declining, student enrollments are falling off, and school bond-issues are failing with some regularity. Even the prestigious pro-education Carnegie Commission[1] has added to the rhetoric of the coming Dark Ages by referring to the 1950s and 1960s as the Golden Age of higher education and contrasting those years with the 1970s and 1980s, which it labeled the Time of Troubles.

Whether one predicts a renaissance or a dark age for education depends largely on whether one is referring to institutions of education or the broader issue of the role of learning in the society. Institutionalized education may well be headed for a Time of Troubles. Whether it will be permanent or temporary, no one knows for sure, but education and learning are vital and alive and are pervading society as never before.

A Substantial Learning Force

The signs of the learning renaissance are all around us. Researchers estimate that between 80 and 90 percent of the adult population carry out at least one self-directed learning project each year and that the typical adult spends about 500 hours per year learning new things from a variety of sources.[2] In city after city, record-breaking crowds have stood in line to obtain tickets to the King Tut exhibits. In January of 1979 America's number-one magazine for the masses, *The Reader's Digest*, selected a book by the director of the Metropolitan Museum of Art for its book section. And, millions have remained glued to their television sets to try to understand human history as revealed in documentaries such as "Roots" and "Holocaust." An estimated one-third of the huge and ever-expanding paperback-book industry is devoted to teaching people how to do everything from fixing the plumbing to fixing a marriage. In my view, these signs of our times point to a renaissance more than they do to a dark age.

Visions of a learning renaissance are equally encouraging when we look at official counts of the number of adults participating in group or organized educational activities of one sort and another. National surveys in the late 1970s estimated that between 17 million[3] and 32 million[4] adults are currently participating in classes, workshops, job training, discussion groups, or some other form of organized instruction. My best guess is that in 1979, one in every four American adults have joined with others in some form of organized learning endeavor. That is a very substantial learning force with a head count two to three times as great as the total number of college students enrolled for degree credit.

Overall, the future looks bright for the emergence of the learning society. Yet just beneath the surface, there lurk some worries. One not often given much attention by colleges enthusiastically looking for new markets of adult learners to fill the seats left vacant by the declining population of 18-year-olds is that the current adult boom may be nothing more than the baby-boom generation creating the old familiar bulge as it pushes through the formal school system. Is it possible that 10 years from now colleges that have expanded their adult programs to accommodate this large baby-boom generation will find themselves as overextended for adults as they now are for 18-year-olds? Some analysts are taking a worried look at the not-very-well publicized statistics that show that participation in adult education slowed to an 8 percent increase between 1972 and 1975, compared with a 20 percent increase for the previous three years.[5] Without question, the baby-boom generation has something to do with the present surge of participation in adult learning, but it is also highly likely that the lifelong-learning movement has a life expectancy far beyond the baby-boom generation.

In the first place, there is the simple demographic fact that the United States is becoming a nation of adults. By the year 2000, says the National Center for Education Statistics, [6] "The United States population will be dominated by persons in their middle years." For most of the years of this century, the United States population has been numerically dominated by young people. With the exception of the World War II years, children under the age of 15 have always been the largest single age-group in the nation. In 1980, however, numerical dominance will shift to those between the ages of 15 and 29. By the year 2000, the largest age-group will be 30- to 44-year-olds, with a rapidly rising curve for 45- to 64-year-olds. In 1970 the United States was basically a "youth culture," with people under the age of 29 constituting a majority (52 percent) of the population. By the year 2000, the United States will become an "adult culture," for people over 30 years of age will constitute 57 percent of the population.[7]

Most people are aware of the baby boom after World War II and the baby bust that followed, but few realize how much the ebb and flow of the birthrate affect what we do and how we think as a society. In the 1960s, for example, most people assumed that the "youth culture," with its high visibility and influence on college campuses as well as in the marketplace, was the wave of the future. In hindsight, it seems apparent that the great amount of attention given to youth and the "new values" of the 1960s was achieved largely from the force of the unprecedented number of postadolescents in the population. In 1964, the year of the Free-Speech Movement, 17-year-olds became, almost suddenly, the single largest age-group in the country. Peter Drucker[8] maintains that anyone who took the trouble to look at the population figures could have predicted the youth revolution on college campuses in the 1960s. While he admits that the particular form of social revolution would have been hard to predict, it should have been anticipated that the sudden shift in age mix to a predominance of 17-year-olds would have profound social implications.

From today's perspective, Drucker is probably right. Throughout its relatively brief history, the influence of the baby-boom generation on American life has been pervasive, affecting schools, recreation, the type of products marketed, and perhaps even the crime rate. As the baby-boom generation grew older, the pressures for educational expansion moved from the elementary grades to the secondary level, from the secondary schools to the postsecondary institutions, and finally to adult education. Industry moved from marketing products such as baby foods to pop records to recreational vehicles to promoting baby shampoos for the personal use of 30-year-olds. The high crime-rate of the 1960s and 1970s is thought to reflect, in part at least, the high proportion of 14- to 24-year-olds in the population, the age group by which most crimes are committed. Even the decline in college admissions test scores has been linked to demographics. University of Illinois sociologist Marcus Felson observed that the decline in college admissions test scores started in 1963 and began leveling off in 1975, the precise years in which those born in the baby-boom years of 1946 to 1958 turned 17. Felson's explanation is that because of their numbers, these children did not get the personal attention at home or at school that would have resulted in better learning.[9] Even the so-called tax revolt can probably be linked to the fact that the predominant age group in the nation today consists of young adults trying to balance entry-level job salaries with the high costs of establishing a family and first home.

Widespread social phenomena such as these are generally attributed by researchers to multiple factors. But without question, the birthrate and the changes of age mix in the population are important factors in social change. Thus, regardless of whether one would like to argue "for" or "against" increased attention to the education of adults, the political reality is that interests are shifting to serving the predominant group in society—which until the end of this century will be adults over the age of 25.

But the lifelong-learning movement is more than mere demographics. Participation in adult learning activities has been increasing more than twice as fast as their numbers in the population.[3] This escalation is probably the reflection of social factors, changing life-styles, and the speed of change itself. One of the factors fueling adult education is the rising educational attainment of the populace.

Survey research is unanimous in concluding that the single most important predictor of whether an individual will participate in organized learning activities is past level of educational attainment.[10] Learning is addictive. The more education people have, the more they seem to want, and the populace is becoming better educated with each passing generation. The average adult over the age of 25 now has 12.3 years of formal schooling, up from 9.3 just one generation ago.[11] Since high school graduates are almost four times as likely to participate in adult education as non–high school graduates, the rising educational attainment of the populace should result in an increased demand for learning activities.

A second social condition that has had, and will no doubt continue to have, a dramatic impact on educational interest and participation is the changing role of women. Between 1969 and 1975, the number of adult women learners increased 45 percent, compared to an 18 percent increase for men.[3] Right now, it is hard to imagine factors that would decrease the demand for education among women unless women become disenchanted with new career opportunities or the trends affecting today's family structures reverse themselves.

A third factor that must be considered is the labor market. Although there is much controversy now over the market value of education, specifically a college degree, there is little doubt that competition for the more desirable jobs will increase as members of the large baby-boom generation find themselves in fierce competition with one another for job promotion. The "promotion squeeze" will probably have a number of ramifications for education:

• First, people whose promotion is blocked in one career line may decide on a mid-life career change. A recent study estimated that there are 40 million Americans in a state of transition regarding their jobs or careers, and that 60 percent of them plan to seek additional education.[12]

• A second option for people whose job promotion is blocked is to find satisfaction in other pursuits, perhaps through learning for its own sake or through leisure-time activities that require new learning. The greatest growth by subject area in adult education in recent years has been in the areas of social life and recreation, closely followed by personal and family living.[3]

• Third, the predicted job competition will probably encourage older people who are in the jobs and younger persons who want those jobs to gain a competitive edge through further education. This personal initiative, buttressed by the increasing tendency of states and occupational licensing agencies to mandate continuing education, will almost certainly heighten demand for adult education.

For all these reasons, increased competition in the labor market is expected to increase participation in adult education. At the same time, competitive labor conditions may make people think twice about leaving their jobs for education. What in fact seems to be happening is that people are hanging onto their jobs and studying part-time—even younger students without families to support.

New Learning Patterns

It looks as though American society is moving away from the "linear life-plan" in which education is for the young, work for the middle-aged, and enforced leisure for the elderly,[13] and toward a blended life-plan in which education, work, and leisure continue concurrently throughout life.[14] We can see the emergence of the blended life-plan in the tendency for formerly full-time college students to reduce course load in order to work part-time and to take time off for travel and other leisure activities. The "good life" today is not likely to consist of all work or all study for the average adult, but rather of a blend of part-time work, part-time study, and part-time leisure.

In addition to changing social patterns, the strong motivation that many colleges now have for attracting adult learners is driving participation rates up. There is ample research to show that making education more accessible increases participation, sometimes dramatically.[15,16,17,18] And, there is no doubt that many colleges are doing everything possible—within the constraints that money, location, and sometimes stubbornly entrenched faculty attitudes sometimes impose on colleges—to make college programs attractive and accessible to adult learners.

The number of colleges and universities offering noncredit courses has more than doubled in recent years, increasing from 1,102 institutions in 1968 to 2,225 in 1976.[19] Furthermore, around the year 1970, even rather traditional colleges began to launch a variety of degree programs and services designed to attract older part-time students. A national survey conducted in 1972[20] found that between one-third and one-half of all American colleges and universities offered programs for nontraditional students.

It is probably a fairly safe guess that, for the next couple of decades at least, most degree-oriented adults will be accommodated in rather traditional college programs, largely through administrative arrangements such as more flexible schedules and more convenient locations. It is important to remember, however, that most adult learners are not currently degree-oriented. Unless the new availability of degrees for adult learners raises degree aspirations (a real possibility in my opinion), noncredit opportunities sponsored by a variety of educational providers are likely to dominate the learning society of the future.

If there is a learning society in our future, what kind of a learning society will it be? Who will be the participants and who will be the providers?

It is difficult to discuss national trends in adult education with much confidence since the National Center for Education Statistics has been tracking participation systematically only since 1969. Reports are published every three years, and we now have access to data collected in 1969, 1972, 1975, and just recently, 1978.[21,22,23] Analysis of the 1978 survey, the fourth anchor point in time, will give us considerably more insight into current trends. . . .

It is already quite clear, however, that adult education in the United States is elitist and getting more so. As a group, today's adult learners are disproportionately young, white, well educated, and making good salaries. Those who still think of night school as a poor-man's college for lower-class immigrants are clearly out-of-date. Today certain populations are significantly underrepresented in organized learning activities for adults; mainly blacks, people with less than a high school education, those with annual family incomes under $8,000, people aged 45 and older, and those living in the central city or on the farm.[3]

Furthermore, the situation with respect to equal opportunity is becoming worse, not better, for all groups except women. The greatest increases in education participation between 1969 and 1975 were made by white women with college degrees and family incomes of $25,000 a year and over. The rate of growth for women was more than double that for men, and adult learning activities for the college educated increased almost twice as fast as for high school graduates. And, the participation for whites increased eight times as fast as that for blacks. As a matter of fact, the proportion of black people participating in adult learning activities has been decreasing over the past six years, in the face of steadily rising participation for whites.[3] Thus not only are white, well-educated people with good jobs already overrepresented on the adult-education scene, they are making much faster progress than their less well-educated peers, and the educational gap between the "haves" and "have nots" is increasing.

It now appears that just as we were beginning to think that we had achieved some success in fighting the battle for equal educational opportunity for 18-year-olds, here this issue is again, raising its ugly head for 30- to 80-year-olds. There is probably more opportunity now for disadvantaged young people to gain access to college than for older disadvantaged adults to continue the kinds of education that would be useful to them.

My personal conviction is that brokering services and education-information centers constitute our greatest hope for shaping the learning society to serve the needs of a democratic society. They are, in fact, the missing link that will help close the gaps between potential learners and educational opportunities and between the educational "haves" and "have nots."[24] The collection of information about adult learning opportunities and its effective dissemination through the counseling, referral, and advocacy programs of educational brokering services have the following advantages:

• Appropriately located, educational brokering services benefit the less-advantaged segments of society somewhat more than today's relatively advantaged adults, who obviously already know about existing opportunities. Thus brokering services begin to address the current inequities in adult education.

• Information and referral centers help colleges and other educational providers utilize their resources more fully, while getting across the message that the learning society consists of a rich variety of learning options provided by schools and colleges, industry and unions, churches and YMCAS, the military and the media, and anyone else who has knowledge to share.

• Well-managed, comprehensive information-systems of available educational opportunities help state and community planners provide for the needs of adult learners and reduce overlap and waste.

It is important for the collective society to make a strong public statement through its state and federal governments that lifelong learning and the full utilization of a wide variety of learning resources are legitimate, desirable, and a necessary goal of the learning society. If no broad social effort is made to acknowledge the desirability of lifelong learning, and adult education is left to the entrepreneurs, such providers, whether educational institutions or other agencies, will cater largely to the ready market of affluent, well-educated adults who will then become the determiners of the kind of education that is available—a distinct possibility that would almost certainly continue the widening of the gap between the educational "haves" and "have nots."

The Most Important Link

Thus far, I have made some basic assumptions about the learning society, none of which seem the least bit controversial to me. I have assumed—on the basis, I might say, of some fairly good evidence—that there will continue to be an escalating interest in lifelong learning on the part of large numbers of adults in the society. I have further assumed that this is desirable, and that we as a society wish to encourage such interest and to provide equal access to a wide variety of learning resources. Finally, I am assuming that adult information-centers and educational brokering services provide the single most important link in addressing the joint concerns of equal opportunity and the effective utilization of learning resources.

The extent to which that last assumption proves valid depends in large measure on how educational counselors do their jobs. If they have good information about university extension classes and inadequate information about other community resources, they nullify the assumption that the learning society will utilize fully a wide variety of learning resources. If an information-dissemination program consists largely of printed lists of available courses for adults, then participation in the learning society is biased toward rather independent, self-directed adults. If a center is located on a suburban campus or in a storefront in the city center, a decision about the nature of its clientele has already been made.

As I see it, the work of education and information services for adults consists of three sequential steps: one, collecting information about the educational resources available; two, reaching the intended audience; and three, assisting clients to identify and obtain the appropriate learning opportunities. The fact that these are sequential steps has probably not been given sufficient attention. Some counseling centers for adults start with Step Three, hanging out their shingle advertising their willingness to help those who come to them. Only after they have been in business awhile does it occur to them that the enterprise may topple because it has an inadequate base of information and because it is reaching only a small or biased group of clients. Other centers may start with Step Two. They identify what is called in the jargon of the day the "intended audience," establish their center in the low-cost housing development or at the local shopping center, and then discover that they lack both the information base and the counseling skills to help their clients. Then, of course, there are the centers that fail to move beyond Step One with their computerized banks of information that are useful only to the most sophisticated adult learners who know what they want and how to use the information to accomplish their educational goals.

At this stage of development of the lifelong-learning movement, I don't think the lack of attention to sequential planning for education-information centers is especially surprising. For one thing, the steps require different personalities for implementation. The individual who is interested and skillful in one-to-one counseling relationships is rarely interested in or knowledgeable about designing an information system that is orderly, complete, and maintained with patient attention to detail. It is probably equally true that Step-Two people, who have personal access to the intended audience, may not know enough about educational opportunities and how to manipulate the system to serve as good counselors and advocates.

My point is that the creation of a national network of effective education-information centers depends more heavily than we have acknowledged on cooperation and coordination among different types of personalities, among the multiple providers of educational services, and among those who need services and those who offer them. In short, there are missing links everywhere, and the chain of lifelong learning in America is only as strong as its weakest link.

For those concerned with Step One, there is the obvious need to create an accurate, complete, up-to-date information bank about the learning opportunities available to adults. Given the size and complexity of this task, I don't see how anything less than a continuously monitored computerized system can serve the needs over the long run. Printed lists are out-of-date before they are printed and distributed, and they are awkward to index so that counselors can locate them using a combination of descriptors such as subject matter, cost, location, credit, and educational level. Furthermore, it is hard to see how anything with less memory than a computer can keep abreast of the increasing numbers of nationwide services and programs. There are now more than 200 external-degree programs, most of which are open to a national and regional audience. In 1978, 95,000 people took the nationwide CLEP examinations, and thousands of adults participated in the television and newspaper courses that were offered across the country. Such national services are bound to increase, and information systems designed to accommodate only local programs are bound to be inadequate. At the same time, the overwhelming majority of adult learners use local resources, and I know of no local community that has solved the problem of information systems at the local level.

Step-One people need a coordinated national center for information collection that would design the procedures for the collection of data at state and local levels and that would assume responsibility for maintaining current information about programs and services available to the national audience. Admittedly, the task seems enormous, but if the airlines, telephone companies, and television networks can do it, it would appear that education can too. My local travel bureau, for example, is now bypassing the printed *Official Airline Guide* and going directly to computerized information. I suspect that before long telephone directories and *TV Guide* may become outdated, too.

For Step-Two people, that is, those concerned about making the connection between the counseling center and the intended audience, there is the common wisdom, supported by research findings, that suggests that the location of the center is a major determinant of clientele. Psychological as well as physical accessibility is important. I suspect that a man seated in a book-lined office in a three-piece suit is not going to reach the same people as a more casually dressed counselor who frequents the laundry room, pool hall, or coffee shop.

Some experience in Sweden would suggest that we in the United States have not done nearly enough to cultivate and utilize peer-group support for lifelong learning. On the hypothesis that the support and approval of fellow workers is important to educational participation, the Swedes established adult information-centers in factories and plants where blue-collar workers form a powerful reference group. This location was found generally superior to housing group locations in generating interest in educational activities. Certainly before we in the United States organize lobbies for financial entitlement for adult learners, we should see what can be done to help United Auto Workers and other unionized laborers utilize their quite generous educational benefits.

Finally, for Step-Three people—those concerned about counseling, referral, and advocacy—there are the research findings that suggest that poorly educated adults want and need more personal assistance all along the route to educational opportunity. They need help assessing their own needs and interests, they need information about learning opportunities, and they generally express more desire than better-educated groups for assistance in making the connection between their educational needs and appropriate opportunities. While the needs of college-educated learners can frequently be met with little more than up-to-date, accurate information, the less well-educated may need personalized help in interpreting and using the information and in talking with educational providers about possible options.

In conclusion, it seems to me that the success of the lifelong-learning movement in the United States is heavily dependent on providing the services that link learners to opportunities. At present, there are many weak and missing links. While each of us needs to be concerned about strengthening our own link in the chain, we need to be equally concerned about strengthening the coordination and cooperation between the links that lead to the learning society.

Notes

1. Carnegie Commission on Higher Education. *Priorities for Action: Final Report of the Carnegie Commission on Higher Education*. New York: McGraw-Hill Book Company, 1973.

2. Allen Tough, *Major Learning Efforts: Recent Research and Future Directions*. Toronto: Ontario Institute for Studies in Education, 1977.

3. Ruth L. Boaz, *Participation in Adult Education: Final Report, 1975*. Washington, D.C.: National Center for Education Statistics, U.S. Department of Health, Education, and Welfare, 1978.

4. Abraham Carp, Richard Peterson, and Pamela Roelfs, "Adult Learning Interests and Experiences," in *Planning Non-Traditional Programs*, by

K. Patricia Cross and John R. Valley and Associates. San Francisco: Jossey-Bass, Inc., 1974.

5. Michael O'Keefe, *The Adult, Education, and Public Policy.* Cambridge, Mass.: Aspen Institute for Humanistic Studies, 1977.

6. Mary Golladay, *The Condition of Education 1976.* Washington, D.C.: National Center for Education Statistics, U.S. Department of Health, Education, and Welfare, 1976.

7. U.S. Bureau of the Census, *Social Indicators 1976.* Washington, D.C.: U.S. Department of Commerce, 1977.

8. Peter F. Drucker, "The Surprising Seventies." *Harper's,* July 1971, pp. 35–39.

9. Marcus Felson, quoted in *Education Summary,* November 15, 1978.

10. K. Patricia Cross, "Adult Learners: Characteristics, Needs, and Interests," in *Lifelong Learning in America,* by R. E. Peterson and Associates. San Francisco: Jossey-Bass, Inc., 1979.

11. Mary Golladay, *The Condition of Education 1977,* Vol. Three, Part One. Washington, D.C.: National Center for Education Statistics, U.S. Department of Health, Education, and Welfare, 1977.

12. Solomon Arbeiter, Carol B. Aslanian, Frances A. Schmerbeck, and Henry M. Brickell, *40 Million Americans in Career Transition.* New York: College Entrance Examination Board, 1978.

13. Fred Best and Barry Stern, *Lifetime Distribution of Education, Work and Leisure.* Washington, D.C.: Institute for Educational Leadership Postsecondary Convening Authority, 1976.

14. K. Patricia Cross, "Museums in the Learning Society." Speech delivered to the annual meeting of the American Association of Museums, Kansas City, May 30, 1978.

15. W. L. Bashaw, "The Effect of Community Junior Colleges on the Proportion of Local Population Who Seek Higher Education," *Journal of Educational Research,* Vol. 7, No. 58, 1965, pp. 327–329.

16. John Bishop and Jane Van Dyk, "Can Adults Be Hooked on College?" *Journal of Higher Education,* Vol. 1, No. 48, 1977, pp. 39–62.

17. James W. Trent and Leland L. Medsker, *The Influence of Different Types of Public Higher Institutions on College Attendance from Varying Socioeconomic and Ability Levels.* Berkeley: Center for Research and Development in Higher Education, University of California, 1965.

18. Warren Willingham, *Free-Access Higher Education.* New York: College Entrance Examination Board, 1970.

19. Florence B. Kemp, *Noncredit Activities in Institutions of Higher Education for the Year Ending June 30, 1976.* Washington, D.C.: National Center for Education Statistics, U.S. Department of Health, Education, and Welfare, 1978.

20. Janet Ruyle and Lucy Ann Geiselman, "Nontraditional Opportunities and Programs," in *Planning Non-Traditional Programs,* by K. Patricia Cross and John R. Valley and Associates. San Francisco: Jossey-Bass, Inc., 1974.

21. Imogene E. Okes, *Participation in Adult Education 1969: Initial Report.* Washington, D.C.: National Center for Education Statistics, U.S. Department of Health, Education, and Welfare, 1971.

22. Imogene E. Okes, *Participation in Adult Education: Final Report, 1972.* Washington, D.C.: National Center for Education Statistics, U.S. Department of Health, Education, and Welfare, 1976.

23. K. Patricia Cross, "Changing Students and the Impact on Colleges." Speech delivered to the Educational Staff Seminar, Institute for Educational Leadership, Washington, D.C., January 11, 1979.

24. K. Patricia Cross, *The Missing Link: Connecting Adult Learners to Learning Resources.* New York: College Entrance Examination Board, 1978.

Part V

A FUTURE
LEARNING WORLD

Bridging the "Human Gap"   Our awareness that we live in a world of limited resources that must be properly managed if we are to survive and thrive was sparked in large part by the first of a series of Club of Rome reports, *The Limits of Growth* (1972). Some ten years later, a follow-up report in the same series boldly proposed that the "world problematique" could be solved through the proper cultivation of the one unlimited resource: human intelligence. Moreover, argued the three authors of *No Limits to Learning* (who came from First, Second, and Third World countries), a *failure* to so cultivate the capacities of human beings would invite planetary disaster.

"Human gap" was the authors' provocative metaphor expressing this challenge to adult education. They urge that the 1980s become a decade of learning in which a new kind of society-wide learning is developed: *innovative* learning, through which people find and absorb new information enabling them both to anticipate and to participate in the decisions that will crucially affect their future.

The metaphor of the gap between the complexity of our problems and our intellectual capacity to deal with them is a widely useful one for adult educators. It can be applied to the situations of individuals who may lack the skills to deal with their immediate environments or with transitions in their personal lives. Organizations or communities may face gaps in coping with a changing social scene or new missions. And, of course, our nation confronts the gap in such areas as increasing productivity and defining our national values and priorities.

Perhaps its most immediate use, however, is in the field of adult education itself. Can we identify the gaps in our own capacities, individually and as a profession, to deal effectively with the new problems of the rest of this century?

This selection is excerpted from *No Limits to Learning: A Report to the Club of Rome,* published by Pergamon Press in 1979.

Bridging the "Human Gap"

James Botkin, Mahdi Elmandjra, and Mircea Malitza

Whoever chronicles the history of the 1970s will see clearly what we perceive only dimly now. Not only is a critical element still missing from most discussions on global problems, but the most striking analyses of the world problematique are diverting attention from a fundamental issue. What has been missing is the human element, and what is at issue is what we call the *human gap.*

The human gap is the distance between growing complexity and our capacity to cope with it. Clearly, one eternal human endeavor has been to develop additions to knowledge and improvements in action to deal with a complexity which, for most of history, derived primarily from natural phenomena. An essential difference today is that contemporary complexity is caused predominantly by human activities. We call it a *human* gap, because it is a dichotomy between a growing complexity of our own making and a lagging development of our own capacities.

Global problems, currently the chief manifestations of complexity, are first and foremost human problems. They are only secondarily attributable to natural causes. As human problems, they inherently encompass all our frailties and potentials. We are not certain whether the issues we identify are complete, correct, or correctly stated. We are still unable to properly assess and respond to the dangerously high levels of risk intrinsic to the world problematique. And it is not only our capacity to cope which is in question but also our ability or willingness to perceive, understand, and take action on present issues as well as to foresee, avert, and take responsibility for future ones.

It is a profound irony that we should be confronted with so many problems at the same time in history when humanity is at a peak of its knowledge and power. Yet to an intelligent being observing from another planet, we must appear absurd. High-energy technologies are still being developed in disregard for the dwindling global supply of petroleum and natural gas reserves and in the face of mounting public and scientific resistances to full reliance on nuclear power. Meanwhile research into

253

more benign and abundant energy alternatives is given belated and insufficient attention. Even during, and partly spurred on by, international negotiations to limit arms, the stockpiling of destructive weapons accelerates to unprecedented levels of overkill among the superpowers and proliferates to the Third World.[1] Age-old discriminations and dangerous practices of domination and superiority continue to haunt a densely populated world which is unable to develop the equitable re-distribution schemes, cooperation, and moral solidarity on which survival of the human species may, for the first time in history, increasingly depend. Such absurd, occasionally stubborn, and often outmoded practices are but a few of the tell-tale signs that mark the human gap. They indicate that, while we live on a new level of risk and complexity, human understanding, actions, decisions, and values remain rooted in a world view that is no longer relevant.

Thus, whereas the "predicament of mankind" as identified by The Club of Rome first emphasized a global problematique deriving from the physical limits and constraints on future growth and development, now the predicament of humanity is increasingly seen as deriving from the human gap. Methodologies are being developed for explaining, analyzing, and formulating proposals to resolve some of the major material constraints of the global problematique,[2] but adequate counterparts are not yet being devised for dealing with the human element.

This report examines how *learning* can help to bridge the human gap. Learning, as we shall use the term, has to be understood in a broad sense that goes beyond what conventional terms like education and schooling imply. For us, learning means an approach, both to knowledge and to life, that emphasizes human initiative. It encompasses the acquisition and practice of new methodologies, new skills, new attitudes, and new values necessary to live in a world of change. Learning is the process of preparing to deal with new situations. It may occur consciously, or often unconsciously, usually from experiencing real-life situations, although simulated or imagined situations can also induce learning. Practically every individual in the world, whether schooled or not, experiences the process of learning—and probably none of us at present are learning at the levels, intensities, and speeds needed to cope with the complexities of modern life.

Distinguishing this notion of learning from schooling does not mean that this report will ignore education which is a fundamental way and a formal means to enhance learning. However, other less formal modes such as family up-bringing, peer groups, work and play, and the communications media are significant and sometimes predominant factors in learning. Further, we shall contend that not only individuals but also groups of people learn, that organizations learn, and that even societies can be said to learn. The concept of "societal learning" is relatively new and stirs some controversy. Some contend that it is merely a metaphor that distorts the meaning of learning. Doubtless the concept of societal learning has limits, but we nonetheless shall maintain that societies can and do learn, and we shall not hesitate to cite evidence of learning processes at work in societies.[3]

The fact that inadequate contemporary learning contributes to the deteriorating human condition and a widening of the human gap cannot be ignored. Learning processes are lagging appallingly behind and are leaving both individuals and societies unprepared to meet the challenges posed by global issues. This failure of learning means that human preparedness remains underdeveloped on a worldwide scale. Learning is in this sense far more than just another global problem: its failure represents, in a fundamental way, the issue of issues in that it limits our capacity to deal with every other issue in the global problematique. These limitations are neither fixed nor absolute. Human potential is being artificially constrained and vastly underutilized—so much so that for all practical purposes there appear to be virtually no limits to learning.

Learning: Success That Turned to Sudden Failure

History shows that in the past human learning has been largely successful. Throughout its cultural evolution, humanity has adapted to its environment—successfully if often unconsciously—shaping its surroundings in ways that ensured survival of the species and that gradually increased the well-being of larger and larger numbers of its kind. Some societies thrived by developing their human learning potential, compensating for inhospitable climate, poor geographic location, or a lack of natural resources. Others, even some with great wealth and power, were too slow to learn: unresponsive to impending changes, they disappeared. But on balance, human learning processes viewed at an aggregate global level have been adequate to meet the challenges as they presented themselves.

Serious doubt must be raised as to whether conventional human learning processes are still adequate today. Traditionally, societies and individuals have adopted a pattern of continuous *maintenance learning* interrupted by short periods of innovation stimulated largely by the shock of external events. Maintenance learning is the acquisition of fixed outlooks, methods, and rules for dealing with known and recurring situations. It enhances our problem-solving ability for problems that are given. It is the type of learning designed to maintain an existing system or an established way of life. Maintenance learning is, and will continue to be, indispensable to the functioning and stability of every society.

But for long-term survival, particularly in times of turbulence, change, or discontinuity, another type of learning is even more essential. It is the type of learning that can bring change, renewal, restructuring, and problem reformulation—and which we shall call *innovative learning*.

Throughout history, the conventional formula used to stimulate innovative learning has been to rely on the shock of events. Sudden scarcity, emergency, adversity, and catastrophe have interrupted the flow of maintenance learning and acted—painfully but effectively—as ultimate teachers. Even up to the present moment, humanity continues to wait for

256 Botkin, Elmandjra, and Malitza

events and crises that would catalyze or impose this primitive *learning by shock*. But the global problematique introduces at least one new risk—that the shock could be fatal. This possibility, however remote, reveals most clearly the crisis of conventional learning: primary reliance on maintenance learning not only is blocking the emergence of innovative learning, but it renders humanity increasingly vulnerable to shock; and under current conditions of global uncertainty, learning by shock is a formula for disaster.

Why does the pattern of learning that succeeded in the past fail in the present? What change in the human condition requires a change in human learning? The changes go much deeper than simply the possibility of annihilation of the human species through war, massive nuclear accident, sudden depletion of the ozone layer, or an irreversible "greenhouse effect." Even in cases less threatening to the survival of life itself, the reliance on reaction, crisis management, and even apparently mild shock can be self-defeating. Because global issues can have unusually long lead times, and because maintenance learning has unfortunately long lag times, an important risk and cost of discouraging innovative learning is that indispensable options may not be available at the time they are needed. There is no room for mistakes inherent in learning by trial and error when the subject is for example large, centralized and costly energy installations. Learning about alternative sources of power must occur before it is forced upon us by high energy prices, petroleum scarcities, or nuclear accidents.

The advent of the global problematique also delineates the end of a period where learning could be denied to a portion of humanity without adverse effects. It is no longer practical to rely on conventional learning at a time when people are increasingly conscious of their rights and of their capacity to support—or impede—measures handed down from above. Irrespective of any consideration of the immorality of restricting learning by race, sex, culture, or nation, no way has yet been devised to generate widescale understanding, cooperation, and participation of some critical mass of the world's inhabitants in the short time period often required. Shock learning can be seen as a product of elitism, technocracy, and authoritarianism. Learning by shock often follows a period of overconfidence in solutions created solely with expert knowledge or technical competence and perpetuated beyond the conditions for which they were appropriate. Should global shock occur, many of the positive accomplishments of science and technology are likely to be discarded in a reaction against elitism and technocracy.

Moreover, because the global problematique affects all four and a half billion people grouped into more than 150 nation states and territories whose boundaries cut across a much higher number of cultures, it demands a type of learning that emphasizes value-creating more than value-conserving. The search for a global consensus on certain key values should not undermine the vital diversity of cultures and their corresponding value systems. At the same time, recognizing the claims of diverse cultures to their own identity also entails the necessity of encouraging joint responsibility for the solution of global problems.

The conventional pattern of *maintenance/shock learning* is inadequate to cope with global complexity and is likely, if unchecked, to lead to one or more of the following consequences: (a) The loss of control over events and crises will lead to extremely costly shocks, one of which could possibly be fatal. (b) The long lag times of maintenance learning virtually guarantee the sacrificing of options needed to avert a whole series of recurring crises. (c) The reliance on expertise and short time periods intrinsic to learning by shock will marginalize and alienate more and more people. (d) The incapacity quickly to reconcile value conflicts under crisis conditions will lead to the loss of human dignity and of individual fulfillment.

The net result of following any one of these paths is that humanity persistently will lag behind events and be subjected to the whims of crisis. The fundamental question that this prospect raises is whether humanity can learn to guide its own destiny, or whether events and crises will determine the human condition.

Bridging the Human Gap: What Type of Learning?

The main purpose of this report is to initiate a debate on learning and the future of humanity, centered around the concept of innovative learning and its chief features. We make no claim that this report provides a definitive statement about learning that will be applicable to all societies. Nor do we assert that innovative learning *by itself* will solve any of the pressing issues. What we do assert is that *innovative learning is a necessary means of preparing individuals and societies to act in concert in new situations*, especially those that have been, and continue to be, created by humanity itself. Innovative learning, we shall argue, is an indispensable prerequisite to resolving any of the global issues. This is not to say, however, that other actions involving political power, technology, economics, and so on will not also make instrumental contributions—although innovative learning needs to underlie and penetrate these and other actions as well. . . .

A primary feature of innovative learning is *anticipation*, which may best be understood by contrasting it to adaptation. Whereas adaptation suggests reactive adjustment to external pressure, anticipation implies an orientation that prepares for possible contingencies and considers long-range future alternatives. Anticipatory learning prepares people to use techniques such as forecasting, simulations, scenarios, and models. It encourages them to consider trends, to make plans, to evaluate future consequences and possible injurious side-effects of present decisions, and to recognize the global implications of local, national, and regional actions. Its aim is to shield society from the trauma of learning by shock. It emphasizes the future tense, not just the past. It employs imagination but is based on hard fact. When the gradual deterioration of the physical or social environment does not move those who should be alarmed, then anticipation either is not present or is not given sufficient priority. The essence of anticipation lies in selecting desirable events and working toward them; in averting unwanted or potentially catastrophic events; and in creating new alternatives. Through anticipatory learning, the future may enter our lives as a friend, not as a burglar.

Another primary feature of innovative learning is *participation.* One of the most significant trends of our time is the near-universal demand for participation. This demand is being felt on the international level as well as at national, regional, and local levels. Nation states, especially (but not only) those in the Third World, are demanding to participate on an equitable basis in the world decisions that affect them—particularly on policies concerning global issues. Groups of every definition are asserting themselves around the world and rejecting a marginal position or subordinated status with respect to power centers. Rural populations are aspiring to urban-like facilities; factory workers seek participation in management; students and faculties demand a voice in administering important school policy; women are demanding equality with men. It is the age of *rights;* and significantly not yet the age of *responsibilities.* An intrinsic goal of effective participation will have to be an interweaving of the demand for rights with an offer to fulfill obligations.

If participation is to be effective, it will be essential that those who hold power do not block innovative learning. Participation is more than the formal sharing of decisions; it is an attitude characterized by cooperation, dialogue, and empathy. It means not only keeping communications open but also constantly testing one's operating rules and values, retaining those that are relevant and rejecting those that have become obsolescent.

Neither anticipation nor participation are new concepts by themselves. What is new and vital for innovative learning is the insistence that they be tied together. Innovative learning breaks down when either is omitted. Without participation, for instance, anticipation often becomes futile. It is not enough that only elites or decision-makers are anticipatory when the resolution of a global issue depends on the broad-based support from some critical mass of people. And, participation without anticipation can be counter-productive or misguided, leading to paralysis (where countervailing forces preclude action to deal with an issue), or to counteraction (where there is backlash resulting in unintended negative consequences).

What are the purposes and values that underlie innovative learning? Two different categories of values will be considered. First, we shall argue that innovative learning cannot be "value free." It is in the conscious emphasis on the role and place of values and their evolution that the borderline between innovative and maintenance learning is most clearly demarcated. Whereas maintenance learning tends to take for granted those values inherent in the status quo and to disregard all other values, innovative learning must be willing to question the most fundamental values, purposes, and objectives of any system. For example, in the debates about energy, it is not enough to ask how to create new energy sources but it is necessary also to ask how scarce energy should be conserved, to which priority uses should it be applied, and by what values should priorities be assigned.

Second and more broadly, this report itself adopts a normative value position. Already the complementary concepts of anticipation and participation have been imbued with a position value. But what are the overall purposes and values of innovative learning and of this report? The first and fundamental purpose is *human survival.* Survival begins with the provision of adequate food, shelter, and health. The planetary agenda would be full just meeting these basic human needs in the foreseeable future; yet, to ensure that these needs are adequately met, innovative learning is essential. To put human survival in the forefront as the first purpose of learning signifies that we are not discussing a metaphysical issue; instead, learning has become a life-and-death matter, and not only for people at the edge of subsistence. Even for those more secure in material provisions, the dictum "learn or perish" now directly confronts all societies—wealthy or poor—even though many of their individual members may still feel insulated from this harshness. Innovative learning for those who oversee the power that can annihilate the human race has become particularly indispensable.

But "just survival" is not enough. The question is survival under what conditions? Individuals are willing to sacrifice their own survival (not to mention that of others) for ideals and causes. *Human dignity* is at the heart of the demands for participation and the great desire to contribute. . . . While dignity will mean different things to different people, we have taken it to mean the respect accorded to humanity as a whole, the mutual respect for individuals in culturally diverse societies, and self-respect.

The concept of learning must be raised to greater levels of visibility, just as ecology was promoted a decade earlier to high levels of prominence. But no team of scholars, however expert, and no combination of public leaders, however charismatic, can provide the final answers. What is urgently required is an open debate on whether there is need to give learning a higher priority in the discussions and actions about the world problematique, and on whether innovative learning is the kind that could help reverse the deterioration in the human condition.

Notes

1. The current strategic weapons arsenal of the world's two superpowers is estimated to comprise the equivalent of over 100,000 Hiroshima-size warheads.

2. See for example, the first two reports to The Club of Rome: *The Limits to Growth* by D. Meadows *et al.,* University Books, 1972, and *Mankind at the Turning Point* by M. Mesarovic and E. Pestel, E. P. Dutton, 1974.

3. To convey the sense of societal learning, an analogy may be useful. A century ago, the concepts of growth and development were applied only to individuals. Today, it has become common usage to refer to the growth and development of societies. Similarly, we may speak of societal learning capacity, and whether a society has the ability to learn quickly or slowly, effectively or ineffectively. A description of how these concepts came to be applied to societies can be found in S. Chodak, *Societal Development*, Oxford University Press, 1973.

The Worldwide Struggle for Adult Education "All over the world, people are experimenting, innovating, creating new structures and approaches in adult education," said Paul Bertelson, UNESCO's chief of adult education, to the U.S. adult educators gathered at one of their recent annual conventions. "And now, for the first time in history . . . professionals can keep in touch with colleagues throughout the world."

The best introduction to the worldwide comradeship of adult educators is a landmark manifesto with the deceptively mundane title *UNESCO Recommendation on the Development of Adult Education*, here described and applied to our American situation by Frank Spikes. His readable summary and commentary make clear why leaders in the field regard the *Recommendation* as a touchstone for progressive thinking. "This is one of the most humanistic statements there has ever been in adult education," says Rosalind Loring, former president of the Adult Education Association of the U.S.A. "It focuses upon the individual, it talks about the learner. It says 'education is inseparable from democracy, the abolition of privilege, and the promotion within society as a whole of the ideas of autonomy, responsibility, and dialog." And Paul Delker, chief of adult education for the federal government, says, "We have much to learn from others—much of the world has been 'there' already, wrestling with theoretical and practical problems of building such a [lifelong learning] system. It may take us a hundred years to make the transition [to such a system in the United States] but the important thing is that we have started—here, now."

This selection was excerpted from an article first published in *Lifelong Learning: The Adult Years* in April 1979.

The Worldwide Struggle for Adult Education

Frank Spikes

In 1976 the world's population passed the four billion mark. This means that 1.6 billion more people lived on the earth in 1976 than did some 26 years earlier in 1950.[1] In terms of land surface, data show that in 1976 an average of 29 people lived on every square kilometer of land on this planet. Adding this current population to an ever-increasing population growth rate, nearly two percent annually; the ever-lengthening life span of the individual—now estimated to be over 73 years on the average in the United States; new advances in communication technology, diplomacy, and the economic arena, leads one to conclude that these four billion souls are quickly becoming a universal, rather than nation-bound and provincial, society of man. Despite the emergence of this universal man, the profession of adult and continuing education has not until recently been able to establish standards and criteria for itself in terms of setting objectives, providing operational definitional bases, or establishing strategies and structures of and for developing relationships between other segments of the educative arena and itself, which would facilitate its practice on a truly international scale.

On November 26, 1976, just such a historically significant document, the *UNESCO Recommendation on the Development of Adult Education* was adopted by the General Conference of the United Nations Educational, Scientific, and Cultural Organization at its 34th plenary meeting in Nairobi, Kenya. This document mandates that:

> . . . member states apply the (following) provisions by taking whatever legislative or other steps (that) may be required, and in conformity with the constitutional practice of each state, (to) give effect to the principles set forth (herein) . . .[2]

Beginning with this charge, the remainder of this article provides the reader with an overview of the salient features of the *UNESCO Recommendation* and offers some suggestions as to why the provisions of this document are important to adult educators in the United States.

263

What is UNESCO?

An understanding of the *UNESCO Recommendation on the Development of Adult Education* is greatly facilitated and enhanced by understanding a bit about UNESCO, its place within the United Nations structure, and its operational charge and philosoply.

UNESCO—the United Nations Educational, Scientific, and Cultural Organization—is . . . one of more than a dozen intergovernmental agencies of the United Nations System, known as Specialized Agencies, which are charged with considering problems within their particular fields of specialization from a universal viewpoint in order to "benefit (the) organization of humanity as a whole."[3]

In some respects UNESCO can be thought of as being successor to the International Institute of Intellectual Cooperation, which was established within the structure of the ill-fated League of Nations; with UNESCO, having much more political charge and support than did the IIIC, which was a privately supported body.[4] Originally founded in 1945 and officially established in Paris on November 4, 1946, UNESCO is comprised of three structural elements—the General Conference, consisting of representatives of member states which in part is responsible for adopting the program and the budget of the organization; the Executive Board, which is responsible for supervising the execution of UNESCO's program and for the administration of budgetary matters; and the Secretariat, which is the day-to-day functional administrative arm of the organization. These three subunits of the main UNESCO organization are concerned with achieving the following operational goals:

• Organizing international intellectual cooperation through the communication of knowledge, the comparing of experiences, and the exchange of ideas through establishing an international network of scholars and specialists who collaborate to solve particular concerns of mankind.

• Providing an international institution through which the world's scholars can, on an interdisciplinary basis, solve problems of world development both through education at all levels, and through effective utilization of natural resources and scientific policy.

• Fostering the moral development of mankind through world peace and understanding by way of advancing education, science, and culture.[5]

It is from this humanistically focused, educationally oriented organization that the *UNESCO Recommendation on the Development of Adult Education* emanated. It was specifically in keeping with the desire of the organization to further the implementation of the second functional area of its operational responsibility that UNESCO produced the comprehensive and powerful document that is the focal point of the remainder of this article. It is comprehensive in the sense that it addresses, in a unified and cohesive manner, a majority of those issues cogent to the process of developing a meaningful and effective adult education and lifelong learning network in nations throughout the world. It is powerful in its humanistic focus, in its concern for the individual as a person and in the attention that is paid to serving populations that have been systematically excluded from life's educative mainstream.

Structure

The *UNESCO Recommendation on Development of Adult Education* consists of an introduction or preamble and ten content specific sections comprised of 67 subpoints, many of which are further subdivided into five or six minor sections. While obviously being too extensive to be recounted word for word in this text, several of the more meaningful and more thought-provoking suggestions of UNESCO follow:

• Education is inseparable from democracy, (from) the abolition of privilege and (from) the promotion within society as are the ideas of autonomy, responsibility, and dialogue.

• The access to education, in the context of lifelong education, is a fundamental aspect of the right to education and facilitates the exercise of the right to participate in political, cultural, artistic and scientific life.

• Education must be considered on a global basis and as a lifelong process particularly in view of the rapid pace of scientific, technical, economic, and social change, for the full development of the human potential to occur.

• Adult education, in the context of lifelong education, is necessary as a means of achieving a more equitable distribution of educational resources between young people and adults, and between different social groups and of ensuring better understanding and more effective collaboration between the generations and greater political, social, and economic equality between social groups and between the sexes.

• Adult education, as an integral part of lifelong education, can contribute decisively to economic and cultural development [and] social progress as well as to the development of educational systems.

• Experience aquired in adult education must carefully contribute to the renewal of educational methods as well as to the reform of educational systems as a whole.

• The universal concern for literacy is a crucial factor in political and economic development, in technological progress and in social and cultural change, so that its promotion should therefore form an integral part in any plan for adult education.

With these philosophical premises in mind, the drafters of this document have first provided a working definition of adult education as utilized in the body of this document by the authors and which has been adopted for use by the member states of UNESCO. While the literature reveals that over time adult education has been defined in many ways, ranging from being equated to the activities whereby the residents of 19th century England were taught to read the Bible[6] to the more recent report of Norman Kurland which suggests that more than 30 terms are present in the literature which describe the modern process of educating adults,[7] the drafters of the *UNESCO Recommendation* have chosen to provide a definition which is both broadly based—one which is thus useful in the various societal contexts of its member states—and one which is in keeping with the philosophical and operational basis of the parent organization. They have suggested that:

> the term adult education denotes the entire body of organized educational process . . . whereby persons regarded as adult by the society to which they belong develop their abilities, enrich their knowledge, improve their technical or professional qualifications or turn them in a new direction and bring about changes in their attitudes or behavior in the twofold perspective of full personal development and participation in balance and independent social, economic and cultural development . . . (it) must not be considered as an entity in itself, it (rather must be considered as being) a subdivision and an integral part of a global scheme for lifelong education and learning.[8]

Based upon this operational/working definition the remainder of the UNESCO text discusses in detail:

1. the objectives and strategies requisite to facilitating the education of adults—including the aims and principles which should govern the process,

2. the content of adult education with regard to its relationship to lifelong education and the specific user constituencies of women, rural populations, the educationally disadvantaged, youth, vocationally oriented users, physically and mentally handicapped persons, ethnic minorities, the unemployed and the aged,

3. methodological, analytical research and evaluative issues relating to the education of adults,

4. the training and status of persons engaged in adult education,

5. the relationship between adult education, lifelong education and the education of youth, and between adult education and work,

6. the procedural and structural considerations salient to the management, administration, coordination, and financing world wide adult education and lifelong learning network and the requisite actions necessary to accomplish these goals. . . .

As can be seen from this rather brief description of the *UNESCO Recommendation,* it is a very comprehensive document in the sense that it addresses most of those issues cogent to the process of developing a meaningful and effective adult education and lifelong learning network in nations throughout the world. Moreover, it provides a powerful humanistic basis in its specifically expressed concern for the individual as a person and pays explicit attention to serving populations throughout the world which have been systematically excluded from the educative process.

Beyond these ideas however this document is important to all adult educators because of the universal view of adult education that it provides. Originating at the 1960 Montreal Conference of UNESCO and being further refined at the Third International Conference on Adult

Education held in Tokyo in 1972, this document is the first world wide standard-setting instrument in the field.[9] Moreover, provided therein are a set of internationally recognized guidelines against which nations can measure the development of their adult education systems and structures. With this world view in mind, the drafters of the *UNESCO Recommendation* have provided a truly meaningful analysis of the major issues relating to adult education and lifelong learning. Likewise, the practice of adult education is clearly integrated into the context of lifelong learning; emphasis is placed upon viewing the process of educating the adult as being a part of a larger cultural, societal, and economic matrix. Hence, wholism of the lifelong education process relative to other aspects of society is the key to the thrust of the philosophical foundation of this resolution. The content, process, objectives, strategies, and relationships of the practice of adult education are viewed as being integral aspects of a total eco-system in which each element is codependent upon other elements of the system and thus are designed to mutually benefit each other during the process of growth and development of the individual and the society. Adult education is thereby seen as being a key structural component of society through which social, cultural, and economic development in the largest sense will be enhanced and facilitated. No longer does the educating of adults assume a peripheral position of adjunct importance. Rather it becomes the central force through which progress of the individual man and woman, and the collective cultures and societies of the world can be advanced.

Supplementing this wholistic world view of adult education and lifelong learning is the equally significant and omnipresent humanistic thrust of the *UNESCO Recommendation*. It specifically stresses that the highest priority be given to educating the disadvantaged learner. Loring[10] has suggested that:

This is one of the most humanistic statements there has ever been in adult education. It focuses upon the individual, it talks about the learner . . . and (it) stresses equity.

The importance of educational equity for all individuals, specifically as related to the underserved constituencies of women, rural populations, ethnic minorities and the physically handicapped is further emphasized in the *Recommendation*'s stressing of the too often ignored principle that:[11]

access of adults to education in the context of lifelong education is a fundamental aspect of the right to participate in political, cultural, artistic and scientific life.

Going even further, UNESCO calls for its member states to provide for adult education programs free of charge to members of underprivileged social groups who, because of lack of funds, would normally be prohibited from participating in such activities.

In addition to the *Recommendation*'s importance as an internationally based, standard-setting document; its importance as providing a wholistic definitional basis for the process of adult education, thereby identifying the relationship of adult education to lifelong learning to other external salient components of society; and in addition to focusing upon the humanism, the individual and the inseparableness of education and educational equity from democracy especially as related to the undereducated adult; the *Recommendation* also provides a useful typology for establishing meaningful adult/continuing and lifelong learning activities at the local, state, national, and international levels through the attention that has been paid to the variety of interrelated issues that are discussed herein and which have been cited in the earlier portion of this article.

Apart from benefitting from the wholism, humanism, and comprehensiveness of the text of the *UNESCO Recommendation* at a philosophical and conceptual level, the implications that can be drawn from this work for practice by adult educators in the United States are great. One of the most significant of these is the impetus that this document gives to establishing a meaningful nationwide system and concomitant policy for delivering, funding, and supporting adult, continuing, and lifelong educational activities in the United States. It is evident that in the past no such unified federal policy has existed and no such model—administrative or fiscal—has been established and put into practice upon which the precepts for practice set forth by UNESCO can be implemented. Delker[12] supported this idea when he recently suggested that with the acceptance of this document:

> We (in the United States) can now begin the shift . . . from the ideal of universal terminal education to the ideal of universal lifelong learning. All the key issues (that) we need to face and work on are here in this document.

At the policy level, this statement, along with the earlier typology of R. H. Dave[13] for UNESCO, offers an integrated model which can be utilized in situating the adult education process into the overall scheme of society. Specifically, these works suggest that:

• Education does not terminate at the end of formal school but is a lifelong process covering the entire lifespan of an individual.

• Lifelong education is not solely confined to education of adults but rather touches base with and thus unifies all stages of education and includes nonformal, informal, and formal patterns of learning.

• The home—through providing a lifetime process of family learning—and the community play a crucial role in initiating and maintaining the process of lifelong learning.

• The effective process of lifelong education embodies elements which are both vertically articulated and horizontally integrated in a manner which seeks systematic continuity; horizontal integration implying "the bringing together of all of the various types of education being provided within the society" to support each other; vertical articulation meaning that the individual brings together in a unified whole all types of educational experiences that have occurred in his or her life.

• Lifelong learning is characterized by flexibility and diversity of content, learning tools and techniques, and allows for a dynamic approach for general and professional education to occur.

If such a universal policy and delivery model is to be adopted, a significant reprioritization of federal funding to support the achieving of UNESCO's goals must be achieved. . . . This is especially true when viewed in light of the present administration's Fiscal Year 1980 budget which the American Council on Education reports to include a cut of 319 million dollars from last year's appropriation for higher education in general and a 16 million dollar cut to a zero dollar level for university community services funding in particular. This same budget recommends a cut of 260 million dollars in student aid funding from the current level of appropriation.[14] Given this situation a truly age-neutral educational financing policy must be developed to accompany any national strategy of lifelong learning.[15] It can be similarly seen that the currently disparate functional areas within the federal government which are now responsible for overseeing the total national educational effort, must achieve a greater degree of unity of function, coordination, and purpose. National models which integrate compulsory education, secondary education, postsecondary education, work and post-work learning activities must be developed, tested, and implemented at all levels. As such structures are developed, movement from the conceptual/theoretical construct level to the application/implementation actional level of these models can and must occur.

At the local program and state level the *UNESCO Recommendation* suggests that several particular issues must be addressed if a true lifelong society is to be achieved, including achieving equality of educational access for all people and redefining the role of education to work, and establishing strategies which would facilitate and enhance the motivation to continue participation in lifelong learning experiences. With regard to the issue of equality of educational access, such questions as: How does the current system of educational organizations affect meaningful participation in a lifelong learning society, and what type of system can be designed to facilitate the ingress and egress of the dropout-prone individual to the world of work must be answered. Likewise if Stern's[16] notion that the amount of education that a person obtains is of greater consequence to the type of job obtained than of the converse can be accepted, the issue of how can effective job structures be developed to encourage the greatest degree of entry into the educational system must be examined. We must also determine how these structures can be developed accurately and effectively to match the needs of the labor market to existing educational resources. Similarly, adult educators must strive to establish effective strategies for relating the values of youth in school to the values of the work place and between youth and the older adult in the work place. Additionally, the question of developing and setting in place structures and methods that will assist the individual to maintain the continuity of his or her early training in later life is also a pertinent one. Finally, how does one, within such a lifelong learning context, become in the highest degree "both the object and instrument in his own development through the many forms of self-education"?[17]

Obviously, the issues and implications for practice raised herein are large ones; ones with potentially vast importance for policy makers at the federal, state, and local levels and even larger implications for society as a whole. Given these dimensions and given the lack of rapidity with which policy and delivery issues relative to lifelong learning in the United States have changed over time, adoption and implementation of the precepts set forth in the *UNESCO Recommendation* will be at best a longterm process, with an even greater longterm consequence for practice and a concomitant lag in adoption by the community of adult education practitioners in the United States. However, what is important, what is significant about this document has perhaps been most succinctly stated by Paul Delker, Chief of Adult . . . Education for the United States Office of Education, who, in speaking about the *UNESCO Recommendation* before the 1977 Conference of the Adult Education Association of the United States, stated that:

> We have much to learn from others—much of the world has been 'there' already, wrestling with theoretical and practical problems of building such a (lifelong learning) system. It may take us a hundred years to make the transition (to such a system in the United States) but the important thing is that we have started—here, now.[18]

Notes

1. *Demographic Yearbook, 1976, 28th Issue.* New York City, New York: United Nations Publishing Service, Department of Economic and Social Affairs, Statistical Office, 1977, p. 115.

2. *UNESCO Recommendation on the Development of Adult Education.* Paris, France: United Nations Educational, Scientific, and Cultural Organization, Adult Education Section, 1976, p. 2.

3. *What is UNESCO?, 8th Edition.* Paris, France: United Nations Educational, Scientific, and Cultural Organization, 1970, p. 9.

4. Gain Franco Popei, "History of the Organization" appearing in *In the Minds of Men: UNESCO 1946-1971.* Paris, France: Universitaires de France Presses, United Nations Educational, Scientific, and Cultural Organization, 1972, p. 15.

5. *What is UNESCO?* op. cit., pp. 22-41.

6. Coolie Verner, *Poles History of Adult Schools: A Facsimile of the 1816 Edition with an Introduction and Bibliographical Notes.* Washington, D.C.: Adult Education Association of the U.S.A., 1967, pp. 1-16.

7. Norman D. Kurland, "A National Strategy for Lifelong Learning," *Phi Delta Kappan,* Volume LIX, Number 6, February, 1978, pp. 385-389.

8. *UNESCO Recommendation,* loc. cit.
9. John C. Cairns, "Recent UNESCO Activity in Adult Education," *Canadian Journal of University Continuing Education,* Volume IV, Number 2, Winter 1978, pp. 32-34.
10. Rosalind Loring, as cited in R. Gross, "Toward a Learning Society: Adult Educators Engaged in a World of Challenge," *Lifelong Learning: The Adult Years,* Volume I, Number 5, January 1978, p. 20.
11. *UNESCO Recommendation,* loc. cit.
12. Paul Delker, "The UNESCO Recommendation on Lifelong Learning." An address given at the 1977 Adult Education Association of the United States Annual Conference, Detroit, Michigan, November, 1977.
13. R. H. Dave, *Reflections on Lifelong Learning and the School.* Hamburg, F.R. Germany: UNESCO Institute for Education, 1975.
14. American Council on Education, *Higher Education and National Affairs,* Volume XXVIII, Number 2, January 12, 1979, pp. 1-3.
15. Norman D. Kurland, "Lifelong Learning Entitlement" in Norman D. Kurland, Editor, *NIE Papers in Education and Work, Number 4, Entitlement Papers.* Washington, D.C.: Department of Health, Education, and Welfare, National Institute of Education, 1977.
16. Barry Stern, *Toward a Federal Policy on Education and Work.* Washington, D.C.: Department of Health, Education, and Welfare, 1977.
17. Paul Lengrand, *An Introduction to Lifelong Education.* London: Croom Helm Publishing, Ltd., 1977.
18. Delker, loc. cit.

Lifelong Learning as Nightmare   The most provocative issue in the field of adult education for the last five years has been mandatory continuing education. Should adults be pressured to participate in learning experiences, whether through social or economic pressure, certification requirements, or legal coercion?

Many adult educators have embraced the trend. "It seems that we are pathetically pleased to be wanted, to be recognized even for the wrong reasons," comments Roby Kidd, "and we have been quick to see that in the short run there may be money to be made by offering programs to people who are legally compelled to attend."

But a growing countermovement within the field has been led by John Ohliger, a veteran adult education philosopher working out of Basic Choices, a think tank in Madison, Wisconsin. "Millions of adults are currently being compelled to go back to school by a burgeoning jungle of laws, regulations and social edicts," Ohliger asserts. "If those who are pushing this trend have their way, it will proliferate until all Americans find themselves forced to enroll in courses all their lives. Already some distinguished leaders in adult education and powerful interest groups like the American Federation of Teachers are advocating policies leading to this direction. Unless something is done to counter the trend, the child born in the United States in the year 1984 will never look forward to getting out of school. From the 'parent-infant development center' which she starts attending at the age of two months with her mother, to the 'geriatric learning center' in which she dies, she will find herself going to school all her life 'for the good of society.' "

The struggle continues, and each of us in the field is confronted with this inevitable question in our program planning and in our thinking: Which side am I on?

This selection originally appeared in 1978 in *Second Thoughts*, the first issue of the newsletter published by Basic Choices.

272

Lifelong Learning as Nightmare

Voluntary Learning and Living for a Free Society

A proclamation put forth for comment and commitment
by a group of adult educators convened by Basic Choices

We are a group of adult educators and others who try to put the following beliefs into practice in our daily lives:

- The primacy of voluntary learning.
- The basic value of free and open discussion intimately integrating thoughts and feelings, reflection and action.
- Working together toward a just society with more democratic control and mutual self-reliance, and less hierarchy, bureaucracy, and external authority.
- Working together toward a world with the best possible balance between maximum free learning and minimum instruction, with a significant place for activities not publicly defined as job-related *or* as learning.

We are encouraged by the activities of many striving to move the world toward these shared beliefs, but we are concerned about certain trends in other directions:

- Adult education is increasingly becoming compulsory by law or social pressure, accompanied by a drive for more certification, credentialing, and professionalization. These trends are burgeoning within political and economic structures dominated by a small minority. Within this framework, knowledge is defined as worthwhile only if it is technical or scientific. Professional elites are increasingly securing monopoly control over access to this knowledge and its development.
- More time and money is being spent on adult education in the name of lifelong learning. Yet these efforts are presently paying off in less economic benefits for most people, less valuable learning, and a decreasing ability to lead the good life.

273

• Greater specialization and fragmentation of work continue while increasingly complex technical development is encouraged in the name of greater personal control over our daily lives. In the face of these trends it becomes clear that we need instead to encourage greater *general* questioning and an examination of the whole and *not* just the specialized parts. We need to control technology and other forces supporting it to foster a better life and to remove some of the growing and unnecessary constraints on our liberties.

To work toward the durable better society which we seek and to counteract these trends we therefore propose to join together, and invite others to join us in these activities:

• Research on the extent of these trends and the structural basis for their growth through new forms of critical analysis, examining especially the links between the political, economic, technological, and cultural dimensions.

• To search for, encourage, and work with positive alternatives for human learning at every level: individual, friendship, family, neighborhood, institutional, local, state, national, and international.

• To engage in collective political action and work with others. This action should include raising basic issues for public discussion in these and other contexts:

1. Opposing laws and pressures for mandatory continuing education in general, and certification, credentialing, and professionalization in adult education.

2. At the same time working toward true public accountability and the growth of genuine personal and social competence.

Using Technology to Break the Shell of "Permitted Ignorance" Buckminster Fuller might be called Mr. Lifelong Learner. His innovative mind is legendary around the world and especially on college campuses. He holds twenty-two U.S. patents for highly practical devices, ranging from a floating breakwater to the celebrated geodesic dome. "He is fondly regarded by millions of his fellow planetary inhabitants as a genius with a comprehensive vision of the humanistic application of technology," said the editors of his collected writings, entitled *On Education.*

Today educators generally recognize that we are poised on the brink of dramatic changes wrought by communications technologies. Education will be profoundly affected by the pervasiveness of minicomputers and microcomputers, by the worldwide range of satellite video, and by the intimacy of cable TV in virtually every home. Already the nation's public TV system and several schemes for an open university based on technology have been launched and are thriving.

Never has the human promise of such technologies been evoked more eloquently than in the following remarks by Fuller. He opens with a vivid metaphor for human beings' assuming unprecedented responsibility for ourselves and our planet. "Suddenly our eggshell is broken, and like the chick, we must make good on our own." Then Fuller predicts a society in which we "are going to have to pay our whole population to go to school and pay it to stay at school." Characteristically, he injects a specific invention of his own into the technological mix: the Geoscope, through which "the consequences of various world plans could be computed and projected."

Finally, he reaffirms the essential individualism of lifelong learning— that each of us has a unique trajectory of interests and that for the first time such distinctiveness can be accommodated, through technology.

This selection was excerpted from *On Education,* published by the University of Massachusetts Press in 1979. It was first published in 1962 in the now out-of-print *Education Automation.*

Using Technology to Break the Shell of "Permitted Ignorance"

Buckminster Fuller

Human beings are born naked and ignorant on board this planet but are given beautiful mental equipment with which, by trial and error, they can gradually learn better how to cope with life. We have not as yet pulled ourselves very far out of that abyss of ignorance. It is important that we realize that we have not. Because of the availability of new communications technology and because we now have a great deal more information, we are supposed to be pulling out very fast, but our reflexes, conditioned by the days of ignorance, are not paying realistic attention to our new information.

We are coming out of a common eggshell of initially permitted ignorance. As with the embryo chick, we were endowed with all the nutriments to nourish us through the period of exclusively subconscious growth. The nutriment for trial and error is exhausted. We are grown. We now know that only our metaphysical mind can and does discover and employ the eternal, weightless, generalized principles governing all Universe transactions. Suddenly our eggshell is broken, and like the chick, we must make good on our own. It must be all or none, and all true to principle.

Every time we educate a person, we as educators have a regenerative experience, and we ought to learn from that experience how to do it much better the next time. The more educated our population, the more effective it becomes as an integral of regenerative consumer individuals. We are going to have to invest in our whole population to accelerate its consumer regeneration. We are going to be completely unemployed as muscle-working machines. *We as economic society are going to have to pay our whole population to go to school and pay it to stay at school.* That is, we are going to have to put our whole population into the educational process and get *everybody* realistically literate in many directions. Quite clearly, *the new political word* is going to be *investment.* It is not going to be *dole*, or socialism, or the idea of people hanging around in bread lines. The new popular *regenerative investment* idea is actually that of making people more familiar with the patterns of Universe, that is, with what people have learned about Universe to date, and that of getting everybody intercommunicative at ever higher levels of literacy. People are then going to stay in the education process. They are going to populate ever increasing numbers of research laboratories and universities.

As we now disemploy people as muscle and reflex machines, the one area where employment is gaining abnormally fast is the research and development area. Research and development are a part of the educational process itself. We are going to have to invest in our people and make available to them participation in the great educational process of research and development in order to learn more. When we learn more, we are able to do more with our given opportunities. We can rate federally paid-for education as a high return, mutual benefit investment. When we plant a seed and give it the opportunity to grow, its fruits pay us back many fold. Humanity is going to "improve" rapidly in the same way by new federally underwritten educational "seeding" by new tools and processes.

Our educational processes are in fact the upcoming major world industry. This is *it;* this is the essence of today's educational facilities meeting. You are caught in that new educational upward draughting process. The cost of education will be funded regeneratively right out of earnings of the technology, the industrial equation, because we can only afford to reinvest continually in humanity's ability to go back and turn out a better job. As a result of the new educational processes our consuming costs will be progressively lower as we also gain ever higher perfomance per units of invested resources, which means that our wealth actually will be increasing at all times rather than "exhausted by spending." It is the "capability" wealth that really counts. It is very good that there is an international competitive system now operating, otherwise people would tend to stagnate, particularly in large group undertakings. They would otherwise be afraid to venture in this great intellectual integrity regeneration.

I would say, then, that you are faced with a future in which education is going to be number one amongst the great world industries, within which will flourish an educational machine technology that will provide tools such as the individually selected and articulated two-way TV and an intercontinentally networked, documentaries call-up system, operative over any home two-way TV set.

The new educational technology will probably provide also an invention of mine called the Geoscope—a large 200-foot diameter (or more) lightweight geodesic sphere hung hoveringly at 100 feet above midcampus by approximately invisible cables from three remote masts. This giant sphere is a miniature earth. Its entire exterior and interior surfaces will be covered with closely packed electric bulbs, each with variable intensity controls. The lighting of the bulbs is scanningly controlled through an electric computer. The number of the bulbs and their minimum distance of 100 feet from viewing eyes, either at the center of the sphere or on the ground outside and below the sphere, will produce the visual effect and resolution of a fine-screen halftone cut or that of an excellent television-tube picture. The 200-foot Geoscope will cost about $15 million. It will make possible communication of phenomena that are not at present communicable to our conceptual understanding. There are many motion patterns such as those of the hands of the clock or of the solar system planets or of the molecules of gas in a pneumatic ball or of atoms or the earth's annual weather that cannot be seen or comprehended by the human eye and brain relay and are therefore inadequately comprehended and dealt with by the human mind.

The Geoscope may be illuminated to picture the earth and the motion of its complete cloud-cover history for years run off on its surface in minutes so that we may comprehend the cyclic patterning and predict. The complete census-by-census of world population history changes could be run off in minutes, giving a clear picture of the demological patterning and its clear trending. The total history of transportation and of world resource discovery, development, distribution, and redistribution could become comprehendible to the human mind, which would thus be able to forecast and plan in vastly greater magnitude than heretofore. The consequences of various world plans could be computed and projected. All world data would be dynamically viewable and picturable and relayable by radio to all the world, so that common consideration in a most educated manner of all world problems by all world people would become a practical event.

The universities are going to be wonderful places. Scholars will stay there for a long, long time—the rest of their lives—while they are developing more and more knowledge about the whole experience of humanity. All people will be going around the world in due process as everyday routine search and exploration, and the world-experiencing patterning will be everywhere—all students from everywhere all over the world. That is all part of the new pattern that is rushing upon us. We will accelerate as rapidly into "yesterday" through archaeology as we do into "tomorrow." Archaeology both on land and under the seas will flourish equally with astronautics. . . .

I think that all the patterns I have been giving you are going to unfold rapidly and that primarily the individual is going to *study* at home. That is in the elementary, high school, and college years. Not until the graduate-work days begin will the individual take residence on campus. I am quite sure that the students of all ages will keep on going to "schoolhouses" to get *social experiences*—or to be "baby-sat." We will probably keep the schools open in the evening because of the growing need for baby-sitters. Real education, however, will be something to which individuals will discipline themselves spontaneously under the stimulus of their own ticker-tapes—their individually unique chromosomes. All people have their own chromosomal patterns. No two persons have the same appetite at the same time. There is no reason why they should. There is no reason why everyone should be interested in the geography of Venezuela on the same day and hour unless there is some "news" event there, such as a revolution. However, most of us are going to be interested in the geography of Venezuela at some time—our own time—but not all on the same day. *Simultaneous curricula are obsolete.* We must make *all* the information immediately available over the two-way TVs ready for the different individual human chromosomal ticker-tapes to call for it.

Welcome to the Invisible College Margaret Mead pointed out that
we are all, perforce, enrolled in an invisible college of continuing
learning—it is the only way one can keep current in an ever changing
world. Here Kenneth Boulding, former president of the American Association for the Advancement of Science, extends this concept even
further. Not only are we constantly learning from one another, but
each of us is also a potential participant in the process of finding new
truth.

Boulding invites us to fulfill three roles as knowledge processors.
First, as Mead stressed, we are learners. Second, we are teachers. Third,
we are part of that process by which humankind comes "to have new
knowledge which nobody had before."

As you will see, Boulding's personal ideal of the invisible college has
a distinct ideological slant. It is one that many adult educators will find
congenial. But even for those who do not, the image of persons of
goodwill joined in a fraternity based on shared knowledge and understanding is one we can all find inspiring.

This selection is excerpted from the chapter "A Strategy for the Transition" in *The
Meaning of the Twentieth Century,* volume 34 of the World Perspective Series
published by Harper & Row Publishers, Inc., in 1964.

Welcome to the Invisible College

Kenneth Boulding

There is in the world today an "invisible college" of people in many different countries and many different cultures, who have this vision of the nature of the transition through which we are passing and who are determined to devote their lives to contributing toward its successful fulfillment. Membership in this college is consistent with many different philosophical, religious, and political positions. It is a college without a founder and without a president, without buildings and without organization. Its founding members might have included a Jesuit like Pierre Teilhard de Chardin, a humanist like Aldous Huxley, a writer of science fiction like H. G. Wells, and it might even have given honorary degrees to Adam Smith, Karl Marx, Pope John XXIII, and even Khrushchev and John F. Kennedy. Its living representatives are still a pretty small group of people. I think, however, that it is they who hold the future of the world in their hands or at least in their minds.

For this invisible college I am an unashamed propagandist. . . . Our precious little planet, this blue-green cradle of life with its rosy mantle, is in one of the most critical stages, perhaps the most critical stage, of its whole existence. It is in a position of immense danger and immense potentiality. There are no doubt many experiments in evolution going on in different parts of this big universe. But this happens to be my planet and I am very much attached to it, and I am desperately anxious that this particular experiment should be a success. If this be ethnocentrism, then let me be ethnocentric! I am pretty sure, however, that it will not be a success unless something is done. There is danger both of the bang of nuclear detonation and of the whimper of exhausted overpopulation, and either would mean an end of the evolutionary process in these parts. If man were merely capable of destroying himself, one could perhaps bear the thought. One could at least console oneself with the thought of elementary justice, that if man does destroy himself it is his own silly fault. He is captain, however, of a frail and delicate vessel, and in the course of destroying himself he might easily destroy the vessel—that is, the planet

283

which carries him, with its immense wealth and variety of evolutionary freight and evolutionary potential. This makes the dangers of the transition doubly intolerable, and demands a desperate effort to remove them. But once we have joined this invisible college, what do we do? Do we join a political party? Picket the White House? Go on protest marches? Devote ourselves to research, education, and propaganda? Or do we go about the ordinary business of life much as we have previously done? Fortunately or unfortunately, according to taste there is no simple answer to this question. Like any other commitment, joining the invisible college of the transition implies a change from the unexamined life to the examined life. What the results of this examination will be, however, and even what constitutes a good grade, is hard to predict for any particular person. What is certain is that we will see and do even old things in a new light and in a more examined manner. . . .

It is a useful question for each one of us to ask, "What changes are taking place in the noösphere, the sphere of knowledge that envelops the globe, as a result of our own life?" We all affect the noösphere in three ways. The content of our own minds is a part of it, so that what happens to our own knowledge and our own images is that part of the noösphere which we can most immediately affect. It is good for all of us to stop occasionally and inquire in what direction the content of our mind is changing, and what the processes are by which this change takes place. We should ask also in what ways do we bring our supposed knowledge to a test—or do we not bother to do this? Do we indulge in any activity which might be described as search—by exposing ourselves, for instance, to unfamiliar sources of information and new points of view?

The second point at which we affect the noösphere is through the information outflow which we make toward others. In conversation, writing, and in the ordinary activity of daily life we are constantly communicating with others, and as a result of these communications their images of the world change. The teacher of course is professionally associated with such an activity, but all of us are teachers whether we like it or not, whether we get paid for it or not, or even whether we are conscious of it or not. The third process is perhaps only an extension of the first. This is the process by which we come to have new knowledge which nobody had before. This process is often regarded as the privilege of a few who are engaged in professional research. The process, however, is not sharply blocked off from the general process of the increase of knowledge in any mind, and a great many discoveries and inventions are still made by people who are amateurs. The more people there are engaged in a search of some kind, who are constantly on the lookout for new and better ways of doing things, the faster will be the general rate of development. The housewife who thinks of a new dish or a new method of resolving disputes in the family, the workman who drops a useful suggestion into the suggestion box, the businessman who pioneers in a new product or method, the government official or politician who develops a new line of policy are all engaged in a creation of new knowledge just as much as the white-coated scientists in the laboratory. The unfinished tasks of the great transition are so enormous that there is hardly anyone who cannot find a role to play in the process.

In a great many areas of life today one sees a certain polarization of the role of the individual, much of which is perhaps quite unconscious but which nevertheless reflects two profoundly different attitudes toward the great transition. On the one hand there are those who despair, who give up hope, and who retreat into nihilism or into the commonplace performance of routine duties. These are the people for whom the pressures and dangers of the great transition are too much, who see so much of the dangers and so little of the potential that they have in effect abandoned the struggle. On the other side are those who still have hope for mankind, who see the enormous potential that lies ahead of us in spite of the dangers, and who therefore seek constantly to build up rather than to tear down, to create rather than to destroy, to diminish the dangers and guide the course. Even among the natural scientists we find some who are concerned with directing their work into significant channels and with playing roles as citizens, others who retreat into a sterile conformity and routine behavior. Among social scientists there are those who are stirred into lively activity both in the pure and applied fields, guided again by the sense of significance of what they are doing and the urgency of man's search for knowledge in this area. By contrast there are others who retreat into sterile methodological dispute or who seek to perform the rituals of science rather than to catch its spirit.

In philosophy there are those who are concerned with new dimensions in the discipline of man's thought, even as they strive with questions that may have no answer, and there are others who relax into a shallow scientism or who erect existentialist despair into an atheistic God. In literature there are those who continue the great traditions by which man uses the exercise of his own imagination to lift himself and achieve self-knowledge—some of these, indeed, are found among the humble writers of science fiction—where others exploit salaciousness in the name of realism and seek to belittle man's image of himself. In art there are those who strive after novelty at all costs and have lost all interest in beauty, and there are those who wrestle with the enormous problem of finding aesthetic standards in a technological age, and who seek to communicate in aesthetic form the enormous danger and potentiality of man's present condition.

In religion there are those who are trying to awaken man to his condition and his modern environment and to develop the great *phyla* of religion in directions which are appropriate to the needs of a developed society. There are others who crudely exploit ignorance in the pursuit of their own power and who seek to give authority to their own prejudices by the invocation of the divine name. In politics there are men who see the necessity for world community and who are engaged within the limits imposed by their own official roles in increasing the probability of peace and the chances of development. There are others who exploit the inner tensions of the masses by projecting hatred on an enemy and who raise themselves to power at the costs of creating disorder and disunion in the world. There are businessmen, managers, and officials who are trying to create humane and workable organizations and to perform the role of the organizer with style and artistry; there are others who are concerned only with minimizing trouble or maximizing gain to themselves. There are housewives and mothers who are raising families of healthy and creative children capable of contributing to a developing world; there are others who are creating neurotics whose value to the society of the future will be negative. There are schoolteachers who create in their pupils a sense of the preciousness of learning and who stimulate their creativity; there are others who use their pupils as outlets for their personal tensions and who kill the love of learning and stifle the creative urge.

One is tempted to end this litany by the good old evangelical hymn and labor song "Which Side Are You On?" This, however, is a dangerous question. It leads to dialectic rather than to dialogue, to preaching rather than to teaching, to self-justification rather than to self-examination, to confirming one's previous prejudices rather than to learning new things. The truth is that each of us is on both sides. The problem is how to raise the one side in all of us and lower the other. I wish I knew an easy answer to this question. Unfortunately I do not. There are many partial answers, but I know no general answer.

The attempt to answer the previous question perhaps leads to another. Is there some point in the great transition at which the invisible college should become visible? Do we need a visible organization like the Jesuits, or the Communist party, dedicated to the ideology of the transition and committed to getting man through it? There is much that is tempting in the idea. It can be argued that the idea of the great transition contains all the necessary elements of an ideology. It has an interpretation of history and an image of the future, a critique of personal and political behavior, and a role for everyone. All that it seems to need is a professional priest-hood who will symbolize the idea, propagate it, organize it, and so shep-herd mankind into the postcivilized fold. That this is a possible "sce-nario"—as Herman Kahn[1] would call it, I have no doubt. But I also have no doubt that it is not the only scenario and I have very great doubt that it is the best one. An elite and disciplined "visible college" looks like an attractive shortcut to the achievement of the ends of an ideology. I think, however, it is a shortcut which has led in the past almost inevitably if not to disaster at least to doing more harm than good or, even at best, to doing good at very high cost. This is an empirical generalization and so belongs to my own definition of folk knowledge rather than to science, and I have to confess that I have no logical proof that an elite organiza-tion dedicated to what seems a noble purpose always does more harm than good. Here is an area where genuinely scientific knowledge has not yet been achieved. I would therefore not rule out the possibility that in the future we may find ways of organizing a self-conscious society of those committed to the transition which will not be subject to those temptations, degenerations, and abuses of power which have characterized all such societies in the past. I furthermore suspect that such societies are most useful when the ideology which they propagate contains strong ambivalences. One needs neither a Jesuit nor a Communist to propagate the multiplication table. I would hope that the concept of the great transition is more like the multiplication table than it is like an ideological position. In that case it is better to propagate it by an invisible college, for the ideas will propagate themselves by their obvious usefulness. They will need very little of the arts of persuasion or of compulsion. Under these circumstances a visible society devoted to propagating this particular truth might well become more of an obstacle than a facility. For this reason, therefore, I have no desire to plant a standard other than the truth itself. It is to this that the wise and honest must repair.

Notes

1. Herman Kahn, *Thinking About the Unthinkable*, New York, Horizon Press, 1962.